Tomboys, Pretty Boys, and Outspoken Women

Tomboys, Pretty Boys, and Outspoken Women

THE MEDIA REVOLUTION OF 1973

Edward D. Miller

THE UNIVERSITY OF MICHIGAN PRESS • ANN ARBOR

Copyright © by the University of Michigan 2011

Published in the United States of America by
The University of Michigan Press
Manufactured in the United States of America
⊗ Printed on acid-free paper

2014   2013   2012   2011   4   3   2   1

A CIP catalog record for this book is available from the British Library.

Library of Congress Cataloging-in-Publication Data

Miller, Edward D., 1960–
    Tomboys, pretty boys, and outspoken women : the media revolution
of 1973 / Edward D. Miller.
        p.   cm.
    Includes bibliographical references and index.
    ISBN 978-0-472-11775-8 (cloth : alk. paper) — ISBN 978-0-472-
03461-1 (pbk. : alk. paper)
    1. Mass media—United States.   2. Nineteen seventies.   3. Mass
media—Technological innovations.   I. Title.
    P92.U5M54   2011
    302.2309′047—dc22   2011000475

In memory of my mother, Jean Baker Miller

Preface
RETROFITTING THE 1970S

I admit it. I became a teenager in the early 1970s, turning thirteen in 1973, the year that forms the scaffolding of this book. The 1970s were my formative years. And as much as one's parents leave an imprint, so does the popular culture. My brain is full of jingles from countless ads and themes from perhaps too many television shows, and I know all the lyrics from *Ziggy Stardust* and *Yellow Brick Road*. After all I learned air guitar in the '70s and bought my first and last pair of platform shoes back then.

I was fortunate to have spent two school years in England during the decade. The first year was in 1972–73 (the year of glitter/glam), and the second was 1976–77 (the year of punk). I can't say I was there at Ziggy's last concert or the first gig of the Sex Pistols, but I can say I saw glimpses of these subcultures through the BBC and the tabloids (and the *New Musical Express*) as well as the television shows *Top of the Pops* and *The Old Grey Whistle Test*. I also witnessed glimpses of these emerging youth cultures in the attitudes and styles of my classmates in pre-Thatcher London. I am quite sure I didn't understand what I was witnessing, but I sensed it was important. I remember some of my schoolmates putting their school blazers on backward and scrawling "Anarchy in the UK" in white chalk atop their makeshift straightjackets. Okay, it wasn't Paris, May 1968, but it was rebellion nonetheless.

I remember seeing the all-girl band the Runaways in 1976 (or was it early 1977?), with the punk band the Damned opening for them. I wasn't sure why I enjoyed singing along with their lyrics in "Cherry Bomb" ("hello daddy, hello mom, I'm your ch-ch-ch-ch-ch cherry bomb"). But it makes sense now. In the recent not-so-great film about them, *The Runaways* (2010), David Bowie is the backstory of the narrative. His image and his music are everywhere in the film: Bowie's androgyny and expressive style and stance inspire Cherie Currie and Joan

Jett to form an all-female band. The Runaways form a link between the glitter era and the punk era, and they were a permission slip (given to them by Bowie) for women and gays and lesbians to enter more audaciously into the arena of popular culture. Young gay men who loved rock music back then may not have had access to "Judy" (or even "Liza") but they did have the Runaways and David Bowie and Patti Smith (I saw her perform in London in 1977, with the Stranglers opening for her).

Living in England those two years served to estrange me from American popular culture. With this book, I am perhaps catching up with the American 1970s. I am fascinated with the era, especially the expression of gender. This is inspired by my mother's intense involvement in feminism beginning in the '70s and my own participation (and at times determined nonparticipation) in the lgbt (lesbian, gay, bisexual, and transgender) culture of the 1980s and 1990s. The questions I ask and the answers I suggest are related to these experiences and omissions.

And this is why in large part I return to the '70s. But why does popular culture—from fashion to music to film—also constantly return to the '70s for inspiration? Does the analog '70s represent the last period before the endless recycling of popular culture? In a word, yes. The originality of the period and the maverick nature (I am reclaiming that word from Sarah Palin and John McCain, thank you) of so many of its important cultural figures have been unequaled since.

Of course, with the arrival of a digitalized culture, a revolution occurred in the delivery and distribution of media. The subsequent rise of person-to-person interaction via new technology has all but supplanted the one-to-many paradigm of so much of media. As a media scholar, and one that struggles against a potential addiction to Apple products (and whatever else that has connectivity and appears cute), I could never say that there is nothing new under the sun: the experience of the quotidian has been altered. And yet it is worth investigating a paradoxical phenomenon: today's media culture appears obsessed with reality at the moment when the notion of a shared reality is all but extinct (we are all soaking in our own subjective bubble baths). The dashing, licentious dignitaries of the 1970s enunciated riveting nonfiction stories, but they did not make claims on "reality" per se. If the focus was on the self, identity was perceived to be elastic not rigid. The meaning and influence of these stars' stories of identity deserve further elaboration; here I offer one attempt to unravel the relevance of part of the '70s to contemporary media.

Indeed my attempt is related to my story—and the way I tell it—but I daresay my concerns are related to what has become a discernible mediatized pastime: remembering the popular culture of yesteryear as a way of recounting—or reinventing—one's experiences in the past. I hope that I can provide the reader with an encounter that is more complicated than watching Fox's *That 70s Show* or VH1's *I Love the 70s*, but part of the reason the '70s won't go away for me is because popular culture won't let go of the '70s. Perhaps this book goes a little way in explaining why.

Acknowledgments

This work has benefited from the collegiality of the Department of Media Culture at the College of Staten Island and the Film Studies Certificate Program at the Graduate Center of the City University of New York. Certain colleagues must be mentioned by name: David Gerstner and Cynthia Chris (who made astute recommendations on various versions of the text) as well as Cindy Wong, Jason Simon, Matthew Solomon, Jeanine Corbet, Sherry Millner, Ying Zhu, and Valerie Tevere. Each has enlivened my workplace life for many years now. Discussions with a former colleague, Vinicius do Valle Navarro, were particularly helpful in refining my thinking about *An American Family.* I first developed the Watergate chapter while I was a fellow at the Center for Place, Culture, and Politics, and the comments of all the participants were helpful, especially those of Karen Miller.

I am grateful to Sally Milner for skilled assistance with the manuscript. For the images, I thank Kristie Falco for her persistent work. I also want to acknowledge Jim Tushinski, Alan Raymond, Todd Kancar, Pati Quinn of Mick Rock Sudios, and Todd Ifft and Buddy Weiss of Photofest. To my good fortune I have worked with Tom Dwyer, Alexa Ducsay, and Christina Milton at the University of Michigan Press on this book. Thanks to the Paley Center for Media and their Scholar's Pass program for help in the research.

My students in the graduate seminar "Documenting the Self: Performance in Nonfiction Film" were responsive to my ideas, and our discussions have influenced the theoretical basis of this book. For the voice in this work, I am duty bound to recognize my students at the College of Staten Island, who continue to challenge me to improve my communications skills. Now, if they could only turn off their cell phones and stop texting (just kidding!).

My father, Mike Miller, ever inquisitive, continues to ask me crucial questions about popular culture and media. My chosen family in New York, São Paulo, and Bexhill-on-Sea has provided me with great support and intelligent discussion over the years: Beth Nathanson, Kathy Tannert-Niang, Frances Sorensen, Jeffrey Stephens-Prince, Sumitra Mukerji, John McGrath, Richard Green, Mark Seamon, and Suze Clemitson. I am so appreciative that Jess Taylor and Gê Viana cleared a spot where I could write in their kitchen during a key moment in the revision. Finally, I am indebted to Ray Montero for inspiring the completion of this project and for providing such wondrous and witty companionship.

Time
Aladdin Sane
Panic In Detroit
Words and Music by David Bowie
© 1973 (Renewed 2001) EMI MUSIC PUBLISHING LTD.,
    TINTORETTO MUSIC and MOTH MUSIC
All Rights for EMI MUSIC PUBLISHING LTD. Controlled and Administered by
    SCREEN GEMS-EMI MUSIC INC.
All Rights for TINTORETTO MUSIC Administered by RZO MUSIC
All Rights for MOTH MUSIC Administered by BMG CHRYSALIS
All Rights Reserved   International Copyright Secured   Used by Permission
Reprinted by permission of Hal Leonard Corporation and
    Tintoretto Music admin. by RZO Music, Inc.

Rock 'N' Roll Suicide
Five Years
Words and Music by David Bowie
© 1972 (Renewed 2000) EMI MUSIC PUBLISHING LTD.,
    TINTORETTO MUSIC and MOTH MUSIC
All Rights for EMI MUSIC PUBLISHING LTD. Controlled and Administered by
    SCREEN GEMS-EMI MUSIC INC.
All Rights for TINTORETTO MUSIC Administered by RZO MUSIC
All Rights for MOTH MUSIC Administered by BMG CHRYSALIS
All Rights Reserved   International Copyright Secured   Used by Permission
Reprinted by permission of Hal Leonard Corporation and
    Tintoretto Music admin. by RZO Music, Inc.

Contents

CHAPTER 1

Introduction

THE BIRTH OF MEDIATIZED REALITY

THE VIEWER AS CRITIC AND CONTESTANT

Contemporary popular media culture is built on the assumption that the stories of so-called real people—as well as the true-life tales of famous folks—are as riveting as anything a writer or director or producer can fabricate from a fictional script. YouTube, the incredibly popular Web site that emerged in 2006, is filled with videos produced by its users and inherits this new tradition inspired by reality television—it turns the media user into both an at-home Simon Cowell of *American Idol* and a contestant who is berated by him. Each of us prowls the virtual American landscape—and our own lives within it—for a dynamic version of reality that is captured by digital technology, whether it's the latest cat video or a group of overtanned twenty-somethings partying on the Jersey Shore. As both productive consumers and domestic impresarios, we are more than eager to present a slice of life and crowd the shelves of a new kind of media library that mixes user-generated content with content produced by corporations. It is not shocking that *Time* magazine's person of the year in 2006 was "You," for by 2006 the heralding of the dexterous techno-consumer had already begun. We not only read magazines online, but we are media authors through crowdsourcing and social media sites, spinning yarns and devising vignettes that seemingly originate from some subjective experience of truth—or a corporate mandate to come up with content.

When did this fixation on presenting episodes of reality—featuring "real" people and not actors—begin? It began in the early 1970s when American media discovered the entertainment value of nonfiction. With this discovery, contemporary media culture began.

REAL STORIES

In the early 1970s major shifts in the culture inspired the entertainment industries to tell nonfictional stories, stories that depicted real life. For example, on January 22, 1973, the Supreme Court made a historic decision in the *Roe v. Wade* ruling. This case legalized abortion nationwide, advancing women's rights. On September 20 of the same year a female tennis player defeated male chauvinism in the "Billie Jean King v. Bobby Riggs" ruling—a profitable televised tennis match named "The Battle of the Sexes." In 1972 Billie Jean King's name had been included in a list of prominent women who had abortions before they were legal in all fifty states. Her inclusion in this list, published by *Ms.* magazine, placed her in the center of debates on abortion, connecting the struggle for gender parity in sports with the larger women's movement. In such ways, legal advances for women became the subject matter of popular culture, with clear heroes and villains; of course, deciding who was the villain depended on the viewer's perspective on the new freedoms granted to women's bodies.

Billie Jean King proved that a grown-up tomboy and female athlete could become a celebrity without presenting herself as traditionally feminine and subservient to the men in her profession. Feminism went prime time with her as a spokeswoman by way of the contest that was staged to prove—or disprove—the equality of women. Her adversary, Bobby Riggs, took on the role of a rather hysterical male chauvinist pig, flaunting an apparently *Playboy* lifestyle (Riggs more accurately described was a rather short grown-up nerd who knew how to use spin—both on and off the court—to his best advantage). In this nonfiction drama, Billie Jean played the role of a more restrained—if "butch"—woman, but she was not above presenting Riggs with a baby pig before the match (he gave her a huge "Sugar Daddy" candy). Both of them joined together to popularize the once elite game of tennis and worked with the network and producer Jerry Perenchio (he had previously funded Joe Frazier boxing matches) to sell the raucous event.

Popular media was shifting in the early '70s, with discussions of sex and sexuality—and the inclusion of forbidden language—moving into the open after power struggles were played out in public. In 1972 comic George Carlin was arrested for enunciating "Seven Words You Can Never Say on Television" in front of an audience in Milwaukee—and in 1973 the Federal Communications Commission (FCC) took radio station WBAI to court for playing the recorded version of Carlin's routine. Yet in 1973 Erica Jong published the best seller *Fear of Flying*, which included the term *zipless fuck*. This term epitomized a new, uncensored way of looking at female pleasure (or attempts at pleasure). No police knocked on Erica Jong's door, and the use of the term showed that many Americans were ready to revisit the public use of curse words and their meanings—even if the courts and police were not ready when it came to their enunciation via broadcasting (bad words are still not used in American broadcasting, except on cable in the later parts of the evening). Even as Carlin and a nonprofit radio station were being rebuked, television culture began to change, becoming more controversial. As Elana Levine writes in *Wallowing in Sex: The New Sexual Culture of 1970s American Television*, "Entertainment television of the 1970s told Americans about the impact of the women's liberation movement, the influence of the gay rights movement, and the outcomes of the sexual revolution through stories and characters, images and sounds, words and silences" (4). This impact was also felt in the magazine industry, pornography, and the popularization of new kinds of pop stars who advocated bisexuality and appeared androgynous and flamboyant.

While feminism and other movements were achieving legal advancements that influenced popular culture, the American economy was in jeopardy. Most notably, the energy crisis started in 1973 because of political strife in the Middle East. Members of the Organization of the Petroleum Exporting Countries (OPEC) were disdainful of the American government's support of Israel and punished Americans by raising the price of a barrel of oil (of course, energy companies didn't suffer—they passed the cost on to the consumer). As a result, Americans waited in long lines for gas. By the end of the year, people were also waiting in line for a new kind of horror film that was extremely bawdy and graphic and popular beyond all expectations. This film, *The Exorcist*, which made rampant use of some of George Carlin's curse words, is not only about a possessed girl about to enter puberty but also about the journey of a demon. The demon, Pazuzo, originates from the sands of Iraq and travels to Washington, DC, to possess an actress's daughter who is about to rebel against her mother and her social milieu. The film is a parable about the economic and psychic moment of the nation, suggesting that the economic downturn apparently caused by members of OPEC and expressions of unbridled female sexuality are somehow linked (see the chapter on *The Exorcist* in Tim Jon Semmerling's 2006 *"Evil" Arabs in American Popular Film*). Coupled with the near collapse of Western masculinist capitalism is the crumbling of traditional patriarchal structures.

The Exorcist warns us that seismic shifts in the economy are felt most strongly in the realm of culture, and in gender construction. When the young Regan is possessed she sounds like a drunken sailor on leave in Sodom. Her innocent, high-pitched voice becomes a gutter-mouthed baritone. What *The Exorcist* shows us is that during an economic downturn identities are vulnerable and gender roles are porous.

In 1973 the U.S. government changed its currency system, abandoning the gold standard forever and entering into a new era in which the value of the dollar is decided by international currency markets. By unlinking the dollar from gold, President Richard Nixon was not only placing the currency system in a state of flux, adding the dollar to the international market, but he was also endorsing the ideas of Milton Friedman, an increasingly prominent economist who became an adviser to the right-wing dictator of Chile, Augusto Pinochet. Pinochet took power in 1973 after overthrowing a popularly elected socialist government with the encouragement of the CIA. Conservative economic and political ideologies encouraged imperial activities—even after the United States' incursion into Vietnam failed to maintain a Western-friendly government there. Indeed the United States did not retreat from the world stage as the unpopular Vietnam War drew to a close—arguably its CIA became more active covertly while the armed forces relaxed their overt efforts to police the world. The nation's economic system began to become more conservative after the trauma of crisis, laying the groundwork for Reaganism and the ideology of the unbridled free market (actually the rise of global corporations). This is an era that is only perhaps ending with the economic collapse of 2008 and the election of Barack Obama.

At the same time as the economic system moved rightward and the focus on governmental social programs was being replaced by a stress on deregulation, paving the way for global corporate dominance, popular culture within the United States was staging a rebellion in the early 1970s. This was a rebellion that focused on displays of nonfiction stories newly found—or reconstructed—for entertainment. These stories featured an entirely new cast of characters.

CAST OF CHARACTERS

My first example would initially appear to be an unlikely inclusion: the Senate's Watergate Hearings. These hearings were televised in 1973 and transformed the shenanigans of the executive branch of government into a soap-opera-like net of competing narratives—especially when the well-dressed, handsome John Dean testified with his stylish, trendsetting wife at his side. The Deans flaunted their youthful attractiveness—and their attraction to each other—as a way of countering President Nixon's all-male, older henchmen, who were trying to lay the blame for a cover-up on Dean, Nixon's former legal counsel. In order to retaliate against the Deans' media savvy and television appeal, Nixon's people spread rumors that John Dean, deemed a "pretty boy" (relative to the rather homely group of men surrounding Nixon), was gay (or that he would say anything to avoid jail because he feared homosexual rape as he was so pretty), and that his chic, sophisticated-looking wife was nothing but a common prostitute. The drama of John Dean's testimony became riveting daytime television watched by many female soap opera fans. At first, these fans were upset that their soaps had been preempted, but many became devotees of the hearings and tuned in every day. John and Maureen Dean were their favorite nonfiction soap opera stars. If the viewers had a chance, they never would have voted Dean and his wife off the show. On their side, the Deans used their telegenic qualities and real-life romance to wage a public relations battle against the president, and won.

Fictional events and real stories intermingled in the early '70s as never before but in structures that today's media users now take for granted. These events and stories continue to have an impact on current media and popular culture. For example, the pioneering reality show discussed in chapter 6, *An American Family,* caused an uproar with its depiction of the troubled Loud family. The oldest son, Lance, wore makeup and hung out with drag queens in a decadent, drug-taking New York milieu. When his mother came to visit him at New York's Chelsea Hotel, the audience saw her anxiety about her son, as well as her attempts to accept his lifestyle—a lifestyle that had never before been shown so openly on television. The controversy around the series predates the craze of current programs that incite real people to perform antics for the camera. Lance Loud seemed to prove Andy Warhol's oft-repeated epigram about fame—indeed his celebrity was fleeting. But he also paved the way for today's reality television stars, showing that anyone can become famous for depicting oneself as long as the subject in question provides a scandal that provokes members of the public and the press to cluck in disapproval. And certainly Lance had his detractors, who decried his "narcissism" rather than applauding him for his rebellious performances of gender and his playful searches for identity conducted in front of the camera.

Like Lance Loud, David Bowie proved that a once ostracized flamboyant man could become a beloved star, thereby traveling a road paved in jewels in large part by such unlikely cohorts as Oscar Wilde (who toured America in 1892 lecturing on aesthetics), Liberace, and Little Richard. In 1973, David Bowie traveled across America first as a character he named Ziggy Stardust and then as Aladdin Sane, personae that inhabit chapter 4. Bowie seemed to celebrate theorist Richard Dyer's description of stardom: "[A] star is an *image* (not a real person) that is *constructed* (as any other aspect of fiction is) out of a range of materials (e.g., advertising, magazines, etc. as well as films)" (1979, 23). Indulging in transmediated artifice, Bowie flaunted an androgynous space-age persona—shocking the country (or at least its mainstream press) and constructing a style of popular expression that highlighted gender ambiguity. His success proves that aberrance is alluring, a suitable brand identity, particularly in the music industry. This lesson has been learned by many, from Annie Lennox to Boy George to k.d. lang, and it is a point that has recently been made again by Adam Lambert's career, launched on *American Idol*—even though Lambert's displays of same-sex desire seem tame in comparison with the theatrics between Bowie and his guitarist, Mick Ronson. David Bowie also revealed that moving images are as important as sound in selling music, anticipating MTV: in 1973 photographer Mick Rock began shooting videos that visualized Bowie's music for promotional purposes.

Another pioneer, though not as well known, who both challenged gender stereotypes and made use of her own story in developing a persona was Alison Steele, New York City's first female rock disc jockey. Like Billie Jean King, she claimed new territory for women's expression and identity. Alison had a deep and smoky voice and called herself the Nightbird. She mixed improvised monologues and recitals of poetry with space-age and tribal sounds. She helped to invent new ways of incorporating real-life experiences into an on-air presentation. Steele elaborated on the free-form DJ style devised in the '60s; she also anticipated the way that the medium would come to be used by talk radio personalities, while other modes of her address, especially her intimacy, would seem odd to today's listeners. Her fans included policemen on the night shift, as well as stoned teenagers, and each was apparently eager to hear the full-length version of the Moody Blues' "Nights in White Satin." Her "earth goddess takes to the skies" persona became legendary.

Although it is often thought of as the time when the rebellious '60s ended, the early '70s was a time when new kinds of stars, personalities from outside the mainstream, became prominent. New voices emerged from the margins, and fictional structures did not accommodate them. In addition, newer ways to structure documentaries and film the news were revised to fit the transitioning culture: real life and real people were getting too eccentric to reassert the norm. The women and men I discuss became symbols of popular media undergoing progressive change that opened up new arenas of representation, even as political and economic leaders reacted conservatively to the changes of the '60s. The economic base and cultural superstructure went their separate ways.

Much of the cultural history of the '70s focuses on the latter part of the decade and ignores the distinctive, nonconformist personalities of the earlier years. These histories have centered either on disco and punk or the indulgence of the "me decade." However, an emphasis on the era as the me decade diminishes the gains fought for and won by gays, lesbians, and feminist women and underplays the new forms of expressiveness and performance that make the beginning years of the decade so dynamic and influential. Accepting that the '70s epitomizes what sociologist Christopher Lasch deemed *The Culture of Narcissism* (1979) delimits a full understanding of the importance of the cultural experimentation that went on during the decade. The first years of the '70s were especially transformative, perhaps in ways that we can only begin to understand now.

The year 1973 has been viewed as the beginning of a more conservative era, a marker that signaled the ending of the rebellious '60s. Most recently, Andreas Killen's *1973 Nervous Breakdown* (2006) argues a similar point, rather persuasively, and indeed 1973 heralds the ascendency of free market ideologues. Yet his book does not focus on the victories won for nascent contestants within identity politics. If 1973 marks the end of a viable counterculture that was centered on rebellious white men who refused the mandates of the system and opposed the Vietnam War, the early 1970s also flaunts the rise of cultural events that highlight feminist women and gay men.

HUMAN CHARACTER

In the essay "Mr. Bennett and Mrs. Brown" Virginia Woolf declared, "[O]n or about December, 1910, human character changed." Woolf chose this particular month because it was just after she saw the postimpressionist show in London, an exhibit that had a profound influence on her and her social and artistic circle. With this oft-cited statement Woolf asserts that it was not only modernism that ushered in a change in how stories were told and images were presented. Indeed, these changes also reflected a shift in the inner organization of individuals.

Innovations in technology in the late 1800s and early twentieth century contributed greatly to this shift in the interiority of people to which Woolf alerts us. Radical changes in the experience of the everyday were provoked by spectacular inventions such as the lightbulb, cinema, and radio. These innovations influenced not only modes of communication and expression but also the construction and conception of the human psyche. New forms of communications technology challenged and changed the psyche. Furthermore the varied responses to these new objects, products, and processes from consumers, users, and producers also served to radically alter how experiences and events were viewed, recorded, and transmitted.

This book posits that in terms of cultural transition 1973 is akin to 1910, though I won't put forward an actual month when this occurred—especially since *An American Family* was shown in 1973 but filmed in 1971. I believe 1973 was the culmination and end of the early 1970s. It was a watershed year in American culture in an era when the politics of identity became paramount. In the early 1970s the change in human character occurred through popular media and centered on the realignment of the genders. Unlike the 1910 moment of transition that Woolf pinpoints, which was an internal one related to "human character," the change in 1973 focused more on visual appearance, gender, and performance. Gay men and women became visible in American media—and effeminate men and mannish women who were not necessarily gay (or out of the closet yet) became stars. The ways in which men and women were represented became varied, challenging some stereotypes while reinforcing others. This change didn't come out of nowhere; it was inspired by the successes of the civil rights and antiwar movements and the avant-garde and experimental arts, yet the women's and the gay rights movements had become increasingly vocal and persuasive, and it was in the early 1970s that these "minority" movements displayed their impact on popular media in a very dramatic and exciting fashion. In the early 1970s the reality star was born. She is fearless when she performs. She invites the camera crew inside her place of work, her dressing room, and her home.

The cultural wars that rage today around abortion, gay and same-sex marriage, and the visibility and representation of minorities are often caricatured so that they appear as a wrestling match between backwoods religious folks fighting overeducated urban, mostly coastal, elites. Yet this cleft between the values and priorities of "red states" and "blue states" became apparent in the early '70s. The cultural wars began with a victory for members of the Left, who were able to translate judicial and legislative victories into the realm of cultural production, extending tolerance and new ways of depicting cultural "others." The Right has been on the attack ever since.

In the early '70s disco began with the popularity of the new Philadelphia soul sound. As documented by Peter Shapiro in his history of the genre, *Turn the Beat Around* (2005), disco not only appealed to gays, African Americans, and Hispanic Americans (and urban Italian Americans) and voiced their aspirations for (self-)acceptance and mainstream success; it was also sung, produced, and mixed by members of these communities. The legendary African American performer of the '70s, Sylvester, who became emblematic of disco (as discussed in Joshua Gamson's 2005 *The Fabulous Sylvester*), emerged from the San Francisco drag performance troupe the Cockettes. He sang in a lusty falsetto and proudly flaunted an onstage persona that bordered on drag, glitter era androgyny, and boyish femininity. Within his community, and beyond, he became a star.

Disco also signaled the rise of the club DJ as a cultural icon and shaman of the technological era: the DJ brought people into a trancelike state in which denizens danced for hours in varying conditions of real and feigned abandon. Indeed, disco's following decidedly did not consist of heterosexual white men, who may have once protested the war but were not likely to surrender themselves to music with many beats per minute and overwhelming percussion. In fact many straight (presumably suburban) white men had formed a backlash against disco by the later part of the decade, repeating the words "disco sucks"—a slogan that was tinged with racial, homophobic, and sexist overtones (see Gamson 184, 185; Shapiro 232–34). In the '70s, disco gathered a far more diverse audience than rock music. The '70s was conservative only if one ignores the realm of popular culture and views protest politics as the primary way in which change occurs. Progressive ideas are also advanced and enacted through performance and play. It was within the realm of culture that minorities gained expression in modes that were not possible in the politicized '60s, even as the radical politics of the '60s had inspired the cultural gains of the '70s.

On television gay and minority characters appeared with more frequency in the early '70s. Black comic Flip Wilson appeared in drag as Geraldine on his highly popular variety show. Sherman Hemsley joined *All in the Family* in 1973 as George Jefferson, Archie's black neighbor, and legendary comic Richard Pryor worked as a guest star on an innovative special, the *Lily Tomlin Show* (cowritten with her lover, Jane Wagner), in 1973. Female characters that took pride in their professional lives, such as Mary Tyler Moore (and her Jewish best friend Rhoda), also became prevalent in the early '70s. Popular culture became sissified, feminized, and more ethnic in the early '70s as the straight, white male counterculture subsided and the Vietnam War ended; with the fall of the hippies, the girls, the gays, and the blacks came marching in. Cultural changes in the early '70s allotted time for Americans who till that time had been virtually invisible in the media.

In the early '70s, fashion changed greatly from the flowing and loose-fitting hippie fashions. In a word, clothing became sexier, exposing and emphasizing certain parts of the male and female body. Young women wore snug miniskirts, hot pants, halter tops, and platform shoes. Men's clothes also clung to thighs and hips, stressing both the buttocks and the crotch, while becoming looser around the ankles in elephant bell-bottom jeans, creating a new male silhouette. Young men also took to wearing platform and high-heeled shoes, pushing out their butts, reveling in a male peacockery that had all but disappeared since the (so-called gay) 1890s. Business suits lightened and brightened in color, and lapels and ties widened, allowing men's haberdashery a new expressiveness, even for more conservative men. In the early '70s, the rising fashion star Yves Saint Laurent was featuring pantsuits for men and women that at first glance were indistinguishable, both modified military and safari looks, though each accentuated the male and female physique slightly differently.

The glitter or glam rock of the early '70s also took on an androgynous style, but this was by no means an asexual look—it was a very adorned and theatricalized appearance that flaunted physical appeal. Clothing was formfitting and unforgiving, stressing thinness but also drawing attention to genitals in its use of velvet and dance-influenced attire, such as the leotard, that was affixed to the body like a second skin. Gone was the natural, makeupless hippie look. Artifice was in (as were flammable synthetics!), newly articulated without harking back to a previous era. Both male and female rock stars and celebrities wore exaggerated makeup, drawing designs on cheeks and emphasizing eyelashes and cheekbones in shading. Fashion in the early '70s was excessive and indulgent, and similarities in style between men and women were highlighted even as the differences between their bodies were underlined, endorsing the ambisexuality and sexual experimentation of the era. In contrast, although the hippies may have espoused free love, their clothing was never especially provocative, nor did it stress individuality; rather it suggested uniformity with others of the hippie milieu. The fashions of the early '70s emphasized individuality, sexuality, and a reluctance to adhere to gender conformity. In this way, fashion marks the shift in American culture from the politics of mass protest to the culture of identity politics, a shift that produced new voices and startlingly new appearances, a shift that is fleshed out in this book.

SEVENTIES THEORY

Each chapter in this book provides an example of this change in American popular media culture through a close reading of a particular cultural event, artifact, or person that portrays the new ways in which gender and sexuality were viewed. This approach is in part also an homage to the era: it is an acknowledgment of the cultural and literary theory that emerged during the '70s, particularly from France. This theorizing made use of the intellectual's newly discovered ability to frame a cultural phenomenon as a textual event, extending the terms of literary criticism to discussions of popular culture and media. My implicit argument here, influenced by Roland Barthes, is that media events are as complicated—and as worthy of interpretation—as the finest of literary texts, a position that energizes Barthes's *Mythologies* (originally published in 1957 but translated into English in 1972) and its interpretations of wrestling, soap detergent ads, and the faces of Hollywood stars. In 1973 Barthes published *Le Plaisir du texte* (translated as *The Pleasure of the Text*, in 1975), which emphasized the place of pleasure and bliss in the experience of texts. I hope to evoke the complicated affectivity and pleasure of American media culture. More explicitly, I lay bare the cultural politics of historic occurrences that took place via media, politics that might not be so obvious and thus require close readings. My hope is that through these specific examples the book provides a larger, if fragmented, episodic picture of the transformations that took place during this era. The current state of media today, with its twin fascination with reality and digital forms of personal expression through social-networking sites and other Internet constellations, becomes more comprehensible through a new reading of the early '70s.

In his 2007 rumination on the twentieth century entitled *The Century*, Alain Badiou divulges his premise.

> My method will consist in extracting, from among the century's productions, some documents or traces indicative of how the century thought itself. To be more precise, how the century thought its own thought, how it identified the thinking singularity of the relation it entertained with the historicity of its own thought. (3)

For rhetorical purposes, the century becomes almost a distinct entity in his book, and each of his case studies serves to illuminate the expressive techniques that occurred during the century (which for him begins with the First World War and ends with the collapse of the Soviet Union and the end of the cold war). In a sense, the century becomes his intended target, part of his audience: the book wishes to alert the century to shards of itself.

Although my book has different purposes and is far less ambitious, I do strive to bring to life the early '70s as a flexible, resilient object that stretches beyond its point of origin. The examples here were not chosen randomly, nor do I expect them to necessarily form a coherent portrait of a few years in American media culture. My hope is instead that the book will begin to reveal key figures that animated American media, allowing the early '70s to be considered unique and crucial. In this sense, these figures—and the response to their activities—produce the '70s, certainly as much as they are themselves products of the time. I do hope to make the '70s aware of itself, that is to say, the part of the decade that deserves to be reassessed in light of the contemporary moment.

For all the transformations that the late 1960s wrought, the early 1970s alert us to the many changes in the popular media industries and the ways that gender roles are depicted in various media. The first years of the 1970s mark a great shift in depictions of femininity and masculinity—and sexuality—as the bodies and behavior of men and women were given new contours and new forms of expressiveness that cannot be called traditional. It took an emphasis on reality in the media to enable a renewed exploration of fantasies of gender.

The early 1970s signaled the rise of nonfiction entertainment, and looking back we can see the beginnings of reality television and user-generated content. What is most compelling is that women and gay men gained a new prominence in these forms of nonfiction media, and this book provides an accounting of the difference the '70s marked in both the visibility and representation of minorities. Why do women and gay men benefit from a rise in nonfiction entertainment, and does nonfictionality enable the expression of voices that traditional fictional forms stifle? I return to this question in the final chapter where I look at *Playgirl* magazine and the films of the gay porn icon Peter Berlin. Both alerted their audiences to the allure of the resexualized male body and the production of personae as the engine for storytelling and the production of desire.

CHAPTER 2

The Watergate Senate Hearings and the Daytime Soap Opera

BACKSTORY

Art Buchwald, a columnist during the Nixon era who deftly used humor to comment on politics, invented an expert named "Siegfreed" (as in Sigmund Freud) in order to discuss the reasons why Watergate became riveting drama, appealing to its audience as political theater. Siegfreed explains to Buchwald:

> Watergate is pure entertainment. It has comedy, mystery, and melodrama. I would prefer that it have a little sex but you can't have everything. People identify with the Watergate characters. They are all clean-cut, short-haired Americans caught up in a soap opera which each insists was not of his making. (7D)

Siegfreed is right. Watergate didn't have sex, but it did have sexiness. Watergate's most famous witness, John Dean, and his wife, Maureen, who appeared five weeks into the televising of the Senate hearings, provided the sex appeal. On June 25, 1973, they became the centerpiece of the proceedings, the stars of the national soap opera.

Other commentators have noted the soap-operatic qualities of Watergate. In his essay "The Danger of Blurring Fact and Fantasy" veteran newsman Daniel Schorr writes, "Great national events—even great national tragedies—have become entertainment" (D1). He cites, as his concluding example, the way the 1973 Senate Watergate Hearings preempted the daytime soap operas. Schorr notes that many soap opera viewers began watching the hearings avidly—even though they were at first upset that their soaps had been taken off the air. Some even contacted the network that he worked for then (CBS) complaining about certain sequences of the hearings or remarking that they liked particular witnesses (or characters) such as John Dean and his "lovely wife."

Schorr's inference is that these daytime viewers were mistaken to watch the hearings as if they were soap operas. Moreover, for him this blurring of genres indicates a larger social ill, one related to the false perceptions of the audience, which allows the public to treat serious issues too lightly. In this chapter I take the opposite point of view—that soap opera fans were astute in how they watched the proceedings—and I take their insights into media culture and national politics very seriously. Today it is taken as a given that successful politicians must have good hair and give even better drama.

The hearings were presented to the audience in ways that were very much like the soap opera genre, especially as soap operas had begun to change in the early 1970s to incorporate issues of the day. The similarities between the soap opera and the hearings became most pronounced with John Dean's testimony. His glamorous wife Maureen flanked him in the Senate room, and they looked like a youthful couple on a soap opera. They flaunted their newlywed status in front of the cameras as a strategy to counter the rather unsexy administration Dean had betrayed. In comparison, the Watergate men were presented as the middle-aged character actors on the soaps who played the parents that struggled to keep their kids from having sex.

The Deans appeared to live a storybook life, that is to say, a life of turmoil in which they survive adversity in part because of their love but also because he is good-looking and she is beautiful and they are both telegenic. They gave the impression they had stepped out of a soap opera and found themselves in another one, though this one was produced in DC, not in Los Angeles or New York, and it was not sponsored by Procter and Gamble but by the legislative branch of government, much to the chagrin of a "competing network," the executive branch.

SOAP WORLDS

The '70s changed the world of soap operas. The new soaps on ABC, *All My Children* (1970–2011) and *One Life to Live* (1968–2012), posed a threat to the dominance of the old CBS soaps, which were sponsored by Procter and Gamble (*Guiding Light* [1965–84] and *As the World Turns* [1956–]). The ABC soaps used contemporary stories and more youthful casts. *One Life to Live* featured African American, Jewish American, Irish American, and Polish American families and did not center on a patrician WASP family like the older shows did. In a groundbreaking story line on drug addiction in 1970, when one of the lead characters became an addict, the show filmed actual group therapy sessions at Odyssey House in New York City. Story lines in soaps began to mimic headlines.

The show also began with a story line of a light-skinned black woman trying to pass for white, who, like Sarah Jane in Douglas Sirk's version of *Imitation of Life* (1959), ignores her dark-skinned mother in public. In 1998, Agnes Nixon, the creator of *All My Children* and *One Life to Live,* discussed how she had difficulty getting the sponsor, Procter and Gamble, to agree to even have a black and a white character live together as roommates in the late 1960s, let alone depicting interracial romance (*Museum of Television and Radio University Satellite Seminar Series* 1998). The new ABC soaps were more liberal in perspective, and their popularity prompted the other networks to change.

All My Children, like most soaps, was organized around a troubled, prominent, upper-class white family and its interactions with another struggling, yet solid, middle-class family (the structure that had become standard in soaps since it was first used in the late 1950s by *As the World Turns*). Yet *All My Children* also dealt with issues of the day such as protests against the Vietnam War and abortion. In 1973, Erica Kane, played then, as now, by Susan Lucci, was the first soap character to have a legal abortion (abortion only became legal nationwide in January 1973 after the landmark *Roe v. Wade* decision).

Elana Levine notes, "The Soaps did occasionally deal with social issues before the 1970s, although these tended to center on illness and disease, unlike the 1970s stories, which took on more explicitly political and sexual issues" (164 n.27). Levine argues that later in the decade soaps became more focused on the problematics of rape, a crime that was being redefined in the wake of the feminist movement. Not all of the soap opera depictions were progressive or supportive of newer definitions of rape as a crime of power and not sexual desire. Most notably, on *General Hospital* in the late '70s, Laura fell in love with her rapist, Luke.

On March 26, 1973, CBS issued forth with *The Young and the Restless* and canceled *Love Is a Many Splendored Thing* and *Where the Heart Is* (the drama of youth beat out love and romance!). *The Young and the Restless* was more visually oriented than previous soap operas, using new lighting techniques, building sets with contemporary furnishings, and choosing new camera angles. The stars of the new soap were younger, photogenic actors. The show maintained the soap tradition of centering on a fractured wealthy family and its interactions with a more wholesome middle-class brood, but its "frank sexuality was new. . . . It brought daytime television directly into the middle of the sexual revolution and the cult of youth that defined the seventies" (Simon et al., 151). Gone were twin beds. Plotlines were built around rape, impotence, adultery, and premarital sex instead of middle-aged or elderly characters coping with illness. *The Young and the Restless*, like the new ABC soaps that challenged the primacy of CBS's daytime television, were fixated on young and attractive male and female leads—and sex was definitely in the air.

Elana Levine writes that *The Young and the Restless* "epitomized the mounting changes in soaps of the 1970s not only because it broke with the conventions of the typical CBS serial, but also because it featured more explicit sex scenes and sex talk than the soaps that came before it" (28). In the first episode, in 1973, a medical student and a waitress loll about on a couch, her hands draped over his thighs inches from his crotch. She shows cleavage, and his pants are 1970s tight. Snapper and Sally discuss their relationship and their lives in the small town of Genoa City. Both agree that their connection is built around sex (and not romance) and their relationship is one without commitment (we soon learn he is also dating the virginal daughter of the owner of the newspaper, who is depicted as a disagreeable patriarch trying to keep his daughter and Snapper apart). Snapper tries to convince Sally to show up late for work, and he starts his seduction. In the early '70s, older folks in the new soaps on ABC and CBS got less airtime and actors that had youthful charisma, like John and Maureen Dean (or like those who played Snapper and Sally of *The Young and the Restless*), became more prevalent.

SENATE COMMITTEE

On May 17, 1973, only a few months after *The Young and the Restless* debuted on CBS, the Senate Select Committee on Presidential Campaign Activities began to investigate the Watergate break-in and cover-up. This committee later broadened its investigation to include other alleged illegal activities of the Nixon White House and ended its first stage of investigation in late August, after 319 hours of its proceedings had been televised. According to Ronald Garay in *Congressional Television* (72), 85 percent of all Americans had watched at least some of the hearings; the citizenry was paying attention to the shenanigans of the executive branch, similar to the way we now stay tuned to the high jinks of amorous starlets or families with too many children or the folks on the Jersey Shore. The hearings laid the groundwork for the release of the White House tapes (the secret recorded conversations in the White House, whose existence John Dean suspected and was later confirmed by White House aide Alexander Butterfield). They also motivated the House of Representative's Judiciary Committee to move toward impeachment of the president; Nixon resigned on August 9, 1974. With these hearings, Americans turned against their president, and the Congress, using television as an ally, reasserted its oversight responsibilities. As Lang and Lang argue in *The Battle for Public Opinion*, "The parade of witnesses and their testimony fascinated the press, politicians and public alike" and the hearings "changed some opinions, especially about the seriousness of Watergate and Nixon's involvement" (93). The beginning of the end of Nixon's political career was performed through a nonfiction drama.

The tales told by the witnesses in the Senate Watergate Hearings—as well as the resulting tensions between the senators—were framed in such as a way as to ensure that they shared much with the genre conventions of the soap opera. For example, the hearings were staged as a search for the truth, for the revelation of secret documents and covert conversations. Soap opera plots also focus on the unraveling of buried truths such as who is the real father of a child or who is plotting against whom (or what are a character's real racial origins). These denouements take months or years to be revealed, and the process engrosses soap opera fans. In the genre, characters that were once evil are offered the chance to reform—or even to come back from the dead. Similarly, characters initially portrayed as good become tarnished, revealing duplicitous motives and criminal behavior. Narratives often revolve around the presentation of appearances versus the clandestine workings of disturbed psyches, much like the characters that populated the many narratives of Watergate. Soap operas, like political dramas, reveal pathologies of prominent people who were once believed to be normal. For example, Viki, a pillar of society in *One Life to Live*, is also Niki (a coarse low-life), as well as many other personas: Viki is revealed to have multiple personalities, and she is later diagnosed as having disassociative identity disorder. Similarly many have speculated on Nixon's paranoia (and criminality) and also George W. Bush's alcoholism and struggles with language as indicators of deep character flaws (others have hypothesized dyslexia). Viewers can rightly assume that their political leaders—and their favorite soap characters—are hiding something; one is always awaiting the removal of the mask and the revelation of the actual visage.

In an interaction during the hearings, as well as in a soap opera scene, dialogue between two characters often revolves around the misdeeds and aberrant behavior of a third, off-camera character and how much this third character knows or is involved in a particular situation. The questioning of members of the Nixon administration similarly often involved the absent character of the president and his level of knowledge of the illegal activities around him. Senator Howard Baker, a leading Republican on the committee, put it simply: "What did the president know and when did he know it?" The guilt—or innocence—of an off-camera character is classic fodder for a soap opera. Such a query also forms the basis of state intrigue. For example, during the administration of George W. Bush, one wonders if he knew that there were no weapons of mass destruction in Iraq and advocated the creation of fake intelligence or whether he actually believed in false reports that had been ordered elsewhere. With Nixon, the Senate committee was determined to find out the point at which he became aware of the cover-up of the Watergate break-in and if, in fact, he had ordered it.

Much of the camera work used during the hearings was very similar to that used in typical soap opera sequences, which follow a strict template. Sequences in the genre begin with a long two-shot that establishes the physical distance between the two main characters (usually within a home or a hospital or another workplace); then there is a medium close-up with the protagonist speaking. This is followed by a reaction shot, often an extreme close-up, of the antagonist with the protagonist's voice heard as a voice-off. In short, in shot formation and sequence, the televised hearings mimicked the style of the soap opera genre, with a strict, predictable rhythm and blocking that keeps characters' movements within a scene to a minimum. In soap operas, if an actor moves to a mark in a scene, he or she will usually stay there for the remainder of the scene; the movement within a sequence is usually reliant on switching between the perspectives of the cameras. In today's soaps, the over-the-shoulder shot predominates in scenes between two characters; in the early '70s, the camera faced the actor in a mid- or extreme close-up.

The camera work at the hearings, which also used close-ups and focused on moving between perspectives, cued the viewer into experiencing the program as a drama, albeit a nonfiction one. Like trained actors, witnesses and their lawyers refrained from direct address into the camera lens, but they always played for the cameras. The sworn testimony of witnesses and questioning by the senators were treated as if they were drama. Everyone on camera—even if they were granted immunity—was guilty of performing in the national soap opera.

Soap operas were broadcast live until the late '60s, and their production history influences how they are filmed to this day. Soaps are now recorded live to tape. Robert Allen wrote in his 1985 *Speaking of Soap Operas* that "while scenes might be recorded out of their eventual sequence in the episode, each scene is enacted and recorded on videotape only once. Editing is done at the time of recording by switching between the shots being simultaneously taken by three television cameras" (66). In other words, scenes are shot as if they are live events; what the viewer may experience as a cut between shots is actually a decision by the director to move to another camera's perspective rather than something spliced together by the editor later. Watergate was also shot using three cameras. The live feed of the Senate hearings and the live tape version of a soap opera are remarkably similar both in structure and in effect; one camera is used to give a perspective of the room, another is set up to focus on the protagonist (John or Maureen Dean), and the third is aimed at the antagonist (one of the senators).

Almost all of the scenes in a soap opera are shot in a studio (scenes are rarely set on location). The studio's sets are almost entirely domestic spaces, and unlike films or nighttime television, sequences do not begin with an outdoor establishing shot. Each scene begins with an interior shot, usually of a large living room, in which two characters are entering or already presenting. Likewise, the style in which the Senate Watergate Hearings was filmed foregrounds that the action occurred in a specific, enclosed space. There are no establishing shots of Washington, DC, or the Capitol Building, which are part of the way congressional hearings are shot today. Watergate was drawing-room fare, and as such it had a familiar look for daytime viewers, particularly since soap opera sets in the '70s favored dark wood and brown leather, similar to the furnishings seen in the hearings, in order to convey opulence and the wealth of their characters. It shunned the use of exterior location shots (which are more common in today's soaps).

Congressional hearings are no longer televised to highlight the theatricality of the event. There is minimal use of extreme close-ups, and instead a split screen is often used, dividing the screen between questioner and nominee. For example, CNN's coverage of the 2005 Samuel Alito Supreme Court confirmation hearings emphasized the tediousness of the event. The screen was often split into six panels (perhaps an unconscious homage to *Hollywood Squares!*). Each panel showed the same moment from different angles (two were of the Capitol Building and the Supreme Court). Although in this format the six panels were dynamic, the image in total was one of stasis (except for the incessant crawl of breaking news and temperatures at the bottom of the screen that CNN started using after 9/11; the crawl has now been replaced by what CNN calls a "flipper"). Throughout the hearing, the camera remained stationary and did not vary its angle on the subject. It didn't zoom in for a close-up very often, and there were no cuts between characters. The distance between antagonist and protagonist was not defined, and reaction shots of the audience that served to animate the room were rare.

As a result, compared to the more traditional camera work used in the '70s to broadcast the government in action, today CNN's use of technical innovation decreases the amount of dramatic tension in the event; the camera work does not emphasize the drama inherent in a congressional hearing. Heavily influenced by recent Web design, CNN's composite image foregrounds the workings of the government as a spectacle for the audience to behold and prohibits the site from becoming one of intimate storytelling. Contemporary broadcast design—on twenty-four-hour news channels especially—obstructs its viewer from becoming close to the event and the event's participants. One stares at a surface and is encouraged to look at the facades of the government. The government appears impenetrable, akin to a Web site on the Internet in which the user can no longer control the mouse and cursor. The viewer is kept out of the crossfire and is never positioned in the middle of the action.

THE NETWORK'S DUTY

As the Senate hearings of 1973 occurred before the popularization of cable television and the rise of twenty-four-hour news cable stations, the major networks' news departments (which have less power within the network structure now) felt duty-bound to present the hearings. This important national event could prove the involvement of the president in either the break-in at Watergate or the subsequent cover-up. Even though in many ways the hearings were set up for the television cameras (there was also plenty of room set aside for newspaper reporters), the networks couldn't break for commercials during the live feed of the proceedings. Yet the hearings stopped for two hours during lunch, and senators took fifteen-minute breaks when they had go to the Senate floor to vote. Industry experts estimated that the networks were "losing" about one hundred thousand dollars in revenue per hour. The networks complained about this loss—even though the FCC informed broadcasters in its 1960 Program Policy Statement that they were entrusted to operate in the "public interest, convenience and necessity" (a key principle of the private use of the public airwaves that was eroded by deregulation in the 1980s).

In order to both serve the interest of the public and avoid losing too much advertising revenue, the commercial networks reached an agreement to present the hearings on a rotating basis. Meanwhile, most public television stations showed a videotaped version at night. Researchers at PBS found that its audience almost doubled during the evening hours, making Watergate the first nighttime soap opera since *Peyton Place* in the mid- to late 1960s. *Dynasty* and *Dallas* followed in the 1980s and focused on the shenanigans of corporate men in the petroleum industry instead of government officials, alluding perhaps to the virtual takeover of the United States by an oil oligarchy.

Unlike public broadcasting, commercial networks' audience dropped by 25 percent during the hearings. Most of the daytime audiences stuck with the government-sponsored programming, but many were disgruntled with the hearings. Some felt that Watergate was inferior daytime fare and yearned for the return of their daily soap operas. The agreement between the commercial networks to rotate coverage lasted from June 5 to September 28; then each network decided when and if it wanted to broadcast the hearings.

This agreement was temporarily interrupted when former White House counsel John Dean came before the committee. Each network showed the full Dean testimony on a live feed, which occurred over five days, June 25–29, one day longer than planned. His testimony served as the climax of the hearings. Dean had earlier asserted that he refused to become the fall guy for the administration, and there was great anticipation around his testimony and the activity of his lawyers to supply him with immunity for it. Dean was found guilty for his involvement in the cover-up. He was ultimately sentenced to only four months by Judge John Sirica of the United States District Court and spent those months in a witness protection program in order to ensure his safety. He feared for his life, and the court took the threats against him and his wife seriously.

In his testimony, Dean implicated the president, asserting that Nixon had discussed the cover-up with him as early as September 15, 1972, in the midst of his reelection campaign. Dean also depicted the culture and

characteristics of the Nixon White House as those of paranoia and excesses of power that involved surveillance and fear of potential plots.
The White House took seriously every real or imagined adversary, using
its power against anyone who was perceived as a threat to the administration. For example, plans were devised by White House employees (in
this case, Howard Hunt) to use prostitutes at the Democratic National
Convention as a way to collect information on Democratic Party strategies. (It was later alleged in an unpublished book entitled "Silent Coup"
that Dean's wife, Maureen, was herself a prostitute. The Deans successfully sued the publisher for libel, blocking publication.)

Howard Hunt advocated direct retaliation against the administration's "enemies" and recommended hiring professional kidnappers to
permanently deport leaders of the antiwar movement to Mexico. Similar
tactics were used within the George W. Bush administration: when someone within the White House revealed that the wife of a former diplomat
who disputed the administration's intelligence findings was a CIA agent
(the Scooter Libby/Valerie Plame case), they were following in the tradition of the Nixon White House. For members of Bush's and Nixon's co-
teries, one attacks one's domestic enemies and does not break bread with
them. This is why Dick Cheney said "go fuck yourself" to Senator Patrick
Leahy, Democrat, of Vermont, when the senator invited Cheney to come
and meet casually with other Democratic senators in 2004.

As White House counsel, Dean actively participated in some illegal,
unethical activities (including payoffs) while apparently making some
recommendations against a few of the more egregiously illegal and de-
vious tactics. He asserted that he was nothing more than a legal errand
boy for the White House. Yet he was also the author of some nebulous
documents, including an August 1971 memo entitled "Dealing with Our
Political Enemies," which encouraged the White House to take advantage of its privileges and its command of the CIA, FBI, and other agen-
cies in order to go after its perceived adversaries.

Back in 1972 White House assertions of innate power were a precur-
sor to recent proclamations of the unitary executive theory during the
George W. Bush administration. This theory disavows any notion of judicial supremacy and asserts that the president must also interpret the
law. The Bush administration reinterpreted the Constitution to flaunt its
authority over the Congress, even after the Democrats regained control
of the Congress in the election of 2006. The rise of the theory of the unitary executive can be seen as a reaction to the protections put in place after the Nixon era, such as the Foreign Information Surveillance Act

(FISA) courts (recently superseded and updated by George W. Bush with congressional support to allow for warrantless wiretapping) and the War Powers Act of 1973.

With the Watergate Hearings, and the turning of the scandals of the president into popular programming, the Congress was able to limit the power of the executive branch. The Nixon government had become a rogue regime, in ways that were similar to George W. Bush's administration smirking at Congress's oversight responsibilities. Today's Congress, unlike the Congress of 1973, has mostly acquiesced to presidential assertions. Congress during the Bush years was not only not doing its job by appearing weak; it was also denying the citizenry good television. Arguably, the citizenry/audience in 2007 wanted the Congress to take on the president via media programming the way it did in 1973. Power struggles between the three branches of government make good programming, and the Republicans in the Senate during the first year of the Obama administration proved to be quite proficient at heightening antagonism, as was seen during the recent struggle for health care reform.

John Dean authored the famous phrase told to Nixon and repeated under testimony: "There is a cancer growing on the presidency." He wanted his boss, and later the public, to believe that he was trying to act like a whistle-blower who was virtually unable to utter a sound. Even against obstacles, Dean struggled to convey that he worked to stop this "cancer" from spreading. His enemies at the White House after the investigation heated up, John Ehrlichman and H. R. Haldeman (sometimes referred to as the "Prussians" due to their Teutonic heritage), alleged otherwise. They accused Dean of being the architect of the cover-up, not its messenger. They also claimed that Dean never truly informed Nixon of the extent of the illegal activity around him.

DEAN'S STORY AND HOW HE STUCK TO IT

John Dean was the son of a Firestone Tire executive in Ohio—certainly a Nixon supporter's demographic, even though Dean admitted attending an early antiwar demonstration. Dean did not excel in his legal studies, but he was ambitious. He married a senator's daughter, and his father-in-law provided him with entry into the Washington elite, even though the marriage didn't last. Dean was fired from his first job at a major firm after only six months due to possible unethical conduct involving applications for FCC licenses, but his connections (and his good looks) ensured that he was still a golden boy. He moved into the public sector. He was hired as minority counsel for the Senate Judiciary Committee. Although he didn't particularly distinguish himself, after one year he was made associate director of the National Commission on the Reform of Federal Criminal Laws. As luck would have it, he then worked on changes to the law that would allow prosecutors to offer partial immunity to witnesses—a provision from which he would later benefit.

In 1969, Dean became an associate deputy attorney general under Attorney General John Mitchell. When John Ehrlichman was promoted from White House Counsel to Chief Domestic Policy Adviser, Dean was asked by him to move from the Justice Department to the White House. Dean took the job, though he was unsure what constituted his duties. He shunned driving around in a White House limo, using his Porsche sports car instead, and dressed in custom-made suits that fit his lean frame well. He was youngish and had a "pretty boy" appearance compared to Ehrlichman and Haldeman, who looked like career military men and were clearly aging. They were tough guys. Dean was more elegant and seemingly more intellectual. They were character actors and, like Nixon, had faces with big features. In contrast, Dean was a leading man with a handsome profile. On daytime television, his type is always the romantic hero—neither too macho nor too effeminate—a lover, not a fighter. He was the stranger who comes to town, gets all sorts of attention, and woos the local girl, to the dismay of the townspeople, who eventually turn on him.

At the hearings his loyal and understatedly glamorous new wife always flanked Dean. Maureen Dean was perfectly prepared for the cameras. At the beginning of the second day of his testimony, she turned to a female reporter sitting behind her to correct her age—the reporter had written in an article she was in her early thirties. Maureen tersely informed the reporter that she was in fact twenty-seven years old. Maureen and John had been married for eight months at this time (he notoriously borrowed $4,850 from a safe that contained unused reelection funds to pay for his honeymoon). She was a former airline stewardess and insurance saleswoman who had been married twice before, once to a bigamist (she had not known of his existing marriage). Her second husband died in a car accident. When she moved to Washington to be with John, she worked at the National Commission on Marihuana and Drug Use. Maureen Dean enjoyed the limelight that the Senate hearings afforded her, even though hers was a mostly silent role. She gained attention by appearing both glamorous and supportive—sitting patiently

John Dean with his wife, Maureen, sit quietly during a lull in Watergate Hearings. (Photo by Gjon Mili/Time Life Pictures/ Getty Images.)

during the proceedings, pouring her husband water, and providing him with hot tea to keep his voice going.

Unlike other witnesses' wives, Maureen was constantly at her husband's side. She smiled or laughed at all his jokes. On the first day she dressed in tones similar to the color of his suits, accentuating her loyalty, and on subsequent days wore sunnier colors such as yellow or red melon in order to brighten up the proceedings and attract some attention of her own. Maureen was a crucial part of the public relations effort mounted by Dean's lawyers—her loyalty to her husband elevated his status and increased his believability. He was no untrustworthy bachelor; he was a devoted husband to a stylish, photogenic wife who showed the cameras that she loved him by the way she kept her unflinching gaze on him.

Maureen later wrote her own book about her early years in Washington, entitled *"Mo," a Woman's View of Watergate* (1975). During the hearings, Maureen was conscious of cultivating an elegant, sexy look that supported and complemented her husband's appearance and manner in every way. They were a powerful Washington couple with a dazzling future as guests and hosts of elite parties. They paraded their obvious attraction to each other in front of the cameras. They were patriotic, young heterosexuals in love, and they looked like soap stars—WASPy, reasonably affluent, and upwardly mobile—and in Washington they were poised to become power brokers and socialites.

Dean proved to be a master storyteller who exuded a credibility factor on television, unlike Nixon, who never quite found the lighting or makeup to give him the right kind of sheen. Media theorist Marshall McLuhan always claimed that Nixon was too hot a figure—meaning Nixon had an intensity more appropriate for radio—and was not suited for the cool medium of television. For McLuhan this was made most clear in the 1960 presidential debates between Nixon and John F. Kennedy. On radio, listeners thought Nixon won the debate, but television viewers thought that Kennedy had given a better performance (perhaps because Nixon was wearing a self-tanning product that began to melt under the harsh studio lights). Nixon was not a handsome man, and indeed cartoonists made great use of his ski slope of a nose. Yet he developed his own presidential stature, and he was successful in the way he evoked the silent majority, which he claimed to represent. He was not beloved, but his patrician devotion to his country contributed to his popularity.

Dean took on the president. In turning against the commander in chief and trying to appear as if he was acting in the interest of the greater good (and not merely saving his own skin), he became a star of the hearings. People began lining up at one in the morning for seats in the Senate Hall. Dean used levity even when talking of illegal activities; he deployed his sturdy baritone and lack of audible regional accent to advantage. He had a slight whistle that accompanied his s sounds (perfect for a "whistle-blower") that served to humanize his otherwise perfect diction. He was just right for media performance. He was immediately recognizable to the television audience. If his hairline was receding, he was by no means bald, which is a decided no-no for newsmen (often leading to some unfortunate hairpieces). His appearance and vocal delivery, if they were lawyerlike, were also youthful. According to Lang and Lang in The Battle for Public Opinion (75), Dean studied his performance during a Walter Cronkite interview in order to avoid coming across as "too cocky, too nervous, too mousy, too young." Sam Dash, the lawyer who advised Senator Sam Ervin and the Democrats on the panel, recommended that Dean stop using his contact lenses during his testimony and put on the horn-rimmed glasses that he had long stopped using. Such devices proved successful. According to a Harris poll, which asked respondents: "If it came down to it, and President Nixon denied John Dean's charges, who do you think has been more truthful about the Watergate cover-up—President Nixon or John Dean?" (Lang and Lang 77), 38 percent found Dean more believable, only 27 percent trusted Nixon, and 25 percent remained undecided. Dean's image makeover allowed him to appear and sound more truthful. The glasses worked—after all a studious bespectacled fellow is considered more trustworthy than a vainglorious pretty boy.

Not surprisingly, Dean has a career in media to this day. He had much to say about the Bush administration in his book *Worse Than Watergate* (2005). He continued his attack on the conservative movement in *Conservatives without Conscience* (2006), which became a best seller, number three on Amazon.com in its first week. In his preface he recounts how he was motivated to return to political commentary by the book that accused Maureen of being a prostitute and him of being the architect of the Watergate cover-up. He successfully reached a settlement with the publisher of this libelous book and realized that he could never successfully leave the political arena after his involvement in the Watergate saga and the enemies he made who would never forgive him. The preface is a tale in which he learns to accept this fate. Although he is still a conservative, he is only heard on liberal media, speaking out against the neoconservatives and the Bush administration on Keith Olbermann's MSNBC show, and was heard on Air America radio before the liberal radio network ended. He updated his Watergate memoir, *Blind Ambition*, in 2009, adding a new foreword.

CAST MEMBERS

The Senate committee was headed by Sam Ervin. Ervin was a southern Democrat from North Carolina and a venerable conservative who espoused prosegregationist views and called himself "a country lawyer." He was also known for his belief that the executive branch of government had become too powerful, especially in relation to the legislative branch. Watergate proved his point. Ervin had remarkably expressive eyebrows, arched in such a way that he appeared to move from surprise to shock with the smallest involuntary twitch on his large face.

Ervin's deputy was Howard Baker, a moderate from Tennessee and a rising star within the Republican Party. He had been on the short list to be Nixon's running mate and turned down requests to become a Supreme Court judge. He had presidential aspirations. In 1973 *Time* magazine essayist Stefan Kanfer remarked on the dramatic potential in the "casting" of the panel: "There has never been a grandfatherly figure quite like Senator Ervin. His face is a cast in itself. . . . Opposing this septuagenarian, Senator Howard Baker, Jr., 47, gives the impression of a leading man who has just come from musical comedy to his first dramatic role. Baker's style finds itself in the magisterial pause."

Baker and Ervin not only had disparate personality traits and ideological perspectives, but they also contrasted visually: Baker was a youngish, chiseled, leading man; and Ervin was a distinguished, if overlooked, character actor who teetered at the edge of caricature. They personified what was then referred to as the "generation gap." Their differences animated the committee, and their affection for each other became endearing. They laughed at each other's jokes and whispered into each other's ears. Columnist Kanfer suggests that the committee was made up of different members of a kinship network (like the powerful family depicted in a soap opera). The hearings often appeared as the squabble of an extended wealthy family, where the female members had been barred from entering the smoking room of the ancestral home. Television coverage allowed women a vantage point onto this heretofore all-male terrain of senators at work. And the presence of Maureen Dean provided women an entry point into this drama. Her chic presence stood out dramatically.

The rest of the committee was diverse and surprisingly multicultural for the Senate—both for the early '70s and for now. The committee featured Daniel Inouye, a senator from Hawaii who had lost an arm in the Second World War and was the first Japanese American in the Senate (in a racist outbreak Haldeman's lawyer referred to him as "a little Jap"). It also included Joseph Montoya, a Hispanic senator from New Mexico, who received some derision in the press for asking somewhat inane questions (e.g., he asked Dean if he was happy). Both were Democrats. The remaining Democrat was Herman Talmadge from Georgia, another southern prosegregationist Democrat. Lowell Weicker, a liberal Republican from Connecticut, quickly distinguished himself as a maverick on the committee. He asked the most pointed questions, reflecting his extensive knowledge of the case (he had hired his own investigation team). A patrician Republican senator, Ed Gurney from Florida, completed the panel. Dean testified that Nixon believed Gurney was the only completely loyal senator. During the hearings, Gurney grilled

Dean, especially on his use of White House funds. Yet later that same year Gurney was indicted for illegal campaign activity and did not run for reelection in 1974.

The Democratic Party was the majority party in the Senate in 1973, and as a result it held four of the seven seats on the committee. However, party membership did not necessarily correspond to allegiance to the Republican president: Weicker was considered the most critical voice on the panel, and he was subject to much surveillance by the White House. Two lawyers joined the senators: Sam Dash (a professorial-looking northerner and son of a Russian immigrant) was majority counsel, and Fred Thompson (a pipe-smoking southerner with lamb chop sideburns that suggested he might also be an Elvis impersonator) was counsel for the minority. Fred Thompson continued to have a dynamic career in the spotlight: he became a senator from Tennessee and also has had a successful acting career, appearing on *Law and Order* as a district attorney. In 2006, Thompson left the hit television show in order to run for president as a conservative Republican, although his campaign was brief.

The Watergate scandal began during the 1972 presidential campaign between Richard Nixon and George McGovern. Although Nixon was ahead in the polls, the Committee to Re-elect the President (first known as CRP and then widely referred to as CREEP) bugged the headquarters of the Democratic National Committee, which was housed at the Watergate Hotel in Washington, DC. On June 17, 1972, African American security guard Frank Wills (the unsung hero of Watergate) was making his nighttime rounds in the hotel and noticed masking tape blocking the lock of a door. He subsequently found that other locks were taped open. He contacted the police. The police followed the trail of masking tape and arrested a group of men—three anti-Castro Cuban Americans who had been involved in the Bay of Pigs invasion (one, Frank Sturgis, had actually started his military career as a pro-Castro revolutionary) and two ex-CIA operatives. Two of the burglars had the contact number of Howard Hunt in their address books. Hunt was a longtime CIA operative and writer of espionage novels who would later be named as one of the "White House Plumbers" (whose job was to plug information leaks in the White House). One burglar was James McCord, a security consultant and ex-CIA agent who admitted to working for CRP. The burglars were breaking into the Watergate not to install surveillance equipment but to fix wiretaps that were not working well. They forgot to cover their tracks in their second break-in.

Clearly the stage was set for implicating the president—or at least his reelection campaign, which was headed by John Mitchell, who had stepped down as attorney general—in the break-in. Yet it took over two years for investigations, both by the press (in particular the *Washington Post* and most notably by Carl Bernstein and Bob Woodward—who themselves became star journalists) and by the legislative and judicial branches of government, to bring about the resignation of the president. The cover-up was successful in ensuring that the details of the break-in were not investigated until after the election. The truth of the event was slow to emerge. The revealing of the engineer of the plot to put the Democratic Party under surveillance—and the solving of the mystery of the cover up—took two years to unfold and was never entirely conclusive. As a result, as with so many events in American history, it remains fodder for conspiracy theorists.

NIXON AND MEDIA

In 1972 television news barely covered the Watergate story. For example, on weekday evening newscasts of the three major networks, Watergate was mentioned only in a third of the broadcasts in the last six months of 1972. Yet in the first half of the following year, after the election, coverage more than doubled and Watergate-related stories received over 23 percent of all news time in '73 (Capo, 597–99). As most Americans relied on television to get their news, and because news coverage had all but ignored the story during the reelection campaign, the networks were complicit with the White House cover-up. The cover-up ensured that Nixon won the 1972 election by a landslide. In 1973, however, the networks were able to turn the Watergate story into a televisual event, rather than just the subject of investigative journalism. At the time of his second inauguration, Nixon received a 68 percent approval rating. Yet American voters had been barred from critical knowledge. The media, particularly television, ensured that voters did not know that the incumbent's administration was implicated in illegal domestic surveillance and obstruction of justice. However, soon after he was reelected, Nixon's administration came under heated investigation.

Nixon's popularity dropped quickly. He suffered not only because of news leaks and investigations but also for his handling of the Vietnam War, which is arguably the backstory of Watergate. The Vietnam War was a conflict that Nixon both inherited and accelerated. Aggression by the United States (in particular the bombings) was not proving successful in ending the war, although it officially ended with the signing of the Paris Peace Accords on January 27, 1973. The conflict in Southeast Asia went on. For example, on the third day of John Dean's testimony (June 27), Nixon was able to sustain his veto of a House bill that defunded the ongoing bombing of Cambodia. The bombing continued.

In Nixon's first four years in office, 20,695 men and women in the U.S. armed forces died in Vietnam. Total casualties of the war from 1965 to 1973 are estimated at over one and a half million people in Vietnam alone. Nixon also expanded the war to Cambodia and Laos, especially via bombing campaigns. Although he had promised to end the war in his campaign in 1968, it is likely that, working through Henry Kissinger, Nixon encouraged the South Vietnamese delegation to back out of the peace talks of that same year, promising them increased financial and military aid. Even if such allegations are not true, Nixon did prolong the unpopular conflict, and the public began to turn against him.

Domestic rebellions and political protest against the war no doubt triggered a response from Nixon to solidify his power and weaken his perceived enemies. Presidential historian Arthur Schlesinger traced the rise of the executive branch and referred to Nixon's administration as *The Imperial Presidency* (1989). Indeed, Nixon increased the number of White House staff in order to insulate himself, and he put his yes-men to work to silence dissident voices. One of the activities of these yes-men was to compile a list of enemies, which was released to the Senate committee by John Dean. The list was extensive. It named almost anyone of prominence who had spoken against the administration, and it included Schlesinger himself, who was by no means a political radical. He was "guilty" of being a prominent liberal.

The Watergate investigation brought the mentality of Nixon and his aides to the public's attention. It ensured that Nixon's government—even as its members believed themselves to be under siege for exercising power that was rightly theirs—also provided thrilling fodder for the media. Exposing the paranoid culture of the White House became a national pastime. After all, providing content for media programming is a crucial part of the president's job description, even if it is not in the Constitution. It is one of the most important aspects of the president's portfolio, especially if he has been reelected. Watergate card games and board games were sold. Watergate puzzles (which featured "bugs"), Watergate dartboards and chess sets, and Watergate comedy albums were rushed into stores. Even Folkways, the branch of the Smithsonian that issues recordings of America's folkloric heritage, came out with an album of John Dean's testimony to the Senate Committee. Nixon's excesses fueled popular culture and the entertainment and gaming industry: in spite of the recession brought about by OPEC and the government's fiscal and energy policies, Nixon's transgressions were good for business.

This role of the presidency—as national emcee—has been especially central since the presidency of Franklin Delano Roosevelt, who used radio to command a nationwide presence. President Bill Clinton, even as the Lewinsky scandal undermined his agenda, remained successful in starring in an unfolding drama. The scandal, however salacious, was perfect for nighttime drama. It reinforced Clinton's lustfulness, which was part of his appeal for the populace. In Nixon's case, Watergate served to highlight characteristics of his political personality—or pathology. Such traits—a Shakespearean mix of ambition and paranoia—had been evident ever since the fake humility of his Checkers speech, when he saved his vice presidency in the face of allegations of wrongdoing. Nixon may not have added sex appeal to his role, like Clinton or Kennedy, but at least he was imperious: he lived as if laws were for the little people. He craved achieving and maintaining power with an obsession that would justify the histrionics of Sir Anthony Hopkins in an Oliver Stone movie called *Nixon* (1994).

BROADCAST DESIGN

The coverage of day 1 by ABC (June 25, 1973) began with newscaster Frank Reynolds explaining to the viewer that this was not ABC's scheduled day to cover the hearings, but because of the importance of the event, the network had decided to broadcast live along with the other networks. Dean's testimony and the numerous leaks that preceded it were receiving more coverage than the conclusion of the visit of Leonid Brezhnev, the Soviet leader, who was in town after a round of meetings with the president. In a concession to its president, the Senate had delayed Dean's testimony one week so that it didn't totally eclipse the summit between the Soviet leader and Nixon.

The coverage begins with Reynolds in a medium shot (we see his torso and face behind a desk) in front of a bold blue background. Behind him the word *Watergate* is repeated in a large white font with a block serif across the background in crowded rows, each repetition of the sturdily presented word separated by a large white dot. This background—and its then-trendy typeface—serves to celebrate the scandal as a media event, not only as a political scandal that the medium of television happens to be covering. Designwise, it lends excitement to the introduction to the hearings and suggests, in its repetition, that Watergate is part of the programming of the network.

Reynolds wears an off-white suit with a wide lapel, a pale yellow shirt, and a dark brown tie with a wide knot. His look reflects some of the changes in men's fashion that occurred in the late '60s and '70s, when the look for anchors became less conservative and men in the media no longer needed to dress like lawyers in dark colors with a traditional cut (a "hip" '70s anchorman was lampooned and celebrated in the 2004 film *Anchorman*). Of course, nowadays men's attire in the news profession has become much more conservative again—even Rachel Maddow has been tidied up for her nightly show on MSNBC. Newscasters look—and act—like solemn businessmen or businesswomen once more (or irate Everymen as on Fox News). The early '70s brought about a loosening of the restrictions on dress, which matched the more colorful use of broadcast design. These changes signaled a transformation in the coverage of hard news, accenting its value as entertainment.

Meanwhile Reynolds's colleague, Sam Donaldson, is outside the Senate's Old Caucus Room. In a long shot, we see his entire frame (and the beginnings of his ill-advised comb-over). He is wearing a silver gray suit, with a pink shirt, and a dark gray tie with a swirling pattern. His suit also has wide lapels, and his appearance shows that the changes in men's haberdashery had influenced reporters' attire as well as that of the anchorman. Donaldson remarks that there is standing room only and "an air of excitement" as everyone is waiting for the entrance of the Senate committee and its star witness. He, too, appears excited.

Donaldson remarks dramatically to Reynolds that "Dean's testimony drives to the Presidency." A dialogue between the two casually dressed young newsmen ensues about the importance of the day and the allegations that might arise through Dean's testimony. Their conversation is also a brazen attempt to encourage the viewer to stay tuned to the ensuing drama. As the conversation finishes, the camera follows the entrance of the venerable Sam Ervin into the wood-paneled room.

In an extreme long shot we see the members of the Senate committee as they assemble in their designated seats at the lengthy and wide conference table, which is covered with a green cloth. This table is across from the witness stand, a small table with two brown leather chairs. The witness's two lawyers sit behind the witness table, and next to them on the right sits Dean's wife Maureen. Reporter Douglas Kneeland of the *New York Times* described Maureen Dean's appearance and placement as if he were writing for the society or fashion page: "His attractive wife, in a light gold dress, her hair done up in an honest bun, was placed behind him at an angle the cameras would frequently catch. The attorneys sat beside her in a less advantageous position for the cameras" (30). One doesn't know how a hair bun could appear "dishonest," but it is worth noting that, for the *Times* reporter at least, her coiffure signified truthfulness and propriety in its austere formation—there was nothing in Maureen's appearance that indicated she was a deceitful prostitute.

The *Times* also reported that Maureen was not only there to provide a background to a medium shot or as a composed presence in a two-shot. She was an active presence. At one point, she passed a note to her husband via his lawyers as he was reading his six-hour opening statement. Apparently the note read, "I know you are conserving your voice, but be as forceful as possible" (in *New York Times* 1973, 30). Maureen also influenced fashion; women contacted chief counsel Sam Dash for information about how to arrange their hair like hers. The pulled-back hair and "honest bun" were a hit. A key part of the success of John Dean's testimony was the presentation of his wife; she sat elegantly on her perch behind her husband. Like him she became a daytime star.

John Dean's two lawyers, Charles Shaffer and Robert McCandless, were also very colorful figures who often appeared in a long shot that placed John Dean in the foreground and located the two lawyers alongside Maureen. Robert McCandless wore large, heavy, black rectangular-framed glasses that dominated his dark-featured face. Shaffer was fair-haired, lean, and dashing—he favored silver-gray suits and brighter ties than McCandless. His glasses were wire framed. The two lawyers listened actively and responded to the proceedings by whispering into each other's ears or by passing notes to each other and then to John Dean. Shaffer was often seen writing notes on his legal pad. The two also made themselves available for interviews during breaks, with McCandless referring to himself as "No-Comment McCandless." Shaffer had been a special assistant to Robert F. Kennedy, and McCandless was Dean's former brother-in-law, so each had a special reason to defend Dean against the Republican media blitz that attempted to cast their client as a turncoat or worse.

Time magazine reported that the Deans and their two lawyers became close during the hearings—and they often shared the same long shot, which made it appear as if all four were a cohesive unit, with John

Dean as its spokesperson. According to the *Time* issue of July 9, 1973, each night the four of them returned to the Dean's Alexandria home, where Maureen made hamburgers for the guys as they watched news coverage of the day's testimony. Each took notes, knowing that their struggle against the president was a matter of public relations and corporate communications. Dean's cocounsels would not let him watch the taped rebroadcasts of his testimony though, which was shown on PBS each night (13). They were more concerned with how the testimony was being reported on the evening news than with evaluating Dean's performance themselves. Then, the magazine reports, after watching the coverage, Dean took a hot bath and Maureen gave him a back rub. Dean reported that he slept soundly each night (presumably after the couple made love). The Deans' attraction to each other—as well as their attractiveness—was a key device they used to influence public opinion.

Maureen recounted the evenings slightly differently—she remembers eating hamburgers with Sam Dash, the Democratic lawyer who advised the panel, eschewing the two lawyers. Maureen disliked McCandless, who tried to get Dean to sign a statement that would entitle the lawyer to a percentage of all future royalties from his books. Perhaps *Time* was seduced by the romance of the Deans that their legal team generated, a team that operated like a public relations firm as well as legal counsel.

During the Dean testimony in the Old Caucus Room, the flock of photographers gathered between the witness table and the senators, in order to get the best shot of the chair and the witness. In Dean's case the witness's wife was also of special concern, and her every movement, even those as simple as putting a cough drop in her mouth, was punctuated by a series of clicks. Television cameras were located in three corners of the room. Although they never appear in any shot, the cameras provided the viewer with a variety of angles, pans, zooms, and shots, and served to define the room, even as they kept the focus on Dean by returning to his face in a medium close-up. His close-up was in a slight profile that focused on the left side of his face but still showed both of his eyes (an important aspect of close-ups).

This camera setup was similar to that used at the Army-McCarthy Hearings conducted by the Senate in 1954. These hearings were set up to investigate whether there was wrongdoing on the part of Roy Cohn in trying to influence the army's treatment of David Schine, another member of McCarthy's staff who had been drafted (it was also rumored that Cohn and Schine were lovers or that Cohn was smitten with the upper-class WASP). Tom Doherty notes in his book on the televising of the Mc-Carthy hearings, "Three cameras were situated strategically about the hearing room: one at the rear of the room, facing the committee at its long table; one behind the committee table and facing the witness table and the spectators; and one at the one side of the room that pivoted at various angles" (200). Doherty adds that the subcommittee permitted "the construction of a three-tiered platform" for the cameras and re-arranged the seating arrangements for the benefit of adding drama, "placing the McCarthy and Army sides right next to each other to ac-commodate camera coverage" (200). In other words, the design of Sen-ate Caucus Room 318 was virtually turned into a television studio for the cameras, serving as a precedent for the ways in which the Senate's Watergate Hearings were filmed.

In starting the Watergate proceedings, Ervin bangs on his gavel on the conference table. After procedural items are discussed, Ervin invites Dean to read from his text, even though each senator already has a copy of the statement—it is clearly for the benefit of the viewer so that he or she can also have access to Dean's "novel." The *New York Times* reporter Douglas Kneeland referred to Dean's remarks as "telling his story to a watching nation," highlighting the fact that Dean's audience is not only in the room but also those tuning in their homes. The use of the word *story* in the headline also underlines the narrative aspect of the over 250 pages of Dean's opening remarks. Dean tells a tale of how he was un-wittingly drawn into the cover-up and increasingly concerned by the ac-tivities around him. He acknowledges his involvement, but he accuses his former colleagues of complicity and obstruction of justice. If he was guilty, others were more so.

Although the camera focuses on Dean's face during his recitation, the broadcast also includes a variety of shots that serve to enliven this reading and provide the responses of the various characters in the room. These shots include an over-the-shoulder shot from behind Dean look-ing at Chairman Ervin (the over-the-shoulder shot is a fixture on the soap opera); a medium close-up of Senator Inouye and other senators, especially Ervin; a two-shot of Dean's lawyers; a pan shot moving from the audience to Dean; an extreme close-up of Maureen Dean; a shot of photographers who are shooting the Deans; and views of the audience that focus on a particular person who is listening avidly. The camera-people used over twenty different perspectives to film the reading of Dean's opening statement. The rather static event is given movement by the camera, adding drama to the witness's reading. Nonetheless the cameras rely heavily on Dean's talking head. They remain on it for periods of up to two minutes, then cut away for up to five seconds to get an expressive reaction shot, and then return to Dean.

During the period of testimony that involved the senators or the committee's lawyers questioning Dean, far fewer shots and angles were involved than during Dean's opening remarks. Instead the cameras focused more heavily on close-ups of either the witness or the interviewer. As in a soap opera, extreme close-ups are reserved for particularly dramatic moments that serve to end a sequence. For example, when Dean is asked by Senator Montoya to discuss his meeting with the president of September 15, the camera moves into an extreme close-up of Dean's face. A few beads of sweat become discernible on the right side of Dean's forehead, emphasizing the intensity of the conflict of emotion he feels in incriminating his president. As Dean continues to speak, the screen cuts to Montoya's response, also shown in an extreme close-up. Previously his face was seen in a medium close-up (one that included his shoulders). The senator looks as if he believes the witness's rendition of the story, as if he has heard it before. This camera usage accentuates that Dean has reached a particularly dramatic moment where his loyalty to the president is completely broken, and that the witness is being truthful, though he is troubled.

Senator Gurney, the president's most loyal senator, grills John Dean on the third day of testimony. He focuses not only on Dean's rendition of the cover-up but also on the circumstances of Dean's firing from a law firm and on the fact that Dean "borrowed" from leftover funds that were kept in a safe in Dean's office. Gurney is relentless, showing some talent as a trial lawyer, attempting to show that Dean is a liar and unscrupulous. In short he tries to suggest that Dean is himself the cancer within the presidency. In his testimony, Dean's uneasiness is not revealed through even the tiniest beads of sweat. Thus, extreme close-ups of his face will not work to reveal Dean's tension. Rather, his hands, which at times begin to fidget, with his right fingers clutching his pen for dear life, show his nervousness. His face and the timbre of his voice remain steady. In reading John Dean's account in *Blind Ambition* it is very clear how conscious he was of the way he was depicting himself and also the degree to which his lawyers—and his wife—were whispering in his ear, offering him directions.

One line of questioning begins with a two-shot consisting of John and Maureen Dean. Maureen sits behind him, and she shifts in her seat, as if to readjust for the camera. In her dress and makeup, however, Maureen looks like she is ready for her close-up (she will get it, but later). She is dressed in a melon-red jacket with a flower adorning the lapel and an open-collared white shirt with a flower pattern, the wide collars atop the lapel of her jacket. Her blonde hair is again pulled back in an "honest bun," which became her trademark look. As she recounts in her memoir, she had originally dressed in a more outré turban that morning. John, however, had told her to change her outfit, reminding her that Middle America was not ready for such an exotic look. Dean's media savvy trumped Maureen's fashion whims, and she returned to pulling her hair back into the simple bun that connoted elegance and control.

After this two-shot of the couple, the camera zooms into a medium close-up of John. This shot is held for one minute, as we hear Gurney in a voice-off (which shows the impact that Gurney has on Dean) ask if he has indeed inherited the cover-up. Dean rebuts, acting as if he doesn't understand Gurney's pronunciation of the word *inherit* (the senator's accent is a very upper-class southern one). He queries Gurney as to whether he said that the cover-up was "inherent." The cameras switch, and we see Gurney in medium shot, looking somewhat irritated, repeat his question and assert that Dean did not inherit the cover-up but rather was in on it at the beginning. We see Dean in a close-up respond to this. As Gurney states that he is now switching his line of questioning, the camera cuts to an extreme close-up of Gurney's papers on the conference table, which then zooms out to an over-the-shoulder shot from behind Gurney.

As Gurney begins his new line of questioning, the camera switches to a medium close-up of Dean and then cuts to an over-the-shoulder shot of the witness, looking from behind him at the court reporters, who sit in front of the senators on the left side. This camera work offers the viewer symmetry and balance, defining the space between and behind Dean and Gurney (as is done in soap operas), as well as focusing on the intensity of their struggle. When Gurney grills Dean about a series of disputed meetings with Mitchell, Ehrlichman, Haldeman, and the president himself (particularly a meeting with the president on September 15, 1972, in which Dean alleges that the president showed that he knew about the cover-up), the screen splits in two, with two medium shots of the adversaries. This split screen hints at the future of how such hearings will be televised. Indeed, television shows such as 24 and films such as *TimeCode* (2000) also rely on composited images (this technique was also used by Andy Warhol and Jean-Luc Godard in the 1960s and Abel Gance and Dziga Vertov in the 1920s). The split screen emphasizes how events that affect each other are occurring simultaneously. The more traditional technique to suggest that two different occurrences are happening at the same time, developed by D. W. Griffiths, is to use crosscuts (cutting between two scenes). The split screen eliminates the need to include the setting of the event and prohibits reaction shots of those who are also part of the incident. In the broadcast, the split screen of Dean versus Gurney is broken when the camera that is fixed on Dean moves to an extreme close-up of Dean's hands. His hands are uncharacteristically moving atop the table, suggesting his nervousness in reaction to Gurney's line of questioning.

In the languages of film and television, extreme close-ups of the hands are often used to signify unease in the person being filmed. They stand in for the emotions of the person when the body being televised is stationary or the face is hiding emotion. The hands in close-up do the work of the face, providing expressivity. Close-ups also suggest an intimacy between viewer and performer, providing the illusion that the viewer is spatially close to the person held within the camera's frame. Close-ups, especially extreme close-ups, provide a perspective that is not available to the viewer in real life—when a face becomes our entire field of vision, we cannot focus on it with the clarity in which we can see a face in a close-up. This unreal point of view allows the viewer to study and perceive a face as if he or she is looking through a magnifying glass, eliminating the visage's background and environment. Soap operas, and indeed many other television genres, rely on the close-up to ensure that stories have emotional intensity. With the use of this device, the actors we see become characters that we "know" because we have seen their heads or hands fill the screen.

When Gurney begins to "cross-examine" Dean on why he used official money for his honeymoon (Dean and Maureen actually had to cut their honeymoon short as Dean was called back to Washington), we see another extreme close-up of Dean's hands, this time focusing on his wedding ring. The camera then zooms out to a medium shot of Dean, so that we, the viewers, can be sure it is Dean's hands we are looking at. After holding this shot for one second, the camera continues to zoom out to a two-shot of Maureen and John, capturing a moment in which she is laughing at Gurney's comment that "$4,850 seems like a lot to spend on a honeymoon." We also hear that the audience is laughing along with her, and Dean is smiling boyishly, perhaps slightly embarrassed. In this sequence of shots, the charm of the Deans is vibrant against the humorless Gurney; the screen switches to the camera focused on Gurney, and in a medium shot we see that he is not amused. The intensity of this line of questioning builds. In another extreme close-up we see Dean's lawyer writing furiously on his pad after Gurney informs the audience that he believes Dean committed a crime by using this cash. The camera zooms away to a long shot that features Dean, his lawyers, and Maureen, allowing the viewer to see their responses to Gurney's accusation. Now it can be seen that this group of four is not amused, and the screen shifts to a medium shot of Gurney, who is pressing his inference that Dean is a criminal and a liar. Dean's response is shown in an extreme close-up. Dean then asks Gurney, "What crime?" The screen cuts to an extreme close-up of Gurney, who responds "Embezzlement," and he continues to ask Dean if a check that he wrote to cover the borrowed money is still in the safe. The medium close-up of Dean is interrupted by the figure of Shaffer, who has moved from his seat; the camera shifts to a two-shot of Dean and his lawyer. Shaffer begins to explain to the senators and the audience that what Dean has done is not embezzlement. In a pointed comment aimed at Gurney, he adds that this is something that the finer legal minds in the room already know. Shaffer succeeds in ending Gurney's insistence.

Maureen gets her close-up at the very end of Gurney's questioning in the afternoon when he returns to the circumstances around Dean borrowing money from the safe. Although this line of question has nothing to do with the cover-up, it is a way to malign Dean's credibility, undermining Dean's key accusation that the president was completely in the loop of the ring of men who obstructed justice rather than outside of it. Gurney asks Dean if he uses credit cards, and if so, why he didn't use them to pay for his honeymoon. (Gurney had produced a subpoenaed bank account statement showing that Dean only had fifteen hundred dollars in his bank account when he took the money.) Dean smiles as he replies that his wife knows he doesn't like living on credit and spending money he doesn't have. We hear the audience guffaw, and the camera moves in to an extreme close-up on Maureen as she giggles demurely. She shakes her head, backing up her husband's assertions of how they manage their finances but also suggesting that she isn't always happy with it. A title appears on the bottom of the screen that reads, "Mrs. Maureen Dean." Her simple theatrics, prompted by her husband's knowing reference to her, highlight the domesticity of the couple and serve to break the momentum of Senator Gurney's questions. Dean, aided by the camera, succeeds in putting forward something intimate about his and his wife's relationship, and once again this serves to charm the audience. The senator is forced to move on, blocked by the smiles and laughter of the enchanting couple. John and Maureen look like the winning couple on the original version of the television series *The Newlywed Game* (1966–74), a game show in which recently married couples answer questions about how well they know each other, with host Bob Eubanks delving into their sex lives to provoke bickering.

As a result, Gurney proves unable to completely discount Dean's believability, in large part because of the way Dean portrays his relationship with his "lovely wife" and the kind of attention the couple receives from the camera. Even though the camera is never able to take up the couple's visual point of view exactly, through the use of close-ups and over-the-shoulder shots from behind Dean, the audience feels "closer" to Dean and his humanizing, lovely, and silent wife. Gurney remains distant. Dean's believability is encouraged by the camera work that highlights the vivid connection between the two stars. The Deans prove irresistible to the daytime viewer via parading their perky, television-friendly, and all-American heterosexuality. Any suggestions that he is gay and she is a prostitute are dissolved by means of their endearing display.

Dean doesn't undergo as many tough questions from the rest of the senators, although Inouye, in a strategic move, makes sure that questions from White House lawyers are heard. Dean has already become friendly with Dash and is about to be invited to Walter Cronkite's vacation home in Martha's Vineyard. He is moving from turncoat to witness to celebrity. At the end of the fifth day, minutes before concluding his testimony, Dean recounts that he needed to go to the bathroom. He whispers to Shaffer, "I've got to take a leak, awful," but Shaffer urges him to finish up and control his bladder. The Republican attorney, Thompson, continues to grill him, once again about the borrowed $4,850. Ervin steps in to defend Dean this time, ending this line of questioning by reminding Thompson that if Dean hadn't reported taking the money, no one would ever know. The session ends soon after, and Dean is able to race to the bathroom. With the subsequent release of the White House tapes, much of what Dean reported to the committee is verified and he and his wife redeem their status as television hero and heroine.

INVESTIGATIONS AND CONSTITUTIONS

Congressional investigations into the workings of the White House are almost as old as the nation itself. The first was in 1792 when the House voted to investigate the failed expedition of Major General Arthur St. Clair into the Indian territory known as the Wabash Confederacy (Indiana, Ohio, Michigan, and Illinois). It was not clear whether the Constitution granted the legislative branch the power to investigate the executive, but the House decided to establish this precedent because of its concern over American losses and the faulty leadership of the general (see Chalou).

It was also not clear if investigations into the army fell under the jurisdiction of the president or the Congress—especially as article 1, section 8, of the Constitution states that the power to declare war and support the army and navy lies with the Congress and article 2, section 2, asserts that the president is the commander in chief of the army and navy. The job descriptions of these two branches of government overlap. The confusion over legislative and executive duties continues to cause difficulties, especially when the president sends armed forces to fight without congressional authority, as happened with the U.S. involvement in the Vietnam War.

In the St. Clair investigation, the Congress did not know if members of the president's Cabinet were legally bound to testify at a makeshift court in either the House, the Senate, or other government commissions. Such constitutional questions continue to baffle protocol in this nation. Controversy occurred when President George W. Bush initially refused to testify before the 9/11 Commission. He subsequently relented but only on the condition that his testimony would not be televised. He also insisted that he appear with the vice president and not be placed under oath. President Bush's view of the committee (that he was essentially outside its jurisdiction) points to the increasing power of the president, beyond what many constitutional scholars would say was implied by the "Founders." Bush further asserted executive privilege in insisting that former White House staffers do not have to testify before the Senate, even after they have been served with subpoenas. In his lawyers' arguments, White House employees are granted the same privileges as the president and do not have to respond to legal documents produced by the legislature.

The increased power of the president has occurred in great part because of the United States' ongoing involvement in war, which has served to write a permission slip to the president to make decisions without consultation. President George W. Bush acted as if he was not duty bound to answer to anyone, even as members of his Cabinet and his close associates were under indictment for assorted crimes. If he earned political capital in reelection, he spent it by ignoring the Constitution as if it were a specialty boutique for urban elites. Instead he went hog wild at the Walmart of unitary executive privilege.

The Italian philosopher Giorgio Agamben argues that at the core of the key foundational documents of Western democracies one can find the mechanism to suspend the rule of law in times of emergency. These emergencies include war, "natural" disasters, and economic chaos. He locates this capability as lodged within the text of the Constitution, which states in article 1 that "the Privilege of the Writ of Habeas Corpus shall not be suspended, unless when in Cases of Rebellion or Invasion the public Safety may require it." As Agamben notes, it is not clear in this statement which branch of government has the right to suspend this process, but he argues that contextually this privilege is that of the Congress as it lies within the article that describes the legislative branch (17). However, historically, presidents have taken advantage of emergency powers that suspend legal procedures. Some of America's most memorialized leaders, such as Woodrow Wilson, Abraham Lincoln, and Franklin Roosevelt—and not only Nixon, who resigned in disgrace— have made use of constitutional vagaries and its provision of emergency powers to justify the suspension of the normal rule of law.

George W. Bush admitted to using surveillance without acquiring warrants. In doing so, he disregarded procedures articulated by the FISA legislation of 1978. Under FISA, the president can, through the attorney general, authorize electronic surveillance without going to the courts, but only for fifteen days. Moreover, he criticized those who challenged him for providing comfort to the enemy. In Watergate, Nixon had no second thoughts about instructing those around him to obstruct justice. For Nixon, domestic rebellions and the Vietnam War vindicated any illegal measures on his part. In his perception, it was necessary for him to be above the law in order to protect both himself and his country.

On November 7, 1973, Congress passed the War Powers Act in response to Nixon's excesses. The act was an attempt to limit the power of the president to engage in undeclared war. Yet under an emergency, the act does allow the president to engage the armed forces in conflict for more than sixty days without congressional approval. Once again, war and emergency privilege the executive branch of government. With the current, seemingly permanent state of war in Iraq and Afghanistan, the executive branch maintains its privilege, upsetting the balance of power that was inscribed by the Founders—even though their documents ensure the upsetting of this balance; thus favoring the president.

Agamben argues, "It is obvious that in a wartime situation the con-flict between the president and the Congress is essentially theoretical" (20), meaning that, during conflict, the president reigns virtually supreme, able to act less like a democratically elected leader and more like a sovereign with inherited powers. Even as Congress may be aware that "constitutional jurisdictions have been transgressed," it usually re-mains inactive in stopping such actions. These transgressions may come under investigation later, but historically the Congress has failed to block the president at the moment in which the leader seizes further power, for such acts appear as if they violate the commander in chief's wartime mandates. Congress provides—or is forced to hand over—a carte blanche to the president.

For Agamben, "President Bush's decision to refer to himself as the 'Commander in Chief of the Army' after September 11, 2001, must be considered in the context of this presidential claim to sovereign powers in emergency situations." He adds that "Bush is attempting to produce a situation in which the emergency becomes the rule" (22). After all, Bush was only the commander in chief of the troops. He was not the commander in chief of the American people; he was their president. De-spite his protestations, the executive branch of government was subject to congressional oversight. Unfortunately, though, the Constitution grants the president imperial-type power during declared or perceived emergencies, and one of Bush's tactics was to continually remind the public of the danger of al-Qaeda in order to justify his grab for power. Obama's strategy is different—and certainly a vocal Republican minor-ity has challenged his domestic policies—but his foreign policy ventures (the continuance and the funding of war) have not been curtailed.

Bush repeatedly stated that the "War on Terror" was a conflict with-out end. This fueled his attempt to secure emergency powers, as implied in article 1 and reinforced in an interpretation of the Constitution known as Unitary Executive Theory. Even as his popularity decreased, Bush's power increased. If we follow this logic, then his suspension of the nor-mal workings of democracy is without cessation as we are always under threat. The normal rule of law is gone. Hence Bush felt empowered to state without apology that he need not ask permission of the FISA court to pursue otherwise illegal surveillance on Americans. Ironically, a citi-zen becomes unpatriotic by reasserting the rule of law through a rather standard interpretation of the Constitution, as the force of law (a term that Agamben uses to describe actions undertaken by the leader that are not the law itself) now resides in the actions of the president and supersedes the law itself. Thus the citizenry is faced with a grave paradox: during the chronic condition of war and the omnipresence of the threat of terrorism, the president operates antidemocratically, arguing that he is forced to do so in order to defend democracy. And as President Obama enters his third year there is no real indication that Guantanamo is really closing or rendition has ended.

For Agamben this also was the citizenry's plight in ancient Rome. Julius Caesar seized power using the rules of the Senate to secure his reign during a time of civil war. He used the Roman constitution to curtail the rule of the constitution. In America, terrorism—and, more exactly, the threat of terrorism and the so-called War on Terror—is being used to perform the same centralization of power.

Congressional investigations into presidential excesses are often little more than ceremonial exercises. For example, the members of the Senate Intelligence Committee knew about the President Bush authorizing the National Security Agency (NSA) to do surveillance on national to international phone calls without gaining approval from the FISA court. It was only after the *New York Times* revealed this activity, much to the chagrin of the Bush administration, that members of the Senate became upset. Even the *New York Times* sat on the story for one year, concerned about its national security implications, rather than immediately assuming its duty to reveal to the public a possible breach of the law.

The news media, under the control of fewer corporations since the 1980s, as Douglas Kellner states in his essay on democracy and media during George Bush's administration, is increasingly reluctant to defend the public's right to informed debate. Instead the mainstream news media present a bias that is in step with corporate ownership. For Kellner, neoliberalism and media conglomeration have "helped to produce a crisis in democracy in America" (31). I would add that the modes in which the government is presented to television viewers, including congressional investigations, have changed dramatically since 1973. Today the modes favor the national emcee, aka the president, even more.

Thus official investigations into the wrongdoings of the executive branch become media pageantry. Media act as a modern court jester that, instead of rousing the king from his bilious melancholia, entertains the populace with the retelling of the king's (mis)deeds. The populace, even if it is outraged by cover-ups and lawlessness, is nonetheless enthralled by the divertissements produced by testimony and cross-examination. The Senate Watergate Hearings, even as they ended Nixon's grab for more power, were also akin to the soap operas that they temporarily replaced. Although Nixon never appeared in front of the Senate commission, he was always its off-camera star, despite scene-stealing performances by Ervin and Dean and Inouye and others. His rants about the entitlements of the presidency reverberated loudly throughout the proceedings. Echoes of his utterances were also heard in the repetitions of George W. Bush.

VIEWERS

During the hearings both the soap opera genre and the soap opera fan were ridiculed. For highbrow-minded critics, soap operas were silly and had poor production values compared to prime-time television and, of course, film. Soap opera fans were either upset that the soaps were interrupted by the most important news of their generation or they watched the proceedings as if they were also soaps and not live broadcasts of the Senate. Either way, soap opera fans were regarded as silly, even though some became hooked on the Watergate investigation, which was considered higher brow entertainment than the typical soap. As Lang and Lang write, the Watergate "fan" was initially reluctant and the daytime viewers "included a disproportionate number of women, many of them a 'captive audience' whose favorite programs had been preempted." They add, "Becoming fascinated, some 'captives' soon became a willing audience" (86).

Writing later in 1973, after the hearings ended, *New York Times* writer Beth Gutcheon defended the genre and its fans. She claimed that soap operas tackle social issues before prime-time television does and depict them more sensitively, especially due to the serial form of the genre. For Gutcheon soaps "do not adopt a patronizing attitude toward women" and include women who work outside the home far more often than other genres of television. Her defense of soaps prefigures the critical reevaluation of soaps that was prompted by the women's movement and feminist scholarship in media. She writes that the soaps "are the only place on television where you may see adult topics—rape, alcoholism, frigidity, the plight of the professional woman who doesn't want children, racism, sexism, even incest—explored in a domestic context as if they were problems that involve real people" (173). Writing in 2007, Elana Levine argues that ABC and NBC challenged CBS's lead in the ratings in the early 1970s by updating the soap opera format, as well as by televising made for TV movies that took on issues of the day (26–27).

Television programming in the early '70s began to deal with more topical issues, influenced by the headlines in its story lines, and it became much more involved in depicting sexuality in order to encourage ratings. Soap operas and their audiences were effective in representing the power struggle between the genders that was part of the popular political culture.

Yet the Watergate drama was not always as progressive as the soaps of the day—in Watergate women were secondary characters that remained silent when the important decisions were being made, like 1950s television housewives. Martha Mitchell, John Mitchell's wife, was outspoken, but she was often depicted as a hysteric or an alcoholic. Watergate was a men's club, and Maureen and John Dean were rays of sunlight during a dark day (they were more familiar to soap opera fans—with their nice white teeth, a dual career family on their way to having children—and they were not without endearing marital squabbles). They were sexy and in love, less interested in power than in setting the record straight so they could enjoy their romance without regret. They were like characters in *The Young and the Restless* who had escaped Genoa City and made it to the nation's capital.

In watching the Watergate hearings, female soap opera fans were looking in at the monkeyshines of men in power—and the heroics of those who were trying to steady the country and find out the truth. Journalist John Beaufort noted in an essay in the *Christian Science Monitor* on July 7, 1973, that it was hard to get any attention from his wife while the Watergate hearings were on. He remarked that when he got a kiss from her, she told him that "it was for Sam Ervin" (14), a man she now found lovable. Beaufort remarks that watching the hearings became a family activity, but his complaint also suggests that female and male viewers had different responses to the proceedings.

The feminist theorist Tania Modleski changed the way media theorists and feminists viewed soap operas by making radically new assertions about both the role of soap operas in women's lives and the narrative structure of shows in the genre. In her pivotal essay "The Search for Tomorrow in Today's Soap Operas," she argued that soaps mimic the rhythm of women's household work. Modleski claimed that soaps might be "in the vanguard not just of T.V. but of all popular narrative art" (87) because soaps offer viewers many characters to identify with and multiple stories that interrelate but do not end, providing distinctive pleasures for the viewer.

Soap opera scholar Robert Allen writes that in Modleski's view "the soap opera represents a narrative form whose construction is diametri-cally opposed to that of the 'male' film and novel" (92). In a soap opera, one becomes immersed in a milieu (usually a small city or suburban town) and a series of endless connections rather than the struggle of a single protagonist moving toward a quick climax. Stories focus on the lives of powerful matriarchs and the ways in which these women navi-gate with authority in male-dominated realms. The lives of these fictional women mimic those of the powerful women who initially created, pro-duced, and wrote the soaps, particularly Irna Phillips (who successfully moved the soaps from radio to television) and Agnes Nixon (the creator of *One Life to Live* and *All My Children*). These soap auteurs also had to learn how to navigate terrain marked out by male network executives.

Modleski's perspective was not that of a media scholar. Her empha-sis was on narrative structures in popular arts (she also wrote about ro-mance novels). Thus, she doesn't examine editing and shot formation (or soundtrack) and how these work to create connections between viewers and the "stories" they watch. Yet her radical insight prompted a thorough reconsideration of a once-ridiculed and "ghettoized" form. Soap operas were often viewed as if they were a contagious or addictive substance—if you watched one episode, you couldn't help but watch the next day's and against the viewer's will he or she became "hooked." Beginning in the '70s, scholars, particularly feminists, began to look at soap operas without judgment and scorn. In fact, scholars' and critics' automatic denigration of the soap opera genre began to be seen as al-most gynophobic and elitist.

Charlotte Brunsdon, in her history of feminist scholarship on the soap opera, writes that Modleski argued that soaps "characteristically con-struct a maternal position for their viewers, which is an engagement with Laura Mulvey's influential 1975 argument that classical Hollywood cin-ema constructs a masculine spectator position" (60). For Modleski, soaps take up the perspective of women and suggest an accommodation to and creation of a distinctive female gaze in counterpoint to the dominant ten-dency of Hollywood films. In a sense, traditional masculinist positions and experience of narrative are excluded in a soap opera.

Modleski's insight also allows us to see that the Watergate Hearings coverage was not merely news footage; it was soap operatic in its daily structure, delayed denouements, and presentation of a web of intercon-necting characters. Its rhythm, similar to that of a soap opera, was in op-position to other programming on television and other news programs. Using Modleski's terminology, we can see that the Watergate Hearings became a feminized form, even though Maureen Dean was one of the few female stars in the series.

Other soap opera scholars note that the active involvement of fans is a key aspect of the ways in which viewers experience their shows. Jane Feuer (in Simon et al.) argues that the assumption that soap opera fans are white female household workers—or unemployed women—is not exactly correct. Viewers include gay men and women of all colors; with the rise of videotape recording (and later the Soap Opera Channel and Tivo), fans can now watch at any time of the day or night. Viewers discuss shows within their own social networks, and some fans write and call the producers of the show and offer their feedback on actors, characters, and story lines. They do not consume the shows passively or quietly. Their responses to a series and its individual episodes serve to complete the show, reminding us of Roland Barthes's notion that the text is incomplete and unfinished without the reader. Soap opera viewers in this way rewrite the broadcasted show, making it an event in their lives.

Modleski's emphasis was that soap operas mimic the rhythm of women's lives and serve as lifelong companions; later theorists who were interested in audience responses to shows argued that the audience's subjectivities and viewing habits actually customized and appended the broadcast product. Soap operas speak and respond to a variety of audiences. The viewer is involved in resituating the already-recited text. The women who wrote Sam Ervin about their favorite characters in the Watergate drama were normal; they felt entitled and empowered to comment on the broadcast product. Their comments became part of the expanded text of the show.

Soaps are stylistically repetitive and predictable, using musical themes to underline poignant moments with cameras moving into an extreme close-up at the end of a scene. Narrative climaxes are delayed, and, although soaps duplicate the calendar at Christmastime (plotlines incorporate the holiday), time moves very slowly on a soap and conflicts and denouements are so anticipated as to make them excruciating. This was true when the genre moved to television from radio and remains so now. The form of the genre has changed but not radically. The story lines, however, have changed drastically, particularly at the beginning of the 1970s. Yet soap opera characters still live in a world where no one watches television (or reads a novel), so it is always, in part, a dreamworld where life is lived without television (unlike the life of the viewer). The Watergate viewer, however, lived a life where television as a medium was crucial, regardless of whether he or she watched the commercial networks during the day or PBS at night.

In the United States, the government is a provider of television programming. Constitutional crises and power struggles between and within branches of government become serialized. With the Army-McCarthy Hearings of 1954 and continuing through the confirmation hearings of Sonia Sotomayor, government provides entertainment to the viewer. Public opinion may be influenced through such proceedings, but the citizenry is also turned into an audience when there is conflict between the branches of government. With the Senate Watergate Hearings, viewers became very involved with the proceedings but not necessarily as participants in the workings of democracy. The explanation for this is not found in the perceptions of the audience per se but rather in how the media, particularly television, presented the proceedings.

The networks complained about losing money because they were showing the hearings, as fifteen minutes of commercial time per hour could not be sold. But they also were given free programming, saving on production costs. This programming was courtesy of the legislative branch of government investigating the excesses of the executive branch. The hearings paved the way for both C-SPAN and Court TV and revitalized a tradition in television that began (and paused) with the Army-McCarthy Hearings. As Tom Doherty notes in his book about McCarthyism and television, these hearings not only ended the career of the senator, but they also served as an argument against using cameras in such hearings. For many years cameras were kept out of the Senate. Doherty argues that even as televising the hearings turned them into a spectacle, it allowed the television medium to act in its own interest. That is, the coolness of television tends to work against antidemocratic demagogues, hot figures such as Joseph McCarthy and Richard Nixon that posed as moral arbiters but were flawed themselves, figures that television had once supported in their rise to power. Doherty writes, "Dependent for sustenance on the very freedoms that McCarthyism restricted, the medium was preprogrammed for resistance. Of course, the commitment to free expression and open access was self-interested; television needed to fill the air time" (18). In televising the Watergate Hearings, network television advocated against the president. It did so by presenting a soap opera set in Congress.

The hearings also restated an unwritten amendment to the Constitution (but one that has seemingly been ratified and accepted by the populace): the president and his inner circle are duty bound to provide national drama, especially by way of scandal, cover-up, and investigation (as well as photogenic children)—and the unabashed display of aberrant behavior. Even though the hearings were not entirely conclusive, they served to weaken both the president and the powers of the presidency, while ensuring that the federal government became prime-time—and daytime—entertainment. In sum, a female narrative form unraveled the malfeasance of men.

CHAPTER 3

Billie Jean King

THE TOMBOY VERSUS THE NERD-JOCK

BACKSTORY

If John and Maureen Dean became young soap opera stars in order to take on an older generation of male politicians, Billie Jean King also saw how participating in a media spectacle could work to challenge male dominance in sports. Like the Deans, she made use of her telegenic qualities and the media as a way to advance a cause. Yet, in 1972, when fifty-five-year-old retired tennis champion Bobby Riggs jumped the fence at a Wimbledon practice court to challenge her to a televised match, King didn't take his offer seriously. She didn't see any advantage to such a match. Riggs was relentless in his challenge, but King repeatedly rejected his offers. Riggs began to talk to other top female tennis players, including the up-and-coming young player Chris Evert, who also turned him down.

Margaret Court, King's Australian rival and the world's number one player, unlike Evert and King, did take up Riggs's challenge. She played Riggs on Mother's Day, May 21, 1973, a few days after the first broadcast of the Senate Watergate Hearings. Court lost embarrassingly in two straight sets. She was ill-prepared, and Riggs psyched her out and neutralized her power game with well-placed lobs and drop shots. Court also had no idea what was at stake in terms of women's tennis and the burgeoning women's movement; in fact she eschewed taking on the role of spokeswoman for the sport. The match became known as the Mother's Day massacre. Court was the wrong woman at the wrong time.

After Court's defeat, Billie Jean King realized she would have to take on Riggs: she needed to correct the idea that even a middle-aged man could beat a professional woman tennis player at the peak of her talents. King also wanted to ensure that she and her colleagues received parity with men's tennis, and, at the same time, she wanted to popularize the sport. She began to see the match as advancing these two goals. For King these objectives were complementary—popularizing the sport would help to publicize her argument for equal pay. If tennis remained elitist, it would remain primarily a man's game. King also knew, as she had warned Court, that the match between herself and Riggs would be a hyped affair. She knew the match was destined to become more show business than sport—and that this could work to Riggs's advantage unless his opponent was media savvy. But King was not only more competitive than the bigger, stronger Court; she was also better suited to indulge in the media-frenzied aspects of the match. Unlike Court, King was a celebrity, and a household name for her brazen tomboy manner, which charmed reporters. She was outspoken about her beliefs about tennis (though she certainly hid her personal life and sexual orientation from the public) and the place of women in society.

Billie Jean King was also a smart businesswoman. Working through Larry King, her husband and business manager, she made sure that the prize money for the "Battle of the Sexes" was increased from $35,000 to $150,000. This was more than her total earnings for 1971, when she became the first female tennis player to make over $100,000 in one year. The match became a huge media event and was moved to the Houston Astrodome, a covered football stadium. If Billie Jean King couldn't advance her agenda by making cogent arguments for equality in behind-the-scenes meetings with those who governed tennis, she would go public with her claims and indulge in a made-for-television event. Her hope was to legitimize female sport by participating in an entertainment event, and, like John and Maureen Dean, she would use the media attention generated by the event to her best advantage by costarring in a well-advertised performance. Much was at stake in her appearance at the "match," and King recounts this stress in her 2008 book *Pressure Is a Privilege: Lessons I've Learned from Life and the Battle of the Sexes.*

Due to this unlikely alliance (and staged conflict) between a short male chauvinist and a trim female athlete, fifty million television viewers turned to their ABC affiliate to watch Billie Jean King beat Bobby Riggs on September 20; a match nicknamed "The Lobber vs. The Libber." This was more than one-quarter of the entire population, an especially high figure considering that the popular 1967 film *Bonnie and Clyde* was being shown on a rival network. Tennis's popularity was already growing in the early 1970s, but this event suggested that the sport's reach could move beyond its clearly defined borders. Tennis could become like baseball, football, and basketball and actually have fans (rather than just aficionados). Indeed, it could actually feature its women athletes rather than choreographing thinly clad cheerleaders on the sidelines (as in football and basketball) to support male camaraderie. The sideline cheerleaders serve to reassert the exclusion of women from competitive sports; the star female athlete challenges this exclusion.

Thus in 1973, tennis was poised to jump from elite sport to a form of popular entertainment. For King, tennis's stature as a sport for the country club set also encouraged its sexism—the sport was still being run by patrician white men—the kind of men who populated Nixon's republican party and worked hard to keep its activities secretive. King wanted to wrest control away from this enclave of purported gentility, an enclave known for its elitism.

Tennis, or more properly lawn tennis, is a very recent game, developed in England in the Victorian era by Major Walter Wingfield in 1874. Lawn tennis took the game of royal or court tennis, which had decidedly fallen out of favor after the French Revolution, back outdoors (Gillmeister, 175). The French game *jeu de paume* was developed in the courtyards of European monasteries in the Middle Ages, and tennis historians see antecedents of the sport in ball games that were played in ancient Egypt, Greece, and Rome. Wingfield's version made tennis available as a pastime for the rising industrial class, a class that had both leisure and land. After all, to have a lawn tennis court requires expansive grounds on which to install such a luxury, and a proper tennis match requires the ability to put aside the demands of work and rest, as a match can last quite a few hours. Thus tennis requires both time and space, a proposition that was not available to the working classes of the time, but these commodities were increasingly accessible to an industrial elite. The tennis lawn must be manicured and tended to, and it became a status symbol to have one's own private court, even if one seldom used it.

Tennis as a game involves the effort of the individual as opposed to the collective activity of a team. Ideologically this makes it a perfect sport for industrial capitalism, which celebrates the maverick entrepreneur or financier as a hero whose singular efforts transform the social landscape. This is similar to the way a tennis court converts wild land into an orderly, structured lawn; in other words it is an encounter with the bourgeois frontier. Traditionally team sports such as soccer (outside of the United States), basketball, and baseball have been more popular and involve the working classes as both fans and participants. Even though megastars emerge from these sports to become brands, the structure of the game requires negotiation and coordination between players.

Even though an individual like Michael Jordan might triumph, it was his team, the Chicago Bulls, that won the championships. After all, in order for Jordan to score, Scottie Pippen had to pass him the ball and Dennis Rodman had to get the rebound. The individual is the winner in tennis; even though he or she may thank (and pay) trainers, consultants, coaches, and corporate sponsors, the player is alone at the end of the tournament receiving the trophy.

As a spectator sport, doubles has never been as popular as the singles variant of tennis (Billie Jean King also worked hard to popularize a new variant of the game—team tennis—with mixed success). Lawn tennis celebrates and makes visible the individual endeavor. In professional tennis today, players are not allowed to consult their coaches during the course of the match (although some are accused of doing so with signals on court), as it is ultimately the individual alone, and his or her strategy, skill, and stamina, that takes on the foe. Tennis is thus the perfect game for the bourgeoisie, which made Billie Jean King's task all the more difficult as a working-class woman determined to make the sport more accessible. Indeed many barriers remain in tennis that relate to accessibility and the history of the game. Many years after the successes of Arthur Ashe and Althea Gibson, prominent African American players Venus and Serena Williams encountered racist responses from spectators and players alike. Indeed double standards were evident when Serena was reprimanded after her threatening speech to a line judge at the 2009 U.S. Open. Her behavior was deemed unprofessional and unladylike, even though years before her time John McEnroe had made it his trademark to argue with linesmen. Until she repaired her public image and apologized, Williams's corporate sponsorships were in jeopardy.

PUBLIC IMAGES

Billie Jean King knew that public image was a key part of the event. She prepared vigorously with her team for the match, but she also made sure to get a suntan before she appeared opposite Bobby in the Houston Astrodome so that she could look the healthy star. She also shot a Sunbeam hair curler ad that ran during the show. King knew her appearance would be a key aspect of her success, not necessarily on the court but as part of the spectacle. She would not let her adversary—and his big mouth—stand alone in the spotlight.

Bobby Riggs probably preferred talking to reporters and espousing his sexist views to playing on court; for him tennis also included all the talk that surrounded the actual match. Riggs's preparation for the match was to contact all existing media outlets and indulge in as much male bonding with sports journalists as possible, even before the details of the match were set. Billie Jean's prematch approach was different from Bobby's—she was twenty-nine years old then, entering the latter stages of her tennis-playing career, and knew how to prepare physically, particularly after defaulting at the 1973 U.S. Open due to a virus (she was harshly criticized for not finishing her match against Julie Heldman). Billie Jean went to Hilton Head in South Carolina, rested, and then trained intensely, avoiding the media. She worked on her strength, particularly in her legs, knowing that quickness would be key in chasing down Riggs's returns. She let Riggs have his fifteen minutes of fame and focused on her own mental and physical preparation. Riggs had no time to train for the match—he was too busy getting ready for interviews and repeating his tirades against woman's lib and women's tennis. He arrogantly overlooked the need to train for the match and was out of shape, especially if he hoped to challenge a revved up King.

Bobby Riggs had won Wimbledon in 1939 and the U.S. Open in 1939 and 1941. After his career as a top player ended, he hung around the tennis world and made money as a gambler and hustler. He was known for challenging his would-be opponents to take him on for money, encouraging them by providing himself with handicaps such as carrying a pail of water or tugging a poodle on a leash while playing. He was wily, opinionated, and attention getting and knew how to provoke his opponents into making mistakes. Bobby was definitely not above using garbage shots (spins and slices and drop shots) to win a point and relied on his opponent to lose in order for him to win. His modus operandi was to frustrate his opponent, for Riggs was unable to overpower him (or her) on strength or fitness alone.

Riggs's jabs against women's tennis, at a time when the game was becoming more exciting and competitive (and definitely less stereotypically ladylike), gave him the attention he craved—and he also wanted more prize money for the senior tennis tournaments. His unabashed—if in part performed or exaggerated—sexism gave him a podium. He claimed with pride (either real or feigned) that he was an "MCP" or a male chauvinist pig, and used this designation to become a celebrity. He rode a growing wave of backlash against the women's movement and wanted to become one of the backlash's spokesmen, especially because it gave him attention and not particularly because he was truly a woman hater or disliked Billie Jean King. In fact Riggs and King had a grudging respect for each other, and, whether or not they discussed it, they forged an alliance by participating in the spectacle.

Riggs's criticism of the women's game was occurring at the exact moment when Billie Jean King and other leading female tennis players like Rosie Casals were arguing for equal pay at the major tournaments. And indeed Billie Jean and others were challenging notions of proper behavior for women both on and off the court. They did not accept the status quo, and they did not act demure. They were as outspoken about their ideas as Bobby, even if their voices were less high pitched than his.

Indeed, King and her allies had begun to succeed. In 1973, for the first time, the U.S. Open made the prize money the same for men and women (Wimbledon only did this in 2007 after Venus Williams did some successful lobbying on behalf of the women's sport). King, after helping to start the successful Virginia Slims Tour, a women's tournament cycle designed to match the men's tournament, also founded a new tennis organization in 1973, the Women's Tennis Association. Ironically, Riggs's big mouth and headline-grabbing, antifeminist diatribes ultimately benefited women's tennis—and, consequently, the wealth and fame of Billie Jean King. Riggs helped ensure that King became a symbol not only of female tennis but of the women's movement itself. Both shared the trophy of popularizing the game of tennis.

Although they were apparently opponents with competing agendas, Billie Jean and Bobby suffered from the same exclusionary tactics that existed in the game of tennis. While Bobby did not come from a working-class background, he did not fit the mold, temperament, or background of the standard tennis player. He was the son of a preacher. At five feet, five inches, he was considered short. He lacked the elegance of John Dean—and he did not have the Hollywood good looks that the Los Angeles Tennis Club favored. Perry T. Jones, president of the Southern California chapter of the U.S. Lawn Tennis Association, who would later stun Billie Jean with his unapologetic snobbery, had discouraged Riggs's entry into the game. Riggs's game and physique lacked the strength and stature that Jones preferred. Like Billie Jean, Riggs was not deterred by this reaction and used his aberrance from the norm to his best advantage.

If anything Riggs played like a "girl"—he used finesse instead of strength and waited for his more powerful opponent to make a mistake. In fact, his first coach was a woman. Eleanor Tennant carefully instructed Riggs to use strategy and placement over velocity and strength. Riggs was chesslike in his approach—he liked to trap his opponent into making a costly mistake—even though his appearance and manner were always loud and flamboyant.

The match between these two outsiders accelerated changes in the game that had been becoming evident since at least the late 1960s. Tennis was changing from a genteel sport favored only by the upper crust. After all, as an amateur sport (King and others referred to it as "shamateur"), tennis attracted mostly white, affluent aficionados who belonged to country clubs and did not rely on prize money for their well-being (tournaments often paid players for participating but not for winning). Players were expected to be well behaved on and off the court and to avoid the celebrity limelight. Although the game was always competitive, it was decidedly polite and mannered—one never argued against line judges and answered the press's questions politely, without humor or attitude.

The open era, which began in 1968, allowed professionals and amateurs to compete in the consolidated U.S. Open and then at other tournaments. It encouraged outspoken or personality-filled male players like the stormy Romanian Ilie Nastase, the burly Argentinean Guillermo Vilas, the elegant African American Arthur Ashe, the disco-dancing Vitas Gerulaitis, the brazen Jimmy Connors, and of course the petulant, bratty John McEnroe. These players were jet-setters and trailblazers who would have been unthinkable in the WASPy game governed by the International Lawn Tennis Association in the early 1960s. Male tennis players began to wear their hair longer and their shorts tighter (one joke was that Nastase's shorts would split if he had to bend too far to get a volley). Tennis stars spent time with actors and models at discos and resorts and became part of the international jet set.

Like the new breed of male stars in Hollywood such as Jack Nicholson, Dustin Hoffman, Warren Beatty, Paul Newman, and Steve McQueen, tennis in the '70s was filled with colorful, rebellious figures who were known as much for their off-court antics as for their playing techniques. These stars were inspired by the counterculture of the '60s and looked more like they had stepped out of the film *Easy Rider* (1969) than a country club or society event. The male rebellion in tennis no doubt helped to inspire women tennis players' rebellion against WASP gentility. The male tennis stars of the early '70s make today's Roger Federer look like a (well-programmed) robot and Rafael Nadal like a shy schoolboy. The on-court theatrics of Novak Djokovic or Andy Murray are tame compared to Nastase's temper tantrums. Even though the game is now more multicultural and international, tennis has become conservative again. Although it is no longer governed so much by genteel organizations, it is now overseen by sponsoring corporations, which are looking for a certain profile in their players and do not want outspoken rebels, preferring players who, no matter how tough they are on the court, can still purr like kittens when they are being interviewed and who always remember to make corporate logos visible for the cameras.

Fame in women's tennis today has become paramount, and much of the emphasis on traditional female beauty seems like a return, almost, to a prefeminist era. Players are often known for appearance and fashionability (led by Maria Sharapova), not necessarily their game. Justine Henin, a number-one player who recently returned to the game briefly, is decidedly dour looking, and as a result she is never seen endorsing products (unlike the Williams sisters, Sharapova, or the two photogenic Serbian players, Ivanovic and Jankovic). So far in her career, Henin lacked the charisma of Billie Jean King and did not exhibit media savvy—she is only a favorite among connoisseurs, and she has never brought new fans to the game, unlike the Williams sisters. Gone now are rivalries such as the ones that existed between Seles and Graf, Navratilova and Evert, or King and Court (indeed a very royal sounding battle). Unlike today's female tennis stars, Billie Jean King was both devoted to her game (many have charged that the Williams sisters do not fully commit to tennis year-round, focusing only on the four major tournaments) and at the same time able to become a popular figure without dolling herself up for male spectators or sports marketing executives like many of today's players, who have prioritized fame and traditional female beauty as part of their brand.

THE END OF THE COUNTRY CLUB

With the "Battle of the Sexes," King writes, "the game of tennis finally got kicked out of the country clubs forever and into the world of real sports, where everybody could see it" (*Billie Jean,* 170). Jerry Perenchio, the boxing promoter who put together the Muhammad Ali–Joe Frazier fight, promoted the match. (He now runs Univision, the largest Spanish-language television network.) Indeed the boxer George Foreman was a VIP in the audience and presented the trophy to the winner. Although the signs of change were already apparent, in one night it seemed that tennis was transformed from an elite sport to a popular one. If Riggs and King were opponents with very different agendas, they also shared this

concern—they believed tennis should be as popular as football or baseball and they became allies to further this goal. Perhaps this goal has
been realized. The U.S. Open has become a very successful and popular
event; in 2007 the total audience was over six hundred thousand, making it the most popular sports event in the country. Importantly, this
record-breaking audience occurred a year after the grounds were renamed the Billie Jean King National Tennis Center, reminding tennis
fans that she had helped to popularize the sport.

The rise of Billie Jean King also signaled a change in the ideals of femininity and the female body. King, who on her own admission had a lifelong attraction to ice cream, made sure she was slim for her matches, but
her trimness included a distinctive muscularity. Her body was worked
out from weightlifting. She did not cover up her aggressive play with
makeup, tight outfits, or a coy, feminine flirtatiousness off court like
many of the top players in her day—akin to how Maria Sharapova's management teams use her blonde prettiness to economic advantage today or
how Serena Williams tones down her on-court intensity when she is interviewed on late-night talk shows. Arguably, Sharapova and Williams
have become celebrities who play tennis. Billie Jean remained a lifelong
tennis player who used her celebrity, and she has become a mentor to
younger players. When Sharapova faced an Australian Open final in
2008, Billie Jean "texted" her these words: "Champions take their chances
and pressure is a privilege." The last four words of the text are the title of
the book that Billie Jean King published later that year, which included a
preface by Holly Hunter, who played Billie Jean King in a made-for-TV
movie *When Billie Beat Bobby* (discussed later in the chapter).

Like John Dean, Billie Jean Moffitt was born into a quintessential
American family—but not one that had its own private tennis court. Her
father, Bill Moffitt, was a fireman for the Long Beach, California, Fire Department. He was hardworking, not particularly ambitious, and liked to
work on engineering projects at home during the weekends. He was in
the military in the Second World War and was a strict disciplinarian (Billie Jean reports that he would spank her when she didn't apply herself in
school). Her father played catch with her—she started out with softball
and then vowed to be a football player. According to Selena Roberts in
her 2005 book on the match between Riggs and King, tennis came later.
When she was ten, her parents suggested tennis because it was a more
acceptable sport for a young girl (53). Luckily the city of Long Beach had
municipal courts and offered lessons, and it satisfied the competitive
spirit that Billie Jean displayed. Also luckily for her, even though her fa-

ther was politically conservative (as a child she remembers him making antigay comments, as well as racist ones), he encouraged her tomboy qualities; perhaps she provided him with a companion for his "male" activities while his son was still too young. His son also became a world-class athlete and was a relief pitcher in major league baseball.

Billie Jean's mother, Betty, worked part time and did home art projects such as ceramics, painting, and rug making. She supplemented her husband's income by working as an Avon lady, selling products door-to-door. She also sold the classic American product of the 1960s and 1970s, Tupperware (housewives gave Tupperware parties and the saleswoman socialized while selling the products). Betty also supported her daughter's aspirations—as soon as Billie Jean took up the game she announced she wanted to be the best in the world. Yet the family was financially unable to completely support their daughter's endeavors—tennis equipment was expensive and required travel to tournaments. Even though Billie Jean began winning tournaments when she was quite young, she literally could not afford the game of ladies' amateur tennis—the per diem and the pay offered amateurs by tournaments were very low, especially for women. Billie Jean's mom made her tennis outfits by hand.

For a number of years, Billie Jean only participated in Wimbledon and the short grass season in the United States, which no longer exists. It wasn't until she met her future husband, a man who had the Hollywood leading-man good looks favored by tennis gatekeepers such as Perry T. Jones, that she devoted herself to the game. Unlike a traditional marriage in the early '60s, in which a woman was often expected to repress her ambitions, Larry King encouraged her to commit to her aspirations and become a full-time tennis player. It was only after 1968, at the start of the open era, that she began to make a large amount of money, even though she was already one of the leading tennis players in the world.

Billie Jean entered the game of tennis when many of the great female players of the 1950s were retiring—players such as Althea Gibson (the first female African American player of note), Maureen Connolly, Doris Hart, and Shirley Fox. This void at the top allowed Billie Jean, as well as other American players such as Karen Hantze and Kathy Chabot and later Rosie Casals (King's doubles partner for many years), to move into the game and command the top rankings. Later a new group of strongly built Australian women players, such as Margaret Court and Evonne

Goolagong, became prominent; they successfully challenged King and the American players and intensified the game.

Billie Jean King had a long—and controversial—career at the top. Her game was aggressive and intensely competitive. To many she played like a "man"—certainly she displayed what the cultural theorist Judith Halberstam described as "female masculinity." King was a serve-and-volley player and did not rely on tiring her opponents with strong ground strokes from the baseline (like Chris Evert, Margaret Court, and many of the baseline players of both genders today). She loved to chase down balls and had a strong lob, great anticipation, and accurate placement. She mixed power with a great touch at net. Her style of game also allowed her to be a very good doubles player; she won doubles (both mixed and women's) as often as she won singles titles.

King's style of play, which foregrounds the serve and volley, is rare today even on grass (the fastest surface), especially since the retirement of Pete Sampras. Amelie Mauresmo was one of the few female players that rushes to the net, and she is at the end of her career (and her aggression was intermittent); Venus Williams is using net play more often as she becomes a more mature player. Among the men, even players with supersonic serves (such as Andy Roddick, who can propel serves at over 140 miles per hour) are reluctant to come to net. Roger Federer no longer volleys at net consistently, even when he plays on grass. In order to stay at the top he has become a baseline player, by default. Baseline players are just too good at producing passing shots. The changes that Margaret Court and Chris Evert brought to the game, with their focus on playing from the baseline, have transformed not only women's tennis but men's tennis as well.

Billie Jean King was a temperamental, opinionated player, and she was also an erratic one—she would often win or lose matches by great margins. She let people know that the U.S. Open was not her favorite tournament—she preferred playing on grass and loved Wimbledon. As soon as she became prominent in the sport she took on the associations and organizations that reinforced the secondary status of women. When these groups didn't provide adequate opportunities or proved unresponsive to the need for change, Billie Jean began her own tours and organizations and publications. She started the magazine *womenSPORTs*, the tour sponsored by Virginia Slims, and the Women's Tennis Federation. With such organizational acumen, her ability to activate allies, and her determination to face down those who tried to block the achievement of her goals, she was not a universally loved figure, though she was certainly a respected one.

Title IX, the federal legislation that banned discrimination in schools, was signed into law in 1972. Billie Jean King was a big supporter of this legislation: it ensured that women on campus had the same opportunities as men to participate in sports sponsored by high schools or colleges. The boom in women's sports, most notably in soccer, tennis, and basketball, is a direct result of Title IX, as it required that schools provide the space and time for women to explore competitive athletics. This boom, in turn, helped to change the notion of the ideal female physique. Worked out and muscular started to become a desired look for women. Women's strength moved from being something felt on the inside to a quality that could be immediately seen in a woman's physique.

Title IX has had an embattled history. Feminist support was not unanimous in 1972. According to Donna Lopiano, executive director of the Women's Sport Foundation, many in the women's movement "thought that athletics was a male construct that taught violence against somebody else, inordinate levels of competition—that it was an unhealthy activity for women—and that we were going to follow in the footsteps of men's values, and not the best men's values at all" (in Roberts, 159). Antifeminists, both male and female, have long criticized Title IX, suggesting that it amounts to reverse discrimination. Their critiques strike a similar tone to those who have attacked equal opportunity legislation.

In 2002, with George W. Bush as president, the National Wrestling Coaches Association filed a lawsuit against the Department of Education, arguing that implementation of Title IX hurt male athletics. In response to this suit, the department created the Commission on Opportunity in Athletics. Supporters of Title IX felt strongly that the commission was stacked with those who did not favor Title IX (many were male football coaches) and that its recommendations would have severely limited the effectiveness of Title IX. Women's sports advocates, including Geena Davis (an actor as well as an archer) and Holly Hunter (who played Billie Jean King in the film *When Billie Beat Bobby*), effectively lobbied the Department of Education and the recommended changes to Title IX were dropped.

The sporting goods industry was far more responsive to Title IX than football coaches. Sports industry sales went up with young women as a new demographic and promised to go up much farther. In 1974, the president of Spalding, Richard Geisler, said, "Suddenly women are into everything, basketball, soccer, track, golf, tennis, softball" (in Searcy). Sales of tennis products increased by 15 percent each year in the '70s, and by 1974, 40 percent of the eleven million tennis players in the United States were women. Title IX's changes in schools meant that many new athletes would emerge (Geisler estimated two million by 1978), and each of these players would need rackets, uniforms, balls, and other sporting accessories. A lucrative new market was opening up. As a result, the sporting goods industry responded well to Title IX and almost immediately began to do market research into the needs of female athletes. Women's sports provided a great opportunity for the apparel and equipment industry, and they were profitable, too, for players' management teams. Until she was outed by a very public lawsuit, Billie Jean King endorsed products for Wilson (tennis rackets) and Adidas (sneakers), as well as Carnation Instant Breakfast, Colgate, Aztec (suntan lotion), and Sunbeam (hair curlers).

APPEARANCES

Billie Jean King eschewed looking too feminine off the court, unlike other players, including Margaret Court and Chris Evert, who assumed more sedate, traditional tennis personalities and looks when they were not playing a match. For example, in the opening of the televised broadcast of the Battle of the Sexes, Howard Cosell commented on King's disregard for emphasizing her good looks. When she entered onto the floor of the Astrodome, Cosell admitted that she was pretty but added that if she would let her hair down and take her glasses off she would be getting offers from Hollywood. In other words, she didn't take the time to look her best for the male viewer. In Cosell's view, Billie Jean King should ditch the glasses and wear more makeup; she should wear clothing that hides her firmness and accents her curves. Cosell's comments were critical of her fashion choices; he was not thinking, of course, that her appearance might be very pleasing to male and female viewers who like athletic-looking, unadorned women. After all, thousands of fans in the Astrodome wore buttons that proclaimed "I love Billie Jean King." No doubt for some, this love had erotic overtones, as well as affection, for a role model.

Indeed even as King makes her divalike appearance on the floor, carried by a group of football players on an Egyptian-style throne, the camera cuts to a man in the stands holding a sign that reads "Billie Jean King wears jockeys." This highlights one of Billie Jean King's transgressions. Not only is she good at a game unabashedly displaying competitiveness; she also doesn't act—or look—like she is supposed to as a woman. She is a gender misfit—she does not perform or look appropriate to her gender. Her demeanor is unlike that of the stronger, taller, broadershouldered Margaret Court. Court took time off when she married to start a family, and she always privileged her husband and marriage over her tennis game, whereas Billie Jean—even though she, too, was married—always made sure that the women's game came first. Billie Jean showed women that they could privilege their careers and lives over the needs and demands of the men with whom they were involved. Not all men appreciated this message—certainly not the man in the stands holding his insulting sign.

When it became news that Billie Jean had had an abortion in 1971 (her husband released this information when she was asked to sign a pro-abortion petition), her status as a rebel was further emphasized. After all, this proved that she had rejected the traditional role of dutiful wife and delighted expectant mother. Her challenge to Bobby Riggs became a challenge to all men, and it solidified her double status: professional troublemaker and professional tennis player. Through her looks and manner and political commitments, she disobeyed the rules of femininity that operated both in tennis and in popular culture. She was a grown-up tomboy who never took to heart the mandate that adopting a culturally sanctioned femininity was necessary for her success. She took her own unorthodox approach—one that helped to make her a success—to the match itself.

The best-of-five-sets match (women usually play a three-set match, but King, feeling confident in her stamina, wanted a five-set match like men play at the major tournaments) took place on the floor of the Houston Astrodome in front of 30,492 fans, the largest audience ever for a tennis match. Socialites and celebrities sat in hundred-dollar seats on the field around the tennis court, specially built for the occasion; the masses paid six dollars for seats in the stands. The celebrities included TV stars Ken Howard and Blythe Danner, who got to plug their ABC television show, *Adam's Rib,* which, like the 1949 film, featured female and male attorneys who oppose each other in court. The country singer Glen Campbell was there, as were Andy Williams and football legend Jim Brown. It was not exactly an A-list Hollywood crowd, yet familiar faces abounded from the worlds of sport and entertainment.

The coverage on ABC used Irving Berlin's song "Anything You Can

Do, I Can Do Better" from the musical *Annie Get Your Gun* (1950) as a theme for the match, replaying the chorus each time the network broke for commercial over a cartoon caricature of the two opponents. *Annie* is the story of another gender misfit, who indulges in the pleasures of male activities but is lost when it comes to the rituals of courtship. Indeed tomboys abound in films and musicals about the settling of the West—from *Calamity Jane* (1953) to *Johnny Guitar* (1954)—suggesting that it was not only land that was up for grabs but also the remapping of gender roles in the expansion of America. Similar gender rights were at stake in the Battle of the Sexes.

The program begins with a carnival-like party in the Astrodome filled with makeshift pregame rituals. Riggs gives King a huge Sugar Daddy candy bar (something she could suck after she lost the match), and King offers Riggs a baby pig (in her autobiography King reassures her readers that the pig went back safely to a farm). As soon as the match starts though, it quickly becomes an intense competition. The tomfoolery of Bobby Riggs quickly dissipates. Riggs becomes sullen and his demeanor tires. Billie Jean barely cracks a smile during the entire match. Her indulgence in the spectacle of the event ends as soon as the match itself begins. She competes in a way that was not possible for Riggs.

The ABC network, which had paid the promoter $750,000 for the rights to the match, begins its program with a series of talking heads from a variety of female and male celebrities, who each voiced their opinion on who is going to win the match. Predictably, most of the men argue that Riggs will win—with some notable exceptions. All of the African American men who are interviewed, save Jim Brown, argue that King will win, due to her superior athleticism. Of course, this is not a scientific survey, but it does suggest that these black men were less invested in the match as a media event and viewed it as part of a struggle for equal rights, akin to civil rights. King will win simply because she is the better player, and this has nothing to do with gender, an argument suggested by Selena Roberts in her book, in which she quotes Gloria Steinem (116) discussing the apparent relationship between civil rights and women's liberation with regard to the match.

Roberts also notes that the actor Cliff Robertson is the sole white man interviewed who thinks that Billie Jean King will win—he bases his argument, though, on hearing that she plays like a man (116), which is to say that she is aggressive, competitive, and powerful. In other words, Robertson can't accept that King is a better player regardless of gender; it is her masculine approach to the game that makes him believe in her victory. Of course, if it is true that King plays as if she were a man (rather than a masculine woman), then also Bobby Riggs plays like a woman. He relies on encouraging his opponent's mistakes and does not rely on physical force; rather he opts for placement. In fact, Riggs is an unlikely representative for mainstream American masculinity. Although he proclaims broadly that he is a male chauvinist pig and does not believe that women's tennis is equal to the male game, he is neither muscle bound nor handsome, and, like King, he wears thick-framed glasses. His hair is unruly, and he walks, as female commentator Rosie Casals continually reminds the audience, more like a duck than a man. He looks goofy, and his effort in the spectacle is more like that of the nerdy character nicknamed the "Toad" on *Happy Days* (1974) than Clint Eastwood's character in *Magnum Force* (1973). Both Riggs and King are remarkably ill suited to represent gender norms, and each is a rebel against the conformity and elitism of the sport of tennis.

The network hired Rosie Casals to comment on the match alongside Howard Cosell and the male tennis player Gene Scott. Each was clearly hired for their partisan position, with Scott favoring Riggs and Casals favoring her doubles partner King. Previously ABC had hired Jack Kramer to be a commentator. Kramer was a real enemy to King. He had refused to give equal prize money to women in the tournament he ran in Southern California and was outspoken against women's tennis. King threatened to drop out of the match if Kramer was allowed to commentate. She was not going to "give him a national forum to spout off his views on the night of maybe the biggest match in my life" (*Billie Jean*, 175–76). For King, if Kramer had been included in the event one of her enemies would be profiting from her endeavors, and thus she refused to agree. The head of ABC Sports tried to calm King down, but she was adamant in her demand: she would not play if he was hired to be a commentator. The network did not officially give in to King; instead Kramer withdrew and was allowed to give a statement before the match that expressed his displeasure at the way he had been treated by King (Kramer received his $2,500 fee). Frank Gifford joined Casals, Cosell, and Scott. Gifford prowled the celebrity seats for interviews during the break—the celebrities were a jovial lot who were busy drinking champagne and socializing and smoking, as well as watching the game. Everyone, it seemed, had placed money on the match. As was written in their contract, Gifford also interviewed Riggs after the first set and King after the second. Of all the commentators Gifford appeared the most neutral.

Cosell could not help but be surprised at how well King was playing and issued forth with comments such as "she's walking like a man" after King stomped the court after making a particularly good point. He also chided Casals for her partisan comments. Indeed, Casals was relentless in making anti-Riggs comments—though she was also often critical of King's play, noting that Billie Jean was nervous at the start and that she was not playing her best in the first set.

Casals's behavior hurt her career as a commentator. As Roberts indicates, "[S]he was virtually blackballed from TV for years" (124). Casals was instructed by the network to make fun of Riggs (his walk, his play, his age, etc.), and she received these instructions in her earpiece. Casals was clearly no fan of Riggs and his antics, and she was more than keen to have King win, but many of her comments that made fun of Riggs himself (and not what he stood for) were written by the producers. Later Casals admitted as much, calling her producer-induced antics "a sideshow" (in Roberts, 124). Cosell also played up the conflict between Gene Scott and Rosie Casals, reminding the audience that he stood between them to keep them from fighting each other, although it is clear that he, too, is taken aback by Casals's comments. Yet, by the end of the match, Cosell does admit that Casals predicted its outcome exactly—6-4, 6-3, 6-3. None of the other announcers could imagine that King would win—let alone in three sets.

The television audience watches Cosell, Casals, and Scott only during the pregame patter (with a rather lecherous Cosell flinging his arm around Casals). As soon as the match begins they are heard as voice-overs commenting on the match. Although the match is ostensibly about equality between the genders, male voices outnumber female voices three to one. The audience does see the third male voice, Frank Gifford, during his brief interviews between sets with celebrities who have the best seats.

Howard Cosell was an excellent play-by-play announcer, but tennis was clearly not his game. As a result he turned to Casals and Scott to further explain some of their comments and to provide perspective on the match. Cosell's voice is one of the most famous in the history of sports broadcasting. The quivering timbre of his staccato baritone can lend suspense to a match of tiddlywinks and bring excitement to the play-by-play of a chess match. Most famous for commentating on the Muhammad Ali fights, his vocal intensity matched perfectly with the theatricality of the prize fighter both inside and outside the boxing ring.

Cosell and Ali became good friends—each benefited from the other's personality and Cosell clearly loved interviewing Ali, setting him up for his witticisms and braggadocio.

The use of Cosell as the lead announcer emphasized that the game was not only a match; it was a "fight" since Cosell was known for covering boxing bouts. Cosell's presence immediately gives the match the importance of an international sports event. He is eager to focus on the showbiz aspects of the match and ready to be charmed by the antics of Riggs, just as he was taken by the rhymed threats of Muhammad Ali. A fight with Muhammad Ali was always a show as well as a power struggle. Cosell was good at egging on sports personalities, which added excitement to an event—making an audience wonder if charming big mouths like Ali—and Riggs—would come through on their boastful predictions.

King quickly dominates the match, and Cosell notes that the humor has gone out of Riggs. Cosell is left to comment on the athletic feats of King, and he does so with unabashed disbelief. He had clearly believed that an out-of-shape ex-athlete in his middle years was destined to defeat a female athlete at the peak of her athleticism just because of his gender. Yet once Billie Jean King shows her aggressive flair, she is no longer female in his purview—he cannot accept a dominant female. For him athleticism and competitiveness are the domain of men, so from this perspective he is forced to describe her as a man. Thus Billie Jean's body is already a transgendered one for Cosell—she has stepped outside the boundaries of what is possible for female corporeality.

Another crucial aspect of the televised match is the audience in the Astrodome. They did not wait until the end of the point to clap and cheer. They yelled and screamed during play (a no-no for which the audience would be chided at a regular tennis event by the chair umpire). The match lost its fanfare and phony ritual as soon as play began. Riggs continued to wear his Sugar Daddy warm-up jacket at the beginning of the match, as his contract dictated, trying not to show that he was sweating. He started off complimenting his opponent's winning shots by yelling a patronizing "atta girl." But when King focused on playing her style of tennis and Riggs was unable to create mistakes in King's play, he, for once, shut up. Although Riggs was silenced, the audience remained loud. As Cosell described the setting for the television audience, the spectators were treating the game like it was football. Both Casals and Scott, who had been paid to disagree and spar, agreed on this point. They liked the crowd reaction, believing that it was good for tennis. In

Close-up of Billy Jean King and Bobby Riggs with the media at a press conference at the Houston Astrodome, September 20, 1973. (Photo by Jerry Cooke/Sports Illustrated/Getty Images.)

one evening, tennis became popular culture. The grown-up tomboy Billie Jean King won the match, but both Bobby Riggs and King—as well as the producers—succeeded in transforming the game of tennis. A woman who struts like a man and a nerdy guy trying to act tough were a compelling duo.

BUTCH HEROES

Judith Halberstam writes, "Before there were lesbians, there were butches." She is discussing film, but it is as if she were writing also about Billie Jean King. Halberstam argues:

> The masculine woman prowls the film set as an emblem of social upheaval and as a marker for sexual disorder. She wears the wrong clothes, expresses aberrant desires, and is very often associated with clear markers of a distinctly phallic power. She may carry a gun, smoke a cigar, wear leather, ride a motorbike; she may swagger, strut, boast, flirt with younger and more obviously feminine women; she often goes by a male moniker: Frankie, George, Willy, Eli, Nicky. She is tough

and tragic, she was a tomboy, and she expresses a variety of masculinities. (186)

With Billie Jean King, we have a woman who has two first names—one a man's name that is also her father's (Billie) and the other Jean, which can also be a man's name when spelled differently (Gene). When she marries Larry, Billie Jean takes on his last name, moving from the more femme-sounding Moffitt to the resoundingly masculine surname King. Billie is like the film women that Halberstam enumerates—and indeed Billie Jean's life is one both exposed to and hidden from the media; she is a butch hero.

When Howard Cosell remarks that King is walking like a man after winning a point, he is also saying—if he had had access to the terminology—that her butch gait is right out of countless movies from *Johnny Guitar* to *Calamity Jane.* In these films the female character's femininity is in question and her masculinity is on display. She walks with a proud swagger, likes to hang out with the guys, and is usually quite charming and popular but is often subject to sharp rebukes because of her marginal status. As much as he is impressed by her play, Howard Cosell continually reminds the audience of Billie Jean King's outsider status and how inappropriately she acts, moves, and looks from a masculinist viewpoint. Yet this "outsider" status is also part of her allure, and, like a film butch, who may be punished by the narrative (or forced to reform), akin to the way the handsome pretty boy vagrant is chased out of town in Tennessee Williams's plays, Billie Jean King is popular because she appears maverick and independent. Like David Bowie (discussed later in this book), King is popular in part because she is a gender rebel, even as she is subject to sexist, homophobic, and "butchphobic" comments. The gender rebel has an allure, but often he or she is forced to suffer for her or his difference.

Billie Jean King was involved romantically for many years with her personal assistant Marilyn Barnett. After their relationship ended, Marilyn Barnett sued her former lover for palimony . . . or "gaylimony," as Billie Jean King later referred to it (Barnett wanted half of Billie Jean's assets, as well as one of her homes). She argued that she had given up her career as a hair stylist in order to devote herself to her former boss's life. In her lawyers' argument, Barnett had been King's real spouse but when the relationship ended had nothing to show for it. The judge ruled in Billie Jean King's favor, stating this was a case of lover's revenge and not the settlement of a real, long-term relationship. The case did not advance the rights of gay people in relationships, but it did force Billie Jean to admit that she had been in a relationship with a woman and to state that she was bisexual. Today King is completely out of the closet, and this unfortunate case became the first step for her in acknowledging publicly what many had assumed all along.

In 1973, Marilyn and Billie Jean were constant companions. When Billie went to Hilton Head to prepare for the match against Bobby Riggs, Marilyn traveled with her—not Larry King, who was busy negotiating the deal with promoters. Larry, whether he knew it or not, functioned as her beard, and as her business manager he profited from her success. A happy, winning Billie Jean was in his best interest, and Marilyn was part of her happiness before their relationship apparently became dysfunctional. Marilyn is mentioned often in Billie Jean King's 1974 book as her personal secretary, but if one reads between the lines, one can see the more intensely personal attachment between the two women. And certainly she spends more time with Marilyn than with Larry; Marilyn goes everywhere Billie Jean goes.

In the Battle of the Sexes, Marilyn Barnett sits closer to Billie Jean King than does Larry King, who is in the second row. When Billie Jean begins to cramp in the third set, Marilyn massages her calf muscle, in front of all America—remember Marilyn is not her trainer, so it is as if they are putting their intimacy on display. Indeed, Billie Jean hugs Marilyn before she gives Larry a rather perfunctory kiss after she wins the match. Although she is still in the closet, she does not refrain from showing that her primary affiliation is with another woman.

LESBIANS IN TENNIS

In her essay "Love-Love: A Content Analysis of the Media Coverage of Lesbians in Sports," Erin Korreck argues that the typical sports broadcaster "masculinizes lesbian athletes and does so because they do not fit the stereotypical image of a 'feminine' woman'"(13). Since sports media find it difficult to describe the lesbian Martina Navratilova (as Korreck showed) using words that are usually attributed to women, terms that are affiliated with masculinity are deployed. Looking at *Sports Illustrated* between 1979 and 1989, Korreck contrasted the ways in which Chris Evert and Martina Navratilova were discussed: 85 percent of the words coded as masculine were used to describe Navratilova (11). Even the tone of the "masculine" words used to describe the lesbian and heterosexual athletes was different: masculine words attributed to Evert were *determined* and *brave* whereas Navratilova's words were *strong* and *power*, accenting Navratilova's physical prowess and her appearance rather than her behavior or effort. The converse was found to be true with feminine words: writers at *Sports Illustrated* used terms such as *pretty* and *sexy* to characterize Evert, focusing on her appearance. The words used to describe Navratilova's femininity included *patient* and *emotional*, referring to her behavior rather than the way she looks. In a bifurcated gender system, women athletes make sense to the masculinist mind-set only when they make an effort to look feminine. Otherwise these athletes are considered to be trangressive, and masculine terms will be used to describe them. A masculine woman shows her femininity only when she makes some form of emotion visible—being affected by emotion remains the domain of women, so the emotive Russian players who often shriek with disappointment, like Elena Dementieva or Dinara Safina, show that they are really girls through some of their "feminine" displays, whereas the more stoic Maria Sharapova displays her femininity not through emotion but through the decided emphasis on fashion that is evident in her on- and off-court ensembles, even though she is broad shouldered and stands well over six feet tall.

In concert with Korreck's findings, when an openly lesbian player from France, Amelie Mauresmo, rose to prominence by advancing to the finals of the Australian Open in 1999, her body—and not so much her sexual orientation—caused an uproar. This uproar was prompted by the reactions from her two final opponents in the tournament when speaking in front of the media. After Mauresmo defeated the higher-seeded Lindsay Davenport, she ran to embrace her girlfriend. Prompted by this display of her sexuality, Davenport, by no means a weakling and tall for a woman at six feet, two inches, told reporters that Mauresmo's strength was overpowering, adding that playing her was "like playing a guy" (in Forman and Plymire, 120). After Martina Hingis beat Mauresmo in the final, she quipped to the German press that Mauresmo "is here with her girlfriend. She's half a man" (120). For Davenport and Hingis, Mauresmo's open lesbianism served as encouragement for them to talk about her "mannish" strength and physique. Hingis was roundly and rightly criticized for her comments, but what is clear in Davenport's and Hingis's remarks is that Mauresmo is not only being chided for her sexual orientation. The physique, strength, and athleticism of the nineteen-year-old newcomer disturbed the top-ranked players—her butch demeanor and "mannish" physique were challenging, and they were phobic in response.

Amelie Mauresmo is a strong-jawed and attractive woman, with very broad shoulders and "cut" arms. Her biceps, however, are not as bulging as Serena Williams's (and her serve is by no means as fast). Yet Mauresmo did not choose to temper her physique with "feminine" fashions as does Williams, who displays a more traditional and very accessorized femininity off the court—Williams also adorns herself with jewelry and wears clinging dresses on the court. Mauresmo's game, like King's, also relied on varying her shots and coming to net. She was not a baseline player who emitted a girlish, soprano shriek every time she hit the ball like Maria Sharapova or, before her, Monica Seles (even the Williams sisters let loose with their own soprano cris de coeur in intense situations).

Mauresmo did not have a two-handed backhand like the rest of the women players (and many men), and in between points she did not have a gait that accentuated her hips like the "femme" players. The combination of her powerful frame and the techniques of her game upset the predominant paradigm in female tennis, which is to balance competition with the appearance of a traditional femininity. The top players exert much energy reminding reporters and fans that they are also girls who like fashion and boys; the Serbian player Jelena Jankovic wears so much makeup on court that it appears as though she is wearing a mask. Mauresmo clearly had no time for such performances and was able to discuss her sexuality openly from the moment she reached prominence, unlike King or Navratilova, who started their careers with their sexuality in the closet. Mauresmo benefited from King's and Navratilova's experiences and ultimately their standing proud as lesbians, even though both King and Navratilova began their careers hiding their private lives in order to protect their careers and endorsements.

As Forman and Plymire note in their 2006 article "Amelie Mauresmo's Muscles: The Lesbian Heroic in Women's Professional Tennis," the response to Mauresmo signaled a change in sports marketing. When Billie Jean King came out in 1981 with Marilyn Barnett's law case, she lost most of her lucrative contracts. When Navratrilova began to discuss her bisexuality in 1980, she knew that she was not going to get the contracts with merchandisers that would allow her to earn the big money. But she also knew that she was still at the top of her game and could rely on prize money (in very large part because of the gains that King and her allies achieved). Navratilova was right—she never received the sports contracts (she did later endorse Subaru however, a car that has been successfully marketed to lesbians)—especially when compared to her heterosexual rival and friend, Chris Evert.

Unlike her predecessors, Mauresmo was able to keep her contracts, most notably with Nike. These corporations stood by her even though she didn't earn a number-one ranking until 2004 and didn't win a major tournament until 2006 when she won the Australian Open against Justine Henin. In this match, Henin was clearly overpowered and outpaced by Mauresmo. Henin withdrew in the second set complaining of stomach flu. Mauresmo seemed more concerned about her opponent and spent time consoling the weeping Henin rather than celebrating her own victory, showing why she is one of the best-liked players on the circuit. She wanted to make sure her colleague was okay before accepting her own triumph. Her concerned behavior was clearly not a display of testosterone-influenced behavior (according to Forman and Plymire tennis fans assumed she was taking steroids [126]), and even after her long wait to win a major tournament she showed a compassion reserved for female athletes. With a Wimbledon victory, also in 2006, she showed no mercy for Henin and put to rest any doubt about the validity of her number-one ranking at the time and the press rumblings that she was a player who chokes in the big matches and that, despite her masculine veneer and contours, she still lacked a competitive (i.e., male) nature.

Mauresmo's body received more attention than her sexual orientation in the media and in discussion groups on the Web. When she emerged in the spotlight, the furor surrounding her physique, her gait, and her manner was entirely reminiscent of the attention given to the "malelike" demeanor of Billie Jean King and the perceived masculine traits of Navratilova. What is clear about the response to King, Navratilova, and Mauresmo is that each becomes a new kind of ideal that is both alluring and threatening—a worked-out body matched by a confident demeanor that is drained of all calculated girlishness. Forman and Plymire argue that Mauresmo's success with merchandisers is one of niche marketing—that she is being presented as a strong lesbian—and that this appeals to a segment of the audience. Hence Nike is not so much going out on limb in supporting a gender rebel or someone suspected of being transgendered. Rather it uses Mauresmo's status as a "butch hero" as a way to sell its product—her perceived "masculinity" trumps her lesbianism.

Although King could not get the same lucrative contracts as an open lesbian in 1973, she was a butch hero all along. Her toned body, her manner and assertiveness, her strut—in short her distinctive female masculinity—were always a major part of her popularity even if some found them threatening. After all, others found her rebel pose alluring and never wanted her to get the beauty makeover that Howard Cosell recommended. And Billie Jean King's efforts and stance have fueled depictions of her in popular culture.

REPRESENTATIONS OF THE KING

In April 2006, HBO Sports premiered *Billie Jean King: Portrait of a Pioneer.* The documentary, produced by Margaret Grossi, uses interviews with friends and colleagues to represent Billie Jean King's impact on the game of tennis—and indeed the role she had in changing gender relations during the 1970s. It features recent interviews with Billie Jean, looking back on her life and her struggles with her identity and the male bias in tennis. Today she is in a committed relationship with her lover, Ilana Kloss, and has been with her for twenty years—they met first when Ilana was a ball girl but didn't get together until many years later. The openness with which the two discuss their courtship and relationship is in marked contrast to the ways Billie Jean once hid her relationship with Marilyn Barnett.

The documentary also highlights the match between Billie Jean King and Bobby Riggs (as does Billie Jean King's 2008 book *Pressure Is a Privilege*) and the influence this popular event had on the game of tennis. The film stresses that Billie Jean and Bobby were friends and remained so until his death—their adversarial stance was for publicity, and each used the Battle of the Sexes to advance their own overlapping agendas. Yet Riggs succeeded just by getting Billie to agree to the match—he had already made his point by beating Margaret Court and was then just after more publicity. King needed to win in order to achieve her objectives; Riggs just needed to show up. Their shared goal was to change the game of tennis forever, surmounting its elitism and introducing it to millions of potential new fans. According to King, when she visited Riggs for the last time, he said, "Billie, we really made a difference, didn't we?" (*Pressure Is a Privilege*, 190).

Tara Mateik's performance piece "Putting the Balls Away" (2008) reenacts the spectacle of the Battle of the Sexes and the media hubbub around the match. Mateik combines video, footage from the event, and a live reenactment of the match. He plays both Billie Jean and Bobby but not simultaneously. Yet in viewing the YouTube version of the performance, one sees the same body playing both characters, and the audience is made a witness to the similarities between the two "adversaries." After all they are played by the same performer and represented by the same body.

During the performance's match sequence, a live Billie Jean King plays against Bobby Riggs, who appears in a video against the back wall (akin to watching a Nintendo Wii tennis match). After a few points in which Billie Jean wins, we see the onstage transformation of the live performer into Bobby (with the help of stagehands), and then Billie appears on video ready to take on the live Bobby. Tara Mateik's reenvisioning of the match becomes an inner conflict of gender, as well as an outer performance of twinned selves, one live, one on video. His performance of the two adversaries underlines the likenesses between Bobby and Billie Jean while italicizing their dissimilarities.

The affinity between Billie Jean and Bobby is also featured in a 2001 film ABC made for TV, *When Billie Beat Bobby*. It starred Holly Hunter as King and Ron Silver as Riggs and was written and directed by Jane Anderson, who also wrote an acclaimed film about a transgendered woman called *Normal* (2003). *When Billie Beat Bobby* focuses comically on the lead-up to the match and then reenacts the battle itself. It also highlights the impact that Billie Jean King's victory has on its imagined female audience. Her victory is depicted as one that inspires women to imagine a different future for their lives.

It also leaves out key aspects of the match and Billie Jean King's personal life. Most important, Marilyn Barnett, a key player in King's life at the time, is written out of the script, and as a result the film puts King back in the closet that she no longer inhabits. In this film there is no attempt to show the "secret" that King hid from her public, and hence no connection is made between her butch behavior and her lesbianism (she is portrayed as charming to a group of male reporters—not as a flirt but as one of the boys who knows how to kid around). Billie Jean's husband is shown not only as her business manager but also as her romantic interest, which was no longer true in 1973—by this time they were really only business partners.

The film doesn't include Gene Scott—the match is announced only by actors playing Howard Cosell and Rosie Casals (Fred Willard, known for his work in the mockumentaries of Christopher Guest, plays Cosell, and Elizabeth Berridge appears as Casals). This omission changes the gender balance of the match greatly—and Casals's anti-Riggs comments are toned down in the film. In sum, though entirely entertaining, *When Billie Beat Bobby* is by no means a docudrama; it is a TV movie based on a real event, though it does use some footage of Frank Gifford interviewing the audience from the telecast of the match.

Nevertheless, Holly Hunter captures King's determination, her restraint, and, when pushed, her temper. Ron Silver is perfect in depicting how Riggs couldn't help but become a caricature of himself, and the actors show the unlikely bond between King and Riggs. At the final point, when it looks like Riggs is about to double fault, we hear Hunter in a voice-over encouraging him to get it over the net so he won't finish the match without a fight. King is concerned for her opponent—she wants him to show his resolve and not his exhaustion, for his sake and in order to enhance the spectacle. Billie Jean King is depicted as being not as single-minded and stern as she appears, and, unlike Rosie Casals, she shows that she actually feels sorry for the guy.

In *When Billie Beat Bobby,* Jane Anderson emphasizes how the match changes the lives of the women who watch it on television. She imagines five separate audiences, cuts between them during the match, and finishes the film with a montage of their reactions to King's victory. There is a young black couple—she wants to watch the match; he doesn't believe that King has a chance and wants to watch the film *Bonnie and Clyde,* which is on at the same time. We also see elderly folks assembled in front of the television at a nursing home—and at first one of the ladies there roots for Riggs because he is older (she changes her mind when she observes his sexist antics). We witness a white family with two boys who eat in front of the television—when one of the kids spills his meal, the wife and mother cleans the carpet instead of watching the television. We see a sorority and witness the young women's intense involvement in the match—and then their joy at King's victory. The final audience we see is a group of men and women assembled at a quintessential American bar. At first the men are boisterous, but when King emerges as the clear winner the women begin to assert their place and cheer.

Anderson shows how, on one evening, the match captured the attention of the country. Yet she clearly believes that the match had an ongoing influence on a variety of households and environments, particularly in relation to how women view themselves in these places and structures. For Anderson, King's victory had an immediate, energizing, and lingering effect on the lives of the viewers—it was not only a media spectacle or entertainment. It was a pep talk to the female audience, telling them to *go for it.*

Anderson demonstrates these effects at the end of the film with the montage of reactions to Billie Jean King's victory. First, we see Casals after Cosell has finally left her alone. In a close-up, she starts to laugh and then begins to cry and her arms go up in triumph as she exclaims, "Yes!" In this we finally get to see the stress that Casals was under all along and how important King's victory was to her, despite her glib comments, which had been encouraged by the producers. The soundtrack begins to feature an upbeat melody that rises in volume, featuring a soulful female vocalist.

This music continues as we see the white housewife crying in happiness, sitting on the carpet in front of the TV. Her two sons and husband are asleep. A title appears on the screen, reading "Will Divorce Her Husband and Go Back to Law School." Next we learn of the influence the match has on the young black couple. In a medium shot, we see the woman, tears on her face, clapping her hands. Her title reads "Will Grow Up to Be a Coach for Women's Pro Basketball." The camera moves to a long shot of her boyfriend, and a title appears that reads "Will Give Women Top Positions in his Software Company." In Anderson's montage, King's victory is a life-changing moment, allowing men to see the validity of women as coworkers in powerful positions.

As the montage continues we then see the women in the sorority, who are dancing to the R & B song on the soundtrack. They move in slow motion and the camera moves in to provide close-ups of various young women in the room. Each close-up is matched with a title that allows the viewer to see the character's dazzling future—one becomes a senator, another a surgeon, another a studio executive, and so on. In Anderson's view, with King's achievement young women are energized to reach their individual goals. We don't know if any of the women become lesbians, feminists, or transgender activists (or workers at a Wal-Mart), but we do learn that their career choices are influenced by King; they move into fields that were then—and still are—male dominated.

To hammer down her point with humor, Anderson's montage finishes with a pregnant woman giving birth. The doctor announces to the woman that her newborn is a girl. Over a close-up of the newborn, a title appears that reads "Future Professional Soccer Player," suggesting that the baby is being born into a new era in which both excellence in sports and individual accomplishment for females are possible. With this sequence the film stresses that the match was a key ingredient in producing a new generation of assertive, professional women who will realize their selfhood through their careers and not through marriage or motherhood—or for that matter, political action.

What the film does not show is that the match also highlighted the reemergence of the butch hero in the figure of the match-fit Billie Jean King. This kind of hero was already a feature in Hollywood films, but with King popular culture had a real-life female hero who was a beloved, desirable icon. She attained this stature because of her stance not in spite of it.

In an episode of *The L Word* that originally aired on January 29, 2006, Billie Jean King made a cameo appearance. *The L Word* was a Showtime drama that depicted the lives of a group of lesbians who live in Los Angeles—a weekly serial with relatively good production values that focused on the sex lives of glamorous-looking women. One of the women was Dana, who died of breast cancer at the end of third season. Dana was a successful tennis player who began the show in the closet but with the encouragement of her friends and girlfriend comes out of the closet in the second season. In the episode entitled "Light My Fire," Dana triumphs in a tennis tournament and after winning a match is interviewed by Billie Jean King (playing herself), who is not only a retired player but in the episode is also a sports announcer. Dana is jubilant at her victory but also clearly delighted to be in the presence of Billie Jean King. King congratulates her on her comeback and then says, "As a professional athlete to come out as a lesbian is really a big risk. Do you get tired of being asked about your sexuality all the time?" Dana agrees, but then says that coming out is easier because of King and then interrupts her own serious response. She tells Billie Jean that she is her hero. They both laugh, and Billie Jean says for the two of them "how embarrassing" it is that the serious interview has become a meeting between a fan and a star. Dana goes on to win the tournament. When she wins, the show cites the "Mauresmo incident" in Australia in 1999. As if inspired by meeting her idol Billie Jean King, Dana passionately kisses her girlfriend Laura in front of the cameras.

Just as Mauresmo's contract with Nike signaled a new era of sports marketing that embraced the display of the powerful female body, *The L Word* episode displays aggressive product placement that shows that today's lesbian visibility is supported by corporate sponsorship. In this episode, the character Dana wins a Mercedes Benz car and uses a Wilson tennis racket—a brand that Billie Jean King used to endorse before she was outed by Marilyn Barnett's legal case. Individual achievement is the scaffolding of corporate sponsorship. Take Nike's tagline "Just do it." The slogan instructs the consumer to take action. Yet its intent is to remind the gay, lesbian, transgendered, or feminist consumer that you never really do it alone; you do it because of your favorite product and the empowered identity that the product gives you as a minority consumer.

This, too, whether she intended it or not, is also Billie Jean King's legacy. In the long road to gain equality, one has to sell products and indulge in media spectacle along the way. One also has to accept this preexisting narrative: the individual is the agent of change, not the group. Of course, Billie Jean King was a maverick—yet she changed the status of female athletics in large part because of the strength of the alliances she developed and the camaraderie that she helped foster among other athletes. Indeed an unlikely ally was Bobby Riggs, who helped to prove her point about women's tennis and the potential for expanding the market for tennis.

The renaming of the U.S. Tennis Association's National Tennis Center as the Billie Jean King National Tennis Center in 2006 was deserved and timely—and the ceremonies that accompanied this event justly paid homage to a woman who improved and popularized the game of tennis. Nonetheless these touching celebrations of the efforts of an individual also serve corporate goals.

To her credit, Billie Jean King let the audience know that "My house is your house." Indeed, the audience for the U.S. Open is diverse and animated, and the stadium names honor Arthur Ashe and Louis Armstrong (who lived nearby in Queens). The ultimate irony is that Billie Jean King never liked the U.S. Open as a tournament and always preferred Wimbledon, a tournament that only provided equal pay for women in 2007, due in large part to the efforts of Venus Williams as representative for the female players. Williams thanked Billie Jean King when she won the tournament in the first year in which women received the same prize money at Wimbledon. She told her mentor, "I love you. I wouldn't be here if it weren't for you" (*Pressure Is a Privilege*, 184).

At Wimbledon lawn tennis traditions remain—all the players still wear white—even though many rituals have been modified. Now players only have to bow—not curtsy—when the queen or her son, the heir to the throne, are in attendance. Other members of the royal family do not have to be acknowledged at all. After all, with the popularization of tennis, it is the triumph of the female or male individual under corporate sponsorship that really reigns supreme. Now the player bows to the corporation, not the nobility.

CHAPTER 4

David Bowie, Aladdin Sane, and America

Like Billie Jean King, David Bowie had started his career in the late 1960s but didn't move into the media spotlight until the early 1970s, after a major image change. Also like Billie Jean, David Bowie directly challenged prevailing notions of gender and did so quite consciously. Unlike King, who had a clearly articulated political agenda, Bowie's challenge was a deliberate way for him for him to achieve stardom. When Bowie sang "Rebel Rebel"(1974) he wasn't referring to a political insurrectionary; rather he was portraying a cross-dresser whose ensemble has been torn, someone like the persona he adopted in the early '70s, one that would bring him "Fame" (another Bowie song, this one from 1975).

David Bowie is now part of rock's aging aristocracy. He and his glamorous wife, the former model Iman, are consummate celebrities—they are elegant and cosmopolitan and succeed in staying out of the gossip pages. Although he is now an elder statesman, Bowie's will never entirely become a nostalgia act no matter how often he plays his old songs; he continues to sound current by reapplying layers and nuance to his identity. However, the drastic changes in his visual style—other than aging—have ceased, and he seems to have stopped taking on characters from other planets—and other sexualities—in performing his songs.

Bowie remains a commanding, intense presence onstage, even without the makeup, mime, and mincing of his youth. After the release of his 2002 album *Heathen,* I was at the outdoor concert at Jones Beach Theater when Bowie opened for Moby (who acknowledges Bowie's influence on his synthesizer-based dance music). As Bowie played, a thunderstorm moved in from the ocean and it began to rain heavily. The stage itself was covered, so Bowie and his band continued to play while the determined and adoring audience got drenched. Bowie was performing when suddenly he pointed up at the sky—and at that very moment a huge bolt of lightning electrified the night. With his grand gestures, it appeared as if Bowie was conducting the light show that rolled above him. This "heavenly" event exemplified the strange appeal and power of Bowie—he was always an x-man, possibly a genetic mutant, or someone who could claim alien ontology having found his way to earth at Roswell, New Mexico. Even though Bowie wasn't the headline act at Jones Beach, on this evening he was the star who controlled the heavens, a celestial being that had come down to earth for a thunderous visit. In comparison, Moby was a mere mortal.

BENDING GENDER

Bowie was never entirely original, nor was he ever completely derivative—and he doesn't always acknowledge the many sources of his sound and look. He is a master of appropriation, setting the stage for such artists as Madonna and Lady Gaga, who scan the world for musical and style trends. In the early '70s Bowie was considered part of the glitter or glam rock movement, which was a style of music that was not of his own design—instead he had accommodated himself to this style of pop music—and with songs like "All the Young Dudes" he became its spokesperson. He also changed glam rock—and then helped to end it. In 1973 his appearances as the desirable androgynes Ziggy Stardust and Aladdin Sane, creatures from other planets who were outrageous and fey, propelled a new kind of youthful rebellion. This rebellion blurred the boundary between masculinity and femininity and celebrated the pleasures of proclaiming oneself bisexual.

This emphasis was startlingly new for English youth subcultures—as Dick Hebdige notes in *Subculture: The Meaning of Style* (1979), Bowie's rebellion had nothing to do with taking up a working-class position that had an embedded or overt politics of the Left or Right—like those of the mods, skinheads, teds, and later punks. Most of these groups' musical genres—even punk with notable exceptions—relied on a certain kind of English "lad-ism," all-male camaraderie united around the plight of being young and working class and, presumably, heterosexual. Bowie's stance elided issues of social class and focused instead on gender—in this way, his stance would appeal to Americans who were in the midst of a great shift in attitudes toward gender and were indulging in new expressions of sexuality. Americans do not feel comfortable confronting issues of social class in their popular culture, except for those tales that repeat the rags to riches theme. These tales are foundational to American mythology and suggest that class distinctions are surmountable. Bowie's otherworldly persona was the ultimate immigrant success story.

Bowie was perfect to take on this role as gender rebel. To start with, he is unusual looking—his eyes appear to be of different color, due to a punch in the eye when he was a child and a subsequent eye operation. He is slim and tall with alabaster skin that verges on looking translucent, rather as one imagines a Martian might look. In 1973, he was not without muscle tone and he had broad shoulders, but his unmanly leanness lent him a youthful and feminine appearance. His slender physique also gave him the ability to wear elaborate outfits and still appear trim. His face was both handsome and pretty—he had the chiseled good looks and strong jaw typically deemed manly, but he also featured a long visage with high cheekbones that is usually regarded as more suitable for a pretty woman. Bowie's teeth were a bit ragged and crowded, hinting at his working-class roots, but his neck was long and seemed to stretch like a reptile's at certain moments—suggesting aristocratic pretension. This pretension denotes the privilege of a private income that affords one self-invention. In sum, Bowie's androgyny—and his masking of social class—was inherent in his body and face, even before he put on a dress and makeup.

BOWIE AND 1973

David Bowie began his career as a pop singer in 1968, but it wasn't until 1973 that he enlisted the trick to his success. That was his year. In England he had three albums in the top one hundred and was a darling of both the media and fans, who imitated his looks and sang along to his strange, confessional lyrics. In 1972, as well as releasing his landmark album, *The Rise and Fall of Ziggy Stardust and the Spiders from Mars*, he established himself as an Andy Warhol–like figure within the music world, becoming an impresario and producer and acting like an enfant terrible with a coterie—or a star with an entourage. He wrote Mott the Hoople's most successful song, "All the Young Dudes," resurrecting singer Ian Hunter's career. He produced comeback albums for Lou Reed (*Transformer*) and Iggy Pop (*Raw Power*) and visited the United States for a short tour. In 1973, he went on the road and tried to become a star in America through a much longer visit.

He released *Aladdin Sane* in April 1973, an album that was directly influenced by his experience traveling in America. Although the album and tour brought him additional fame and more critical acclaim for its adventuresome musicality, they did not bring him all the success in America he wanted. He wanted to extend his popularity beyond the devoted cult following that his previous album had produced. This cult following would not explode until he changed directions in 1975, mimicking and adapting the rhythm and blues sound that was based in Philadelphia (a city where he was especially popular) with the album *Young Americans* and the single "Fame," cowritten with John Lennon. His movement toward R & B and soul music is already hinted at in *Aladdin Sane,* and the album marks the end of his glam rock period.

In America, Bowie's affiliation with glam/glitter was not especially advantageous to him as this pop movement never really caught on in the heartland of the United States as it had in England. Still American rock critics loved to discuss Bowie's appeal and the meanings of his songs and his stance—Bowie was rich in symbols, signs, connotations, and contradictions. He was far more provocative than most of the corporate heavy metal or the emerging Los Angeles sound that was finding its home on FM radio and the predictable pop that was common on AM. Finally, for the first time since the summer of love, journalists had something to muse on—after all, how much could be written about the top single of the year—Tony Orlando's "Tie a Yellow Ribbon Round the Ole Oak Tree?" How much more could be written about new albums from the bands prevalent on FM such as English bands that indulged in virtuosic guitar and keyboard solos and bummed out lyrics; Yes, Pink Floyd, or Emerson, Lake, and Palmer, or even Black Sabbath or emerging American FM acts like Steely Dan or the Eagles? Bowie's complexities and contradictions stood out, and he legitimized the existence of social critics in the guise of rock journalists.

American funk music was dynamic at this time (with bands like the Ohio Players, Tower of Power, the Isley Brothers, War, and Parliament/Funkadelic), and disco music was just starting out. Yet due to the racial stratification of American radio, funk was having a difficult time finding its place on the bandwidth and was still being ignored in the rock press. Bowie, however, did not ignore American music, especially the sounds that were emerging from the black and gay communities, and by 1975 his pose and musical style began to reflect these influences.

Bowie was born David Jones in Brixton, South London, an area later known for its large West Indian community. His dad was a Yorkshireman who married an unmarried woman with a child; their first child together was David. His dad was a ne'er-do-well and a former club owner who later moved into middle-class respectability by working his way up to become a publicist. His mom worked as an usher in a movie theater. She resisted middle-class respectability and, like many in her family, suffered from mental illness; clearly Bowie was a child of both of them—ambitious, troubled, unconventional. As a teenager, David persuaded his father to buy him a saxophone, and spurred on by a growing love of music (initially Elvis Presley, but then Charlie Parker and other jazz musicians) he began music lessons, encouraging his fascination with American music, which continues to this day.

David Bowie's fascination with America may have begun with music, but it quickly spread to an obsession with American culture: its myths and social realities, its celebrities, and its influence on the rest of the world. Two of his most famous songs, "Young Americans" (1976) and "I'm Afraid of Americans" (1997), portray his contradictory feelings toward the nation and its people—as does a less well remembered song entitled "This Is Not America"(cowritten with Pat Metheny and part of the soundtrack for the 1985 film *The Falcon and the Snowman*)—but many of his other songs take on the United States as subject matter. His first tour of the States, supporting the album *The Rise and Fall of Ziggy Stardust and the Spiders from Mars,* propelled this fascination. Bowie refused to fly and traveled the country with his band in a Greyhound bus. This journey resulted in the musically more adventurous—and more "American"—album *Aladdin Sane.*

Aladdin Sane is not as heralded as *Ziggy Stardust* or as memorialized in rock histories, yet it is an album that takes on America as a subject matter. Bowie becomes an acute social observer of the land of Lou Reed and Iggy Pop and attempts to bring soul and jazz influences into his rock-guitar-based music. This required new percussion, new background vocalists, a new pianist, and the increased use of saxophone. In sum, this transition would prove to break up the English band that had brought him to stardom. By the end of 1973 Bowie had dropped his band, mimicking the narrative in the album *Ziggy Stardust,* which tells the story of a rock savior who leaves his bandmates behind as he reaches stardom.

David Bowie's 1972 Carnegie Hall debut in New York was sold out. It included four hundred reporters and critics (some of whom had been previously sent over to England by RCA records to see a Bowie tour in England). He was promoted as a major new force in rock. Yet during the same tour, across America's expanses, concert dates were canceled due to low ticket sales and Bowie played for just over one hundred fans in an eleven-thousand-seat hall in Saint Louis. In Phoenix, he also played for a small audience in a huge hall, apparently made up of a large contingent of drag queens.

Bowie proudly declared himself bisexual, and in January 1972 he told one reporter from England's *Melody Maker* rock newspaper that he was gay and always had been (in 1983 he refuted his own assertion). He appeared in women's clothing onstage and in press photos. Bowie loved fashion as much as ideas and music, and with such an emphasis he can be credited with helping to end the hippie era once and for all. With his ascendance, for a few "golden years" rock's politics focused more on new poses of sexuality, and butch women like Suzi Quatro and Joan Jett (in the protopunk all-girl band the Runaways) and effeminate men like Elton John and David Bowie all but dominated the airwaves. Many of Bowie's public declarations about his sexuality were part of the pose he held for publicity. Indeed, it does appear that Bowie spent more time in bed with women than men even in his bisexual glam rock years, but the fact that he insisted on this pose—if only for career purposes—was very influential to young men and women struggling with their identity.

Bowie and his American wife Angela (Angie) had a son, and she too, alerted the media to her bisexuality, which she insists was more true to her sexual nature than his. Ironically, their heterosexual union made bisexuality and androgyny fashionable. Thus, the threat to the parents of Bowie fans was never in his overt political views; rather it was in the performance of his pansexuality and the prettiness of his face with a bit of makeup on it. Most of his biographers remark that he was promiscuous, particularly in the very productive years of 1972–74. Yet his romantic life in the 1970s centered on two women: his wife Angie and an African American singer, Ava Cherry, who was also Angie's friend and lived with the two of them for quite a while. It was also rumored that he was involved with the cross-dressing performer Wayne County, who later became Jayne County. Most famously, Angie claims—or rather, brags—that she walked in on her husband and Mick Jagger in bed.

Whatever the "truth" of his orientation, Bowie became a star in part because he presented himself as an effeminate man who reveled in his own beauty. Bowie's preoccupation with foregrounding his deviance—and in flaunting the homoeroticism of his close male friendships with Iggy Pop, Lou Reed, and later Mick Jagger (to say nothing of his onstage simulated fellatio of bandmate Mick Ronson's guitar)—played on the success of the burgeoning gay rights movement. He also helped to make it fashionable for a certain kind of male peacockery and dandyism, pushed to the margins of society since the jailing of Oscar Wilde, to reemerge into the mainstream of popular culture. Mick Jagger displayed a vainglorious strut and pose, but Bowie turned style into a movement. Now men could proudly display all their feathers (and satins and velvets) and invest in presenting themselves as bisexuals, whether or not they acted on it. His ability to proclaim his difference was a remarkable shift in the gender politics of the day and was galvanizing for all the sissies, drag queens, sexual deviants, and nonconformists who were teens in the early 1970s, such as Boy George and Annie Lennox.

Yet Bowie's success in 1973 was not only explained by the presentation of his sexuality. The secret of his 1973 transformation into a rock star, beloved by critics and fans alike, was found in the marketing of his psyche and libido through a theatrical character he devised. As Philip Auslander notes, he "sought explicitly to perform rock *as theater*" (106, italics in the original). His movement into rock as musical theater required a break from his hippie past. The hippie movement was too drenched in American sincerity to indulge in the more English traditions of pose, artificiality, and excess. As Auslander succinctly writes, "Ziggy Stardust was a figure of alterity, not authenticity" (132). Bowie had already chopped off his hippieish hair in 1971; he had already gone to New York and hung out with the Warhol crowd and celebrated the aesthetics of decadence in his lyrics; he had already reshaped his Anthony Newleyesque crooning (113), combining an indulgent vibrato with hard-edged rock and reflective ballads that changed tempos with a catchy chorus (such as in the classic "Ch-ch-ch" in the chorus to his 1971 song "Changes"). Indeed, he had seen the play *Pork*, which traveled to London and was based on phone conversations between Andy Warhol and "superstar" Brigid Berlin; he had imagined "Life on Mars" on the 1971 *Hunky Dory* album and the plight of the space traveler in 1969's "Space Oddity" (which became a hit again in 1973). America and its Apollo space program and the demimonde of New York enthralled him. Yet fame still eluded him.

In 1969 David Bowie had begun to explore in music and words one of his major themes of glorious alienation: the saga of those who felt they were not really of this Earth even though they were also entirely English. To elaborate and illustrate this picaresque tale—the journey of a misfit who abandons himself desperately to pleasure in order to gain salvation—Bowie turned to theatricality, wearing makeup and dresses to accentuate his innate androgyny. He had studied mime with the avant-garde gay performer Lindsay Kemp, which sharpened his gestures and facial expressions (Kemp's troupe took the stage during some of Bowie's performances in 1972). Bowie knew that bringing in outside influences enhanced rock music. His influences were especially diverse, including ideas and visual inspiration from the high arts of jazz and Kabuki and the literary experimentation of William Burroughs. Other influences were from popular culture such as comic books and pornography. These disparate citations proved compelling to audiences, but it was not a mass following, rather a selected niche. All of these ingredients, attitudes, and poses brought him attention, but they did not add up to being a star.

David Bowie became a star when he decided to act the part—and he named this star Ziggy Stardust. The album *The Rise and Fall of Ziggy Stardust and the Spiders from Mars* was released in June 1972. It was a concept album, telling the fractured tale of a pop star named Ziggy, an alien from Mars, and his band. He arrives on Earth (like the character Bowie later played in Nicolas Roeg's 1976 film *The Man Who Fell to Earth*), a planet that has only five years left. Ziggy can offer the planet salvation, and he must come to terms with being a messiah. Ziggy was a figure of ultimate desire, mesmerized like Narcissus by his own image yet also intoxicated by the sound of his own voice and guitar. This character was at once a celebration of a rock star and a caricature of one—and Bowie invested himself in this performance, which mocked rock culture and at the same time indulged in it. Bowie confessed to being seduced by Ziggy as well and often insisted on being referred to as Ziggy in interviews at the time. When he killed off Ziggy, he and the character had almost merged into one. In taking on a persona that he invented—a denizen of the demimonde who was notorious for his lovemaking and narcissism and unbridled death wishes—David Bowie made himself a star. He colonized his own invention, conquering the terrain he had helped to map out.

His stardom was always postmodern—it was a simulation of stardom brought about by his own willful representation. Bowie became famous but not for being famous in the way that was predicted by Marshall McLuhan or Andy Warhol and feared by sociologist Daniel Boorstin (Boorstin railed against the kind of mediated pseudoevents of celebrity in which Bowie seemed to revel). Rather Bowie became famous by playing a character that was already a star in a narrative that Bowie, and his manager, constructed. Ziggy Stardust's fame was transferred back to the actor who played him. Bowie, by revealing the details and the differences—as well as the gluing together—of the private self with the public persona, made himself into the star he had always wanted to be. Suzanne Rintoul suggests in "Loving the Alien: Ziggy Stardust and Self-Conscious Celebrity" (2004) that Bowie's technique of becoming a star may be the standard maneuver, but Bowie/Ziggy is "a performance of celebrity" that "reveals the machinery behind the prefabrication of what an audience longs for or needs." Ziggy is the result of Bowie's research into the audience and media culture of the time by way of an elaboration of an identity that is drawn to save but cannot silence inclinations to destroy. To use contemporary marketing terms, Ziggy was the corporate logo of the Bowie product, but as Rintoul argues, Ziggy is also "a Bowie parody."

Ziggy was a fleshed-out character, and Bowie played it with the vigor of a method actor, yet he admitted that Ziggy Stardust and (later) Aladdin Sane were inventions, flights of his fancy, and dramatizations of his own self-involvement brought to the stage, in part, to sell the music. Bowie's confessions to trickery were part of the trickery itself. In 1973, as Bowie was enjoying the stardom that Ziggy Stardust had brought him, he quickly killed Ziggy off in London, in the famed concert of July 3, 1973, leaving a shocked audience in disbelief by announcing he would never tour again. What Bowie meant was that Ziggy would not appear again. Bowie was just getting started with playing his personae.

Meanwhile, a new persona, Aladdin Sane, emerged from the fall of Ziggy Stardust. Both creatures were orientalist fantasies, Ziggy was part Kabuki performer who wore clothes made by Kansai Yamamoto, an emerging designer whose clothes were influenced by traditional Japanese theater. Aladdin Sane was a magical, deranged boy from an imaginary Middle East who loved jazz piano—and he moved Bowie farther away from the glam rock sound of Ziggy Stardust. Both characters were designed to be objects of desire for all who encountered them. As Bowie wrote in the lyrics of "The Jean Genie" (which appeared first as a single and then on the album *Aladdin Sane*) even if Aladdin Sane and Ziggy Stardust were from an orientalist planet far away, they were also imbued with a healthy dose of Western narcissism—for the Jean Genie "loved to be loved." Whether or not he was capable of loving another was never clearly decided, but Bowie was most happy when he and his characters became desirable, something to be gazed on and craved by both young men and young women who imitated Bowie's style.

For Bowie, stardom always had a correlation with the celestial, and hence the beloved star is never entirely of this planet. Witness the song titles from *Ziggy Stardust:* "Starman," "Star," "Lady Stardust," and of course "Ziggy Stardust." In Bowie's imagination, rock stars come from the heavens; they are divine creatures that exceed humanity. Rock stars, in their inane decadence—such as the rock icons that Bowie worked with in 1972 and 1973, Lou Reed and Iggy Pop—no matter how lofty and attractive, no matter how bent on destruction through drugs and self-brutalization they were, in Bowie's eyes came to this planet as saviors willing to sacrifice themselves to fans. They offered themselves as sexual fantasy and entities with which fans could identify. Their self-destruction was part of their allure, and their rock star skinniness, paleness, indeed their corporeality—both energized and devastated by drugs—were incredibly sexy, even if they were not built for arduous sex acts. For Bowie, being a celebrity was mundane, but becoming a star connected him to a pantheon of otherworldly beings with which he found an affinity—this affinity was in the elevation of sleazy sexual behavior that defended him against the gloom of everyday life in the crumbling cultures of 1970s England and America.

David Bowie released *The Rise and Fall of Ziggy Stardust and the Spiders from Mars* in June 1972. The name Ziggy is in part an homage to Iggy Pop, who had become friendly with Bowie by this time. Iggy Pop was the lead singer of the Stooges, a garage rock band from Detroit, and a great influence both on glam rock and on punk rock with his onstage antics and singing style. But if Ziggy was from Venus, then Iggy was from Mars. If Bowie was cooked, to borrow a title from anthropologist Claude Lévi-Strauss, Iggy was raw. Bowie was the calculated aesthete, and Iggy was the wild man, an urban primitive. Rather than wearing ornate velvet or sheer kimonos, Iggy often wore his skin by going shirtless, unbuttoning his leather trousers to expose his genitals, and flaunting his muscled, scarred torso. Iggy was notorious for cutting himself and bleeding onstage—and he often let loose with animalistic howls, rolling around in his primal nature. His band was drenched in three-chord rock with lyrics that celebrated the cruelty and ecstasy of lust, most famously in the restricted splendor of "I Wanna Be Your Dog" (1969). Even though in many ways he was Bowie's opposite—Bowie was composed and rehearsed and Pop was instinctive and unpredictable—the Stooges' emphasis on short songs, a strong backbeat, repetitive guitar riffs, and yelling, almost sarcastic vocals was a direct musical influence on glam rock.

The name Ziggy is probably also a tip of the hat to the '60s model Twiggy. She was also celebrated for her androgyny and her slender look—she epitomized the chic, modern, London look of the mid-1960s just before the hippie look took over. With Twiggy, the modern super-model was born, creating a new female ideal—boyish in physique, without curves, and with just the mere suggestion of a female breast. Twiggy was both gamine and entirely stylish with her schoolboy short hair and huge, saucer-shaped eyes framed by dark makeup and extra-long lashes. Twiggy showed up on the Bowie album *Pinups,* released in late 1973, a shot that revealed the similarity between Twiggy's and Ziggy/Bowie's looks.

In England, the *Ziggy Stardust* album jumped to number five on the charts, but in the States it never rose above seventy-five in the top one hundred albums. Yet it stayed on the American charts for seventy-two weeks and went gold in 1974. The television network VH1 considers it to be one of the top one hundred rock albums of all time. Its influence on punk rock and the ways in which it deepened and complicated the rock trends of glam rock are immeasurable. Every song has become a classic. The album follows *Hunky Dory,* which established David Bowie's place in the burgeoning glam rock movement (more often referred to in the United States as glitter rock). Glam never became popular beyond the major cities of New York, Los Angeles, Boston, San Francisco, and Chicago. Bryan Ferry and Roxy Music did gain a large cult following in the States. But other English acts, such as T-Rex, Slade, Gary Glitter, and the Sweet, which dominated the pop charts in England in the early 1970s, never developed an American following.

BEFORE BOWIE

David Bowie was by no means an inventor of glam rock, nor did his early work in the late '60s influence it. Yet *Ziggy Stardust* is often consid-ered archetypical of the trend in rock music, even though it was an al-ready moving train Bowie jumped on. If glam rock had an inventor, it was Marc Bolan of the English band T-Rex, as Philip Auslander argues in his book *Performing Glam Rock* (2006). Bolan took the lead in develop-ing glam rock's mix of strong guitar riffs with catchy melodies and rela-tively dreamy, if incoherent, lyrics. Bolan moved away from the hippie look by wearing tight fantastic clothing and makeup and adorning him-self with glitter, though he kept his long frizzy hair. In rock, this was a great shift from looking downscale in jeans while playing impossibly virtuosic music such as in progressive rock with bands like Yes or Pink Floyd or Led Zeppelin. Bolan was a beautiful pop idol. He played guitar-based music that was often sculpted into a three-minute single that was easy for fans to sing with its strong backbeat and intensely catchy lyrics and melody.

The American cult performer Jobriath was already staking out some of the territory that David Bowie would move into. He referred to himself—as did the promotional material of his record company—as a "fairy." Jobriath celebrated his sexuality through music and movement—and he sneered at Bowie's sexual posing. Rock critic Greil Marcus notes that Jobriath was "the real queer" whereas Bowie was "the phony queer" (in O. Hall), and Elektra records decided to market Jobriath according to his difference. Like Ziggy, Jobriath was convinced that he was not of this Earth. He felt he was from outer space, for sexual deviants are above castigation and the sexual conventions of planet Earth as they are divine creatures with shamanic overtones. Jobriath's emphasis on his sexuality, also stressed by his management, did not pay off—after all Jobriath was not an exotic from England. Rather he was a homegrown "radical fairy" who nonetheless proved to be influential.

Lou Reed also laid the groundwork for David Bowie and glam rock. He was the lead singer of New York's Velvet Underground, which emerged from the Warhol Factory of the mid-1960s and featured the impossibly beautiful German model/chanteuse Nico. If West Coast music of the late '60s (particularly from San Francisco) celebrated the hippie lifestyle from free love to ingesting LSD, the Velvet Underground indulged in the demimonde, the pain/pleasure of taking heroin, and the sadomasochism inherent in obsessive sexual and romantic entanglements. Their music moved from dronelike, half-spoken incantations to repetitive guitar riffs counterpoised with lyrics influenced by avant-garde poetry and performance. As Lou Reed and the Velvet Underground stood firm against the hippieish music of the late '60s, while devoting themselves to experimenting with the rock form, they became a very strong influence on '70s rock that wanted to break away from the confines of heavy metal and progressive rock clichés. Their live performances drew on traditions other than rock music and incorporated experimental film and video, dancers, and intense strobe lighting. David Bowie was thus greatly indebted to Lou Reed and took it upon himself to resurrect Reed's career. Bowie also brought him to the stage in some of his performances for an encore of the classic Reed song "White Light/White Heat."

The New York Dolls emerged during Bowie's glam years and were also an influence on Bowie's incarnations of Ziggy Stardust and Aladdin Sane. The band formed in 1971, playing brash garage-band-influenced rock that was unheard of at the time while dressing like transvestite prostitutes in high-heeled pumps, ripped stockings, fingernail polish, overly rouged cheeks, and trashy wigs or teased out hair. They were anything but elegant, and they delighted in looking and acting sleazy. Singer David Johansen, like the rest of the band, was presumably heterosexual, yet he delighted in putting forward a swishy "barbiturated" sexuality to the delight of his audiences (and probably himself). The tension that was created when drug-addled tranvestites played pared-down, noisy, hard rock proved irresistible for many who were looking for rock to return to its energetic, rebellious roots.

Although Bowie did not accept Alice Cooper as an influence—he grew tired of being asked this question by American interviewers—Cooper did provide some of the foundation that Bowie then took as his own. Like Iggy Pop, Cooper was from Detroit, and he rose to fame in 1968. Cooper was heterosexual, and there was nothing camp or fey in his performances, but he did take on a woman's name and he wore makeup and women's clothing in order to adorn the metal rock 'n' roll that he sculpted into catchy singles. He was intensely theatrical—notorious for throwing a live chicken into the audience, which apparently then tore the bird apart—and his look and stance prefigured shock rockers like Marilyn Manson and prepared the way for lesser rock acts like the very costumed and themed Kiss to become popular with an American audience. Alice Cooper influenced glam rock not only with his costumes but also with his emphasis on playing guitar-based rock that was designed for a 45rpm single—not only a 33rpm album. Alice Cooper had bona fide hits heard on AM radio that celebrated teenage rebellion like "I'm Eighteen" (1970) and "School's Out" (1972). Later in his career, he also had a hit with the oddly profeminist ballad "Only Women Bleed" (1975).

By the early 1970s, a new group of teenagers became rock 'n' roll consumers. They were no longer satisfied by the love and peace sentiments of the late 1960s. White teenagers were being denied access to the delights of funk music, and as the era of Motown glory was ending it left only Marvin Gaye and Stevie Wonder as mainstream successes. Glam rock took up the estranged sentiments of this new teenager and celebrated his—and her—plight. This audience still wanted to buy singles (45s), eschewing the album-oriented, progressive rock heard on FM radio, but they did not necessarily want the sugarcoated excess of pure bubblegum pop like that provided by the Archies. Writing in 1978, after the beginning of punk, rock journalist Ken Barnes looked back on the relative success of glitter/glam rock.

> Glitter rock was mostly a sham, but what a glorious one! Flashy costumes, strident guitars, monolithic beat—glitter was exciting, records tailormade for disinherited kids. Its fashions revolted against an overall denim dullness, while musically it was a vital reaction (lifesaving, it seemed at the time) against a deadly boring, prematurely matured music scene. Glitter brought singles back to prominence. With the Beatles disbanded, the Stones and Who aging, largely inert, and seldom disposed to release singles as in the past; and newer superstars (Led Zeppelin, for instance) even less disposed, the 45-oriented (by disposition and economic status), British teenage population was hard up for music and idols, and glitter supplied both in profusion. Glitter was the first great rock & roll awakening of the '70s, synthetic or not, and even if the music sometimes sounds hopelessly dated . . . there's an immense amount of gratitude and respect owed to it. ("The Glitter Era," n.p.)

Glam rock returned rock to its rebellious roots when the progressive rock bands of the 1960s were becoming corporations that played in large halls. Glam drew on pop music with its chantlike choruses. It also drew on progressive rock, with its emphasis on the guitar as the lead instrument, but it sounded and looked like neither. Flared jeans and peasant blouses were not suitable attire for this newer generation of rebels; neither were the overt politics of rebelling against governments and foreign policies. Rather the revolt was centered more on the body and its portrayal and presentation through clothing, makeup, and hairstyle. The body and face became tableaux for a radical new mode of self-presentation that was heavily influenced by the performers that fans loved. Huge platform shoes and boots were in, as were tight satin and velvet clothing and high-water, rolled-up jeans and spiky, dyed, short hair. Joseph Roach in his 2007 study of charm and charisma, *It*, writes that "the eye of the beholder seeks out the highest features as focal point for its gaze, marking all the head as stage, and the features on it only players." Thus one can't underemphasize the importance of hair as glam's crowning achievement. Roach continues, "More intimate than clothing and yet more reliably prearranged than countenance, hair represents a primary means of staking a claim to social space. . . . Social hair is performance" (127). With Ziggy and his romantic plight, Bowie transformed glam rock, providing it with its story of origin in a newly imagined (outer) space, a story painted onto Ziggy's face and made theatrical and enigmatic by his blonde, spiky hair.

TALES OF ZIGGY

The *Ziggy Stardust* album opens with "Five Years." The song begins—and ends—with a simple drumbeat. The drumbeat increases in volume for the first sixteen seconds of the song. A strum of guitar accompanied by a piano chord introduces the half-sung lyrics, which capture the apocalyptic vision of the early '70s as much as they introduce the story of Ziggy/Bowie. The twin fears of nuclear war and ecological devastation of the planet prefigure this solemn realization that Ziggy's adopted planet has a limited life span, and Ziggy/Bowie details the actions of the new earthling with shock and awe. As he crowds his brain with experiences and observations, he yearns for the comfort of his mother. Although the song is not overtly political, Bowie asserts the nobility of the dispossessed and marginal versus the panic of people who hold symbolic power when they are faced with disaster. When a girl "goes off her head" and starts to "hit some tiny children," a person of color comes to the children's rescue: "if the black hadn't pulled her off, I think she would have killed them." When Ziggy sees a cop who "kissed the feet of a priest," Bowie incants "and a queer threw up at the sight of that," clearly siding with the viewpoint of the "queer" repulsed at the complicity of the police and the church.

From observing the world, the lyrics move on to looking back on Ziggy/Bowie and the shared dilemma of a performed identity. Ziggy and Bowie are both always in danger of feeling as if they are in a staged drama, as opposed to entirely inhabiting their experiences and feeling the intensity of emotion. Bowie sings, "it was cold and it rained so I felt like an actor, and I thought of ma and I wanted to get back there." The song then moves into repeating the increasingly intense refrain, "We've got five years," with a mounting string accompaniment adding to the intensity for the remaining minute and fifty seconds. This repetition becomes increasingly plaintive, as well as theatrical, highlighting the paradox in much of Bowie's singing: he invests himself in his notes, sounding intense, and at times his singing is almost tortured in a near scream. Yet there is always an emotional distance in the deployment of his vibrato and his ability to croon—and this technique lets the listener know that Bowie is also indulging in playing a character. In "Five Years" this style is contrapuntal to the stark, solemn confessional lyrics that suggest a concerned social commentator.

The rest of the album is not so filled with desolation, but it continues the story of Ziggy Stardust. The next song, "Soul Love," which also begins with a simple drumbeat, speaks of the promise of love. Yet the narrator in the song, presumably Ziggy, is unable to feel the heights of the emotional love that he can sense others have access to—one wonders if Martians are the ultimate narcissists, unable to surrender to love. The album continues to elucidate Ziggy, his life, his band, his relationship with his body, and his doomed pursuit of love, as well as his relationship with his fans and his fans' relationship with his music.

Of course, a concept album was nothing new in rock music—the Beatles' *Sgt. Pepper's* (1967) and the Who's *Tommy* (1969) were concept albums (another, the Who's *Quadrophenia,* was released in 1973). What distinguished *Ziggy Stardust* was that its emphasis was not on musical storytelling per se. Rather the album is a long character study, moving back and forth from Ziggy's point of view to songs about Ziggy such as "Ziggy Stardust" and "Lady Stardust"—each offering a different point of view on Ziggy. In the song "Ziggy Stardust," he is a rather butch, egotistical monster almost out of control, and in "Lady Stardust" he is a femme, immaculate, and endlessly charming chanteuse. Such songs provide different portraits of a made-up cultural figure and the milieu he created. The album is not a "rock opera" in its musical structure (there are no musical themes carried throughout the album, no overture, and no supporting characters that could have led to it one day becoming a film). Neither is it fantastical or hallucinatory like *Sgt. Pepper's.* The *Ziggy* album uses the invented figure as a surrogate through which Bowie can reflect on and indulge in stardom, rock idolatry, and the appeal of androgyny and gender ambiguity during the economic boom in postwar England and America (although the United States staged wars in Korea and Indochina).

The album ends as dramatically as it begins, with the anthemic "Rock 'n' Roll Suicide." Unlike "Five Years," which is written in the first person, "Rock 'n' Roll Suicide" is written in the second as a direct address, evoking and trying to prevent the imminent suicide of Ziggy, reminding him that "he's not alone." This song often finished Ziggy's live performances, and onstage Bowie and the audience enacted the lyrics: the song repeats the line "Gimme your hands, cause you're wonderful." As Bowie sang these lines he extended his hands to the audience, who in turn offered their outstretched hands to touch their beloved. It was as if

David Bowie attends to the needs of Mick Ronson's guitar. (Photo copyright © Mick Rock, 1972, 2010.)

his fans were willing Ziggy/Bowie back to life, each celebrating the wondrous other—and also hopefully continuing the show. The song becomes both a celebration of the sacrificial demise of the rock star from Jim Morrison to the not yet dead Sid Vicious, but at the same time it offers the devotion and mingling of identifications between star and performer as a reason not to kill oneself. The fans breathe life back into the body of the star, the diva/divo. The concert becomes a ritualistic act of revivification of the rock deity.

David Bowie went on tour immediately to promote *Ziggy Stardust.* He came to America in September, traveling with a large entourage of forty people. His management company, MainMan, set up offices in New York (and later in Los Angeles), and two performers from the Warhol play *Pork,* Leee Black Childers and Tony Zanetta, were hired as vice president and president. Bowie's manager, Tony DeFries, worked hard to gain Bowie publicity before he arrived in the States, and he succeeded in fine-tuning Bowie's appeal as a gender rebel. As Bowie biographer Christopher Sandford states, DeFries's schmoozing with the press ended in numerous headlines that "warned" Americans to "Lock up your sons—Ziggy is coming" (92). Bowie was not just coming to America; he was setting up shop there. He was immigrating—and in the next two years he spent as much time in the States as he did in England.

The first show took place in Cleveland on September 22, 1973. For this tour, Bowie added an American avant-garde jazz pianist, Mike Garson, to the band's lineup. Garson, a scientologist who tried to convert Bowie's band, the Spiders, was supremely talented. His playing mixed honky-tonk with cabaret and the latest techniques in improvisation, and he became a major part of the appeal of *Aladdin Sane.* In this part of the tour, though, he was not in the foreground—rather the guitarist Mick Ronson continued up front (both musically and visually) except in certain songs such as "Changes," which relies on piano embellishments to make its musical points.

The day after the concert in Cleveland, Bowie began working on the next album, *Aladdin Sane.* Bowie and the band traveled on a chartered Greyhound bus (Bowie refused to fly, which is rather odd for an "alien"), and his experience on the tour is represented in this album. The song "The Jean Genie" is derived from an impromptu jam on the bus, and it became one of Bowie's greatest hits with its tempting riff and his spoken verses, which alternate with the sung chorus. The song depicts a gloriously sleazy and appealing character. Apart from its obvious reference to the story of the magical genie in the bottle from the Arabian

Nights, Bowie also has said the song is about Iggy Pop and shows his fascination with this figure. Bowie said of the song, "I'd just met Iggy. He was this character out of Detroit and I was trying to verbalize him in some way. I wanted to respond to the kind of image I had of him, which changed as I got to know him" (in Welch, 92–93). Others have suggested that the song is a reference to the French writer Jean Genet, who was also famous for his involvement in the demimonde of criminals and hustlers. Indeed the name of the song and its depiction of a persona who relishes his outsider status could be a depiction of Genet, Iggy Pop, or Bowie himself.

Bowie also wrote the song "Panic in Detroit" on this tour, after a night on the town with Iggy Pop. It offers another portrait of the American singer. In this song Bowie casts him as a desirable political rebel, a homegrown Che Guevara, who hides his gun and is the survivor of a revolutionary group, "the National People's Gang." Bowie sings over the classic American Bo Diddley beat and soulful backing vocals. Conga drumming augments the intensity of the song. Mick Ronson's slashing guitar work crashes and slices over the beat, and he lends the song a feeling of impending chaos, of police retaliation against the failed, if glorious, revolutionary leader. Iggy Pop thus is played out as a mythic character, a mirror for Bowie.

Whether or not Bowie fell in love (after all, he insisted he was incapable of this emotion in song after song), it is clear that he was fascinated with Iggy Pop, and this fascination has erotic overtones and undertones. The album *Aladdin Sane* is evidence of Bowie's involvement with the American singer. It documents his changing perception of this enigmatic character, who is both a sexy revolutionary leader from the ultimate American city of Detroit and a magical genie let loose from the bottle and wreaking havoc wherever he goes. Clearly Bowie is mesmerized by his antics and attitude. Bowie views Iggy as a rebel in instinct, spontaneity, and wildness, whereas his own stances, even if they have more grace, are also always rehearsed and calculated. If Bowie represents the ego, he casts Iggy Pop as the unconscious. Or Iggy Pop was the genie that enchanted and enlivened Bowie's Aladdin.

Bowie's most important date on the tour occurred when he debuted, like every aspiring singer who wants to conquer America, in Carnegie Hall. The September 28, 1972, concert was a great success, and the tour was extended by eight weeks even though some dates had to be canceled due to lack of ticket sales. Bowie, however, was especially popular in Philadelphia, and a third show, on December 2, was added after the first two were sold out. The entire tour was a mixed success; RCA, his record company, didn't make much money, as Bowie's entourage was large and prone to expensive parties, charging everything to the record company. It was clear that Bowie didn't make real inroads into the larger American audience; instead he secured his attraction to a cult of followers. However, he had the chance to work and hang out with his American idols, Lou Reed and Iggy Pop—and Pop came under the surveillance of Bowie's management company, MainMan, which had opened up a Los Angeles office in part to look after the reckless American singer.

ALADDIN MOVES TO AMERICA

Bowie returned to England in December 1972 but he didn't stay away from America very long, returning on February 6, 1973. He arrived with a new song list that included songs from the yet to be released album *Aladdin Sane,* which he had finished in the weeks spent in England. Bowie's onstage character had begun to change from Ziggy to "A Lad Insane" (Aladdin), and he changed outfits five times during his concerts. He later mused that "Aladdin" was really Ziggy in America.

> It was just me looking around and seeing what was in my head. It was the result of my paranoia with America at the time. I ran into a very strange type of paranoid person when I was doing Aladdin. I met some very mixed up people and I got very upset which resulted in Aladdin. I knew then that I didn't have much more to say about rock 'n' roll. (in Welch, 56)

Aladdin was born of Bowie's experiences on his first American tour. Aladdin was as much a mood, a reaction to travel, a personification of a travelogue, as he was a character. The songs move from celebrating (and parodying) being a rock star and savior to social observation and estrangement in response to an America that both horrified and enchanted him. For the Englishman, America was already outer space.

The character of Aladdin premiered on Valentine's Day in 1973 at the Radio City Music Hall. The concert was a multimedia affair. It began with transgendered composer Wendy Carlos's electronic music from the film *Clockwork Orange* (1971). As Stephen Davis writes in *Rolling Stone,* "[S]everal layers of curtains parted to reveal a giant screen on which was projected an animated film of the cosmos rushing at light speed at the viewer" (1973). Davis describes Bowie's midair entrance.

A single spotlight opened up on a set of large concentric spheres welded into a cage and suspended 50 feet above the floor of a stage, in the middle of which was standing a stern and staring Bowie clad in a black silver garment, the first of what would be five different costumes that night. (in Harvey)

His costumes became skimpier with each change, as he performed an ersatz striptease for the audience, revealing his legs, part of his buttocks, and one nipple. He emphasized his lean frame as an object of desire, enjoying its display, serving as a counterpoint to his songs of suicide, paranoia, and alienation—exposing the eroticism in desperate characters and the salvation of lust. The concert ended with "Rock 'n' Roll Suicide." During this song, a girl jumped onstage, grabbing Bowie. Bowie fainted midsong. Some among the audience thought that was part of the act (and some feared he had been shot [Thompson, 68]), but Bowie was actually suffering from exhaustion. The nurse who diagnosed him blamed his excessive makeup—she said the cosmetics blocked his pores, inhibiting the normal activity of his face and body! (Harvey). While Bowie didn't tone down the makeup, he did sleep for twelve hours in order to prepare for the next night at the hallowed hall.

For the Aladdin tour, Bowie's management had learned from their mistakes. Bowie only played in venues where he and Ziggy had sold well. As a result, the Aladdin tour was more successful than Ziggy's, although it was stated that Bowie dropped to just 110 pounds. For someone just over five feet, ten inches, this is dangerously thin, suggesting there was little nutrition in his diet, and a lot of amphetamines. The tour moved on to Japan in April. The album *Aladdin Sane* was released that month.

The album cover is one of the most memorable in rock's history. Due to its use of seven colors, it had to be printed in Switzerland. The cover consists of a photograph of Bowie in a medium close-up against a white background. His hair is bright orange. His face and bare shoulders are Kabuki pale, but his cheeks and temples are rouged. Bowie's eyes are closed. A lightning bolt in red and blue divides his face starting on the right side of his hairline. The bolt moves diagonally down his face, crossing his left eye, traversing his cheek, and then extending down to the extreme left side of his chin. His bare shoulders show off an enticing, feminine décolleté. A substance resembling mercury sits atop his right clavicle, with part of it dripping over the bone, serving to underline his otherworldliness. Below this on his chest, the photo appears overexposed, and the bright whiteness of his skin matches the background color of the image.

Bowie's visage borders on looking like an animated image of a science fiction or cartoon character, one that is drawn rather than photographed. The lightning bolt makes literal Bowie's emphasis that he is a man divided, split apart by his pursuits, insights, and actions. Bowie has stated that Aladdin Sane is a character that was also in part based on his schizophrenic brother, and this image supplements the commonly held notion that schizophrenia renders the psyche dual and cleaved. Yet the cover image also depicts someone who is not entirely human—and in fact Aladdin is more unearthly than Ziggy: Ziggy hid his alienness by looking like a blonde rock star who appears to be at home in a dark urban setting. The cover of *Aladdin Sane,* however, is a head shot of an actor from outer space. He is impassive, almost imprisoned with himself; his makeup and adornment serve as protection from the world he can barely discern—or wants to escape. He seeks solace from the multiple, imagined gazes on his pale flesh. His hair is an impossible red color, almost that of a flame; his expression is on the border between indifferent and solemn. The cover serves to define the character and experience of Aladdin Sane as much as the songs on the album. If *Aladdin Sane* was a portrait of America, it was portraiture that stressed the fantastical, almost nightmarish reality the singer encountered—from the delights of the sleazy streets of New York, to insurgents in a collapsing Detroit, to the aging glitterati of Los Angeles furtively looking for prostitutes. Aladdin's America was both magical and horrific.

The album opened with "Watch That Man," a Rolling Stones–influenced romp that offers a snapshot of a celebrity party with some unsavory characters, particularly the host, who is perhaps the most unsavory of them all. Bowie's vocals are somewhat buried in the mix, following a technique used by the Stones in the early '70s, deliberately giving the album a rough, unpolished sound. Background vocals and saxophone riffs invigorate the hard-rocking song, one that indulges musically (it's a party song after all) in what it condemns lyrically.

The track that follows is the title track. The full name of the song is "Aladdin Sane (1913–1938–197?)." As the critics noted, 1913 and 1938 are the years before the two world wars broke out, and thus, in the title, Bowie suggests that war is imminent again in the 1970s. The song was written when Bowie was on his way back to England after his first American tour. Bowie biographer George Tremlett (90) suggests that the song was inspired by a book that Bowie was reading, Evelyn Waugh's novel *Vile Bodies,* which satirically describes the decadence of young people who dance and party away, ignorant of the encroaching Second World War. Indeed, the song does invoke the smart set, whose members are overly involved with who is sleeping with whom, in denial that the charms of opulence are fleeting when war is looming.

> Watching him dash away, swinging an old bouquet—dead roses
> Sake and strange divine Uh-hu-hu-uh-hu-hu you'll make it

In the song, a young man is taken off to a war that no one understands or sees as part of daily life, much like how the War in Afghanistan appears to be beyond the purview of many contemporary Americans even with our endless media choices, unless one has a loved one fighting there or one watches programming or reads newspapers originating from another country.

Although Bowie's lyrics in the verses use William Burroughs's cut-up style (where lyrics are assembled nonsequentially from a group of possible selections), they are also redolent of a bygone era. His singing is embellished by his use of falsetto and vibrato, but the song is Mike Garson's as much as it is David Bowie's. Bowie invited the pianist to indulge in an original long jazz solo. The piano becomes evocative of the dying culture of which Bowie sings, beginning with glissando flourishes that suggest sophistication and decadence, evocative of Jazz Age extravagance. The piano solo is almost foreign to the pulsing bass line and rock drumbeat of the song. Garson's playing then becomes frenetic, increasing his use of tremolo and trill. He moves up to the higher keys, and his playing becomes almost shrill, signifying near panic as Bowie returns to the question posed in the chorus: "Who will love Aladdin Sane?" As the song finishes, Bowie sings the lyrics from "On Broadway," again trying to evoke another era and location for the song.

With the lyrics, his crooning singing style, and Garson's piano, Bowie makes links in this between the 1970s and earlier eras of excess, times when the young and attractive avoided the obvious and blinded themselves to the clear warning signs in the political climate. In America in 1973, Aladdin confronts a culture in which the young and self-designated fashionable are all doing massive amounts of cocaine, barbiturates, amphetamines, and opiates, ignoring the ongoing war that Nixon refuses to end and the economy that is collapsing (due to rising oil prices and conflict in the Middle East). In this song, Bowie condemns this decadence, yet at the same time he celebrates and portrays its allure. This celebration and critique provide the creative tension that motivates the album.

"Drive-In Saturday" evokes the sexless future, even as it refers to the drive-in theaters that once populated America and served as a site for so many seductions. This song begins in waltz time, yet it is a dystopic vision of a mediated America. The young have lost their sex drive and have to go to the movies on Saturday to see onscreen what lovemaking is all about—otherwise they will have no idea how to experience erotic love. Bowie wrote this song while traveling through the desert in Arizona, and he is picking up on a chaste aspect of the American landscape, where the young are still taught abstinence and are instructed to divorce emotion from bodily expression. Bowie observes this contradiction in American life between the horny young people populating the coastal cities and those in the apparently repressed hinterlands who inhabit what an outsider could perceive to be a sexless bubble. Also Bowie is suggesting that Americans are constantly trying to experience the epic not through their own lives but through that which they view onscreen, as spectators. He knows this, in part, because he is a "resident" alien and was raised elsewhere.

Side one finishes with the rocking song "Cracked Actor," embellished by Bowie's harmonica playing, which harmonizes with Mick Ronson's guitar. The song tells the tale of an aging actor in search of anonymous sex with a male prostitute. According to Chris Welch (60), Bowie imagined this song as his own future after looking out from a limo at sordid interactions on Hollywood Boulevard. The song is catchy but merciless in its indictment of someone who has given up on love and uses purchased sex as its substitute.

Side two of the album opens with the song "Time," which is barely a rock song. Rather it is a Bertolt Brecht/Kurt Weill brooding on aging in a culture filled with the love of commodities and unwrinkled faces and firm bodies. Bowie's encounter with America is also an encounter with an infatuation with youth and the desire for youthfulness as a form of merchandising. "Time" stages the dilemma of aging in such an environment. Musically it relies on the piano of Mike Garson, and lyrically it centers on the personification of time as an evil nemesis.

> Time—He's waiting in the wings
> He speaks of senseless things
> His script is you and me, boy

In the song time is spoken of as being akin to a masturbating prostitute and is described through the haze of drugs and alcohol, in order perhaps to soothe its ravages. (Yet such a lifestyle only ages a rockstar more—just look at the craggy faces of so many aging guitar heroes prone to drug use in their younger days. . . .) For Bowie, time is personified as traitorous and faithless, seemingly affording a person a way station from the hardships of an edgy and excessive life, but in truth providing none—time provides no rest areas when it is measured by what occurs to a youthful body. Aging proves to be unavoidable and unconquerable; and youth is doomed from the get-go—it looses its magnetic allure, and substitutes plastic surgery for sheen. The song "Time" allegorizes the plight of the pretty boy alarmed by wrinkles, thinning hair, and a deepening voice, a plight that is also Aladdin's/Bowie's. He fights a loosing battle with decadent elegance, surrounded by rolled up $50 dollar bills reserved for chopped up white powder and flute glasses filled with overpriced champagne.

Bowie half sings the verses. He emphasizes the word *boy* at the end of the first two stanzas, and again his attraction to and repugnance for the sleazy world of prostitutes and johns reveals itself—and his fascination with this world is analogous to his relationship with America itself. The third stanza makes reference to Billy Murcia of the New York Dolls, who had recently died of a drug overdose, and Bowie suggests that Time demands sacrifices from the young and reckless in order to maintain its control over human activities. The "you" that Bowie/Aladdin Sane addresses in the song is presumably male (he refers to him as a boy), and in the final verse he speaks of his inability to inhabit their dreams; instead they can only abandon themselves to the moment. Bowie's delivery is campy. When he sings the line "You—just scream with boredom," he shrieks the word *scream* in his falsetto, mimicking the sound of a crazed drag queen he has no doubt encountered in the streets and at the parties of urban America.

The chorus consists of "We should be on by now," followed by a very catchy series of La, la, las, on which the entire band joins in, evoking a drunken sing-along. The words have two obvious references. The first is of a band waiting backstage for their queue to go onstage and Aladdin/Bowie's feeling that he should be in front of his audience performing—almost as a form of salvation, of delaying the ravages of time itself. The second reference is to waiting for drugs to take effect, so that the high can provide illusions, illusions that can serve to hide the presence of "Time." Intensely theatrical, the song paves the way for the less sublime "Bohemian Rhapsody," an even campier song by Freddy Mercury of Queen. Both songs show that some of the most loved rock songs are not rock songs at all but are replete with structures and techniques borrowed from opera, musical theater, and cabaret. They only masquerade as rock songs.

Side two of the album also includes "The Prettiest Star," a ballad that was written before most of the material on *Aladdin Sane* and as such doesn't delve into the sleaze, drug taking, and contradictions of America. Rather, it takes up an earlier obsession of equating worldly fame with celestial bodies, meaning that to become a star on Earth elevates one above the grime of Earth, a theme that enlivens *Ziggy Stardust*. Fame accentuates beauty and eliminates all the tedious aspects of everyday life. Bowie/Aladdin follows this song with a version of the Rolling Stones' "Let's Spend the Night Together," and it provides new possibilities for the song as a same-sex seduction. The song also lays bare the influence that the Stones have on this album musically (in its hard-rocking moments at least). Bowie adds some lyrics to the song: insisting to his beloved that "their love comes from above, " again emphasizing the celestial aspects of carnal attractions. Still this remake is the least successful song on the album, in part because he can't wrest it from the arms of Mick Jagger and the kind of impact the song had in its initial release in 1967.

After "The Jean Genie," the album finishes with "Lady Grinning Soul," a balladic love song that again features the piano flourishes of Mike Garson, linking it with "Time" and the other songs on the album that rely less on Rolling Stones–like rock structures. The song reveals the ease that Bowie has in singing ballads—after all the dramatic indulgences, his singing is his trademark, making him an unlikely rock performer and a more natural theatrical singer. Bowie can get away with a love song, and border on sounding sincere, while always revealing that he is perhaps more enchanted with the timbre of his own crooning, plaintive voice. Nonetheless, with "Lady Grinning Soul," he finishes *Aladdin Sane* by moving away from the drug-drenched sleaziness of much of the rest of the album. He once again invokes the redemption of love that he so consistently denies as a possibility. This tension is heightened while he is staring out alternately at a chaste and God-fearing rural America or a horny, seedy urban America from the window of a hotel room, a hired bus, or a limo, seeing himself reflected in the shenanigans of hustlers, johns, and aging actors. Bowie's point of view is always distinctive, and his pose is often subversive to gender norms.

GENDER AGENDA

In her influential book *Gender Trouble* (1990), Judith Butler writes, "*In imitating gender, drag implicitly reveals the imitative structure of gender itself—as well as its contingency*" (117, italics in the original). Butler insists that our everyday public actions related to gender—our displays of perceived masculinity or femininity, even of androgyny, actions that we may think of as part of our authentic selves—are always in part a parroting of activity that we have witnessed. These perceptions leave an imprint on us. Drag draws attention to and exposes the artifice involved in everyone's "performance" of their gendered selves and the degree to which we are all repeating lines from gendered scripts that are marked as male or female.

For Butler, acting appropriately as a man or woman is never encoded in our DNA or determined by our balance of hormones designated as masculine or feminine. Gender appearance and behavior are learned, and learned through each of us mimicking the actions, the gestures, the gaits, and the cadences of others. One becomes distinctive only through a series of detours through observing and repeating—and also rejecting—the public personae of those one encounters. It is in this process that one learns how to perform gender. A young man may have the genitalia and physique that "prove" he is male, but this does not determine his gender performance; rather the outfit he wears and how he wears it have as much bearing on how he will be perceived both by others and by himself.

David Bowie deliberately took it on himself to upset gender norms—and not only by insisting he was gay (he wasn't) or bisexual (he probably only went through a "phase"). His public performances in his glam rock years, as the character Ziggy or Aladdin, involved a rejection of expectations about how to portray and frame his body. These transgressions—his bitchiness, his campiness, his adoption of orientalist attire and space-age kitsch as a form of drag—were as successful as they were calculated. For Bowie, the sound of his voice—and his voice is a pleasing, controlled, theatrical, and versatile one—was not enough to develop his following, nor was it enough for him to maximize his performance. His work emphasized the visual, as does drag; it elaborated on and embellished the surface of a person as a way to both reject and hint at the truth of the person behind all the makeup, feather boas, and kimonos.

Rock critic Greil Marcus argues that a rock icon "divides the society between those who are disgusted and condemn it and those who are excited—maybe secretly, maybe not secretly—and find it appealing and attractive" (in Gilbert, 30). An icon has to be controversial, and in many cases the controversy is centered on the performance of gender; most recently Lady Gaga proclaimed her bisexuality (rumors circulated that she was transgendered and had a penis). Whether or not this term has anything to do with her behavior, it is part of what she is selling: difference. Successful rock stars do not conform to standard displays of masculinity and femininity—even macho heavy metal bands grow their hair long and indulge in makeup (though they always insist on sounding "male"). In *Just Kids,* her recent recounting of her early days with Robert Mapplethorpe in New York, Patti Smith recounts how much more attention she garnered when she changed her hairstyle from a hippieish Joan Baez look to a more androgynous Keith Richards style (2010). As Bowie learned, teenage rebellion and media attention are often focused on challenging and parodying gender norms. The public craves femmey boys and butchy girls, even if some profess to be repelled. As an insouciant Boy George stated after his band won a Grammy for best new artist in 1985, "Thanks America, you've got style, you've got taste, and you know a good drag queen when you see one."

Judith Butler argues that "the giddiness" of the drag performance is related to "the recognition of a radical contingency in the relation between sex and gender in the face of cultural configuration of causal unities that are regularly assumed to be natural and necessary" (137–38). Drag performance is pleasing and funny because it creates a cleavage between expectation and reality and it places in jeopardy the assumed unity between appearance and actuality in relation to sex and gender. This disruption is a pleasurable one, both to enact and to behold, as everyone is at some point issued a mandate to conform to gender rules, but only some enact a rebuke through either performance or lifestyle (or both). David Bowie became a star by investing himself in a disruption of the gender system. He scribbled across the normal signature of a man; it became an inscription of feather boas.

THE VOICE IN DRAG

Bowie's androgyny and calculated use of artifice were perhaps most pronounced in his appearance, but they also extended to his style of singing. He is a rock singer influenced by cabaret, musical hall, and ballad singing, a cross between Mick Jagger, Little Richard, and Anthony Newley (with hints of Judy Garland thrown in). He often mixes half-sung words with vocal lines in which he deploys his vibrato, ensuring that theatricality—and not only the expression of emotion—is foregrounded in his vocals. Shelton Waldrep describes Bowie's singing as

> a type of singing that almost over-signifies to remind listeners repeatedly that what they are hearing is a self-conscious performance of a character and emotion (singing to make you think about singing) that

yet connects to many listeners because it is not closer to how they experience emotion than music that attempts to be "naturalistic." (116)

Bowie's vocal style is indulgent and excessive and self-conscious: he
croons.

Waldrep asserts that Bowie's use of falsetto is also indicative of his
use of a "queer vocal erotics" (116). Yet Bowie never commits to his
falsetto throughout an entire song—or an entire career—unlike such gay
singers as Sylvester, Jimmy Somerville, or Klaus Nomi. Instead, as Waldrep notes, he uses his higher register "to create a momentary change in
chord or tempo, rather than to signify queerly the way it does for someone like Little Richard" (116). The falsetto is one of the techniques that
Bowie has access to—and one that can highlight the dramatics of his
voice. It shows that he will extend his range beyond traditionally held
distinctions between registers that are marked as male and female.

When men use their falsetto voice, they do not necessarily sound female—rather they are taking the steps that enable them to reach notes
that otherwise would not be available to them. In moving the origin of
their voices from the chest to the head, they are not reverberating as androgynous or asexual per se. In fact, the falsetto can be an intense voice
of male seduction—think of Marvin Gaye's use of falsetto in the song
"Let's Get It On."

The falsetto enables the male voice to move into high passion and
drama. In Western understandings of the voice, high notes portray a
heightened state, whereas low notes are employed to convey melancholy.
The falsetto voice does not imitate the soprano voice, but it does accom-
plish what a female voice is allowed to do—express precise, and at times
frenetic, emotion or a heavenly constitution. Male voices are restricted not
only by the organic production of the voice but also by social customs that
encourage them to remain restrained. When the voice moves up into the
head, it conveys excess and artifice and extends the borders of the male
voice. Bowie indulged in the vocal excess and artifice of the falsetto as part
of his performed rejection of traditional masculinity.

Yet Bowie's gender performance, one that rejected convention, became easier to digest because he framed it as if he were becoming another character. Furthermore, the character was not of this world; he was
a fairy from another world—not a homegrown, earthbound queer. Like
Jobriath and Klaus Nomi, Bowie was an androgyne. Thus he could not
possibly be from this planet, because on planet Earth the divide between
the genders is virtually a law. Bowie enacted a radical estrangement,
embracing and flaunting and staging over and over his own feigned for-

eignness. This foreignness was expressed in insisting that the difference between male and female—as well as deciding which gender he most desired (at least publicly)—was not his concern for he was not bound by earthly distinctions. Yes, it was an act, but it was an act that had major repercussions in terms of extending what could be possible in popular culture. The teenage girls loved him, and so did many of the boys. He became a sex symbol, in part for upsetting gender norms and in part for writing lyrics about sex as a monetary transaction and love as an impossibility that fame can trump.

David Bowie's stance was particularly influential on two gay rock critics. In his essay on glam/glitter, "The Androgynous Mirror," for *Rolling Stone*, Jim Farber writes of his own embrace of the rock genre as a way to both proclaim and mask his sexuality. He writes, "In the mix of male and female friends making up my glitter coterie, I was the only one who was gay (and the only one who knew that I was gay)." "Glitter's zone of ambiguity" protected him, he says, from "[his] own fears and sheltered [him] from the world's judgment" (145). Thus glam rock—and Bowie's emphasis on bisexuality—did not encourage him to come out as a gay. Rather glam rock provided Farber and other gay and lesbian teenagers with a freed-up zone where all sorts of sexual play were permissible. This zone was without the social mores of the larger culture. As I remember from my own high school years, it was preferable to be bisexual (at least at the *Rocky Horror Picture Show*), but being gay still meant being ostracized. Bisexuality was made cool by male rock stars and female tennis stars.

The British rock journalist John Gill takes a harsher look at Bowie and the sex/gender limitations of glam rock in his book *Queer Noises* (1995). For him David Bowie's proclamation of gayness in the early 1970s "was just another role for Bowie, who wasn't, of course, even David Bowie, really, but David Jones of south London playing at being a media star called David Bowie" (107). Yet Gill acknowledges that "while Bowie long ago dropped the pretense of even bisexuality, an aura of queerness has clung to him to the extent that he is probably the only heterosexual on the planet who has so much space devoted to him in the world's gay media" (107). And of course, Gill himself devotes much of his book to David Bowie's queerness and doesn't discuss Jobriath or Klaus Nomi, gay performers who influenced Bowie (some might say Bowie ripped them off). After all, Bowie's influence on popular culture continues to be easily discernible and visible.

Gill acknowledges that "Queer David" of the early '70s

created a breathing room both for queers and for those who weren't sure about their sexuality or their feelings about the sexuality of others. I knew and know heterosexuals whose attitudes about sexual difference were radically altered by the atmosphere of glam rock, particularly by the field of ambiguity staked out by David Bowie. (110)

There is great irony here. The glam rockers—not only David Bowie, but also Marc Bolan, Bryan Ferry and Eno of Roxy Music, Iggy Pop, Lou Reed, and the New York Dolls—were virtually all heterosexual. Yet they all flounced about like a bunch of poofs, transvestite prostitutes, or effeminate Martians. Yet both Farber and Gill attest that their influence on gay youth was considerable—they created a "space" where young people could explore their sexuality. For Gill, Queer Bowie created "breathing room"; for Farber, Bowie's androgyny helped construct "a zone of ambiguity." Both critics thus use a spatial metaphor to describe the effects of Bowie and glam rock on their own ability to achieve a gay identity—Bowie provided them and others with room in which they could become themselves. Bowie created space where there was none before—he brought a little bit of outer space to planet Earth and secured its place on the map. Bowie's outer space was a zone where gender mandates were nonexistent. Within this zone, youths could explore their sexual preferences without rebuke. Yet at the same time Bowie was only playing a role that he thought would bring him stardom.

The rock critic Lester Bangs was less impressed—and less influenced—by Bowie's use of personae and his abrupt changes in musical direction. After Bowie gave up glam rock and turned to soul music in 1975, Bangs deployed a racist and homophobic vocabulary to describe the calculations in Bowie's transformations. First he described Bowie's attire as "Afro-Anglican drag." He continued to cynically contextualize Bowie's moves, which he saw were strategically designed to bring him a black and gay audience.

Everybody knows that faggots don't like music like David Bowie or The Dolls—that's for teenagers and pathophiles. Faggots like musical comedies and soul music. No gay bars have "Rebel Rebel" on the jukebox; it's all Barry White and the big discotheque beat booming out while everybody dances his or her ass off. I'm not saying that Black and gay cultures have any special mysterious affinity for each other . . . what I'm saying is that everybody has been walking around for the last year or so acting like faggots ruled the world, when in actuality it's the niggers who control and direct everything, just as it always has been and properly should be. (123)

For Lester Bangs, Bowie's move to soul and disco was not due to a great love of the music and style or any affinity he might have for African American culture. It was another terrain to conquer, a bandwagon for him to jump on in order to expand his audience. For Bangs, glam rock never became affixed to gay culture; it was geared toward teens experimenting with their sexuality. Gay culture looked outside rock for its music—and turned to the black popular music tradition in order to find its musical identity. Hence disco. Once again Bowie followed, but he comes off like a trailblazer in part because of his visual appearance and in part because he sang like he hated rock music and loved balladic seduction.

BOWIE ON FILM

Two films have had an ongoing impact on the way glam era David Bowie is perceived: D. A. Pennebaker's *Ziggy Stardust and the Spiders from Mars* (1973, recently remixed for DVD) and Todd Haynes's *Velvet Goldmine* (1998). Pennebaker's film is a documentary about Bowie's last performance as Ziggy Stardust/Aladdin Sane (he performs songs from both albums and changes outfits to accommodate both characters—and he shocks his audience by announcing that this is his last concert). *Velvet Goldmine* is a fictional homage to the glam years and features a character, Brian Slade (who plays a character Maxwell Demon), who fakes his own death onstage and subsequently loses his fan base.

D. A. Pennebaker is one of the most renowned and important filmmakers working in the direct cinema style. He often examines rock music and celebrity in his films. He directed the landmark *Dont Look Back* (1967), which documents Bob Dylan's first tour in the United Kingdom and features the young musician's cantankerous interactions with the British press. Pennebaker is fascinated with the backstage area as a site of transformation and with seeing performers prepare for the audience. His films often are anchored by the tension between the public and private personae of celebrity—and the performances involved in both. In *Ziggy Stardust,* much of the backstage preparation, as Pennebaker captures it, is related to makeup and wardrobe changes. In these scenes, Bowie is emotionless and passive as his makeup artist and costume assistant help him—it is a solemn and ritualistic change from David Bowie into his space-age characters. We see the central place of theatricality and artifice in his performance as it is taking place in mundane fashion. When Bowie's wife Angela comes to the dressing room to wish him luck before the concert, she is livelier than he and is clearly playing for the camera. David Bowie remains motionless and remote—he is in a liminal moment, between two identities. He appears almost lifeless, especially in relation to Angela's upbeat persona. These backstage scenes (we also see him during costume changes when the band is engaged in solos) provide a great contrast with those in which we see Bowie onstage, where he is in command, using mime or grandiose gestures, and gradually wearing less clothing and flaunting his body.

The shots of the audience also reveal much about his fan base. The audience is primarily female and quite young. By 1973, he had become a heartthrob for young female teenagers. They know all the lyrics to his songs and imitate him in their dress and use of glitter, makeup, and footwear. Bowie is an object of desire for them, and they are almost religiously involved in his performance, imitating him. Of course, the focus on female fans may be the result of the cameraman's choice of reaction shots, but we do see rows of young female teenagers—teenyboppers— who stand enthralled watching Bowie. Guitarist Mick Ronson is clearly also beloved by the audience, and though he is never center stage when Bowie is singing, the lighting designer of the show makes sure he is visible to fans.

Bowie and Ronson cavort onstage like lovers, fully invested in the roles of butch (Ronson) and femme (Bowie). And of course, famously, we see Bowie going down on Ronson's guitar during his solo in "Suffragette City" to the delight of the female fans in the audience. What we witness in the film is how the female fan is energized by this performance of male homosexuality. This display of feigned desire is delightful and inspirational for them—and sexually involving—even though Bowie and Ronson are miming actions that exclude them as possible partners for the star and his partner. Bowie's onstage antics show how alluring a prancing, effeminate man—or if you will, a drag queen—is to a female audience. The space that Bowie creates, the space that was so useful for gay rock critics Gill and Farber, is also one that is inhabited by scores of girls who have just recently become teenagers. They may be attracted to him, but they also identify with Bowie's rejection of traditional depictions of sexuality. In Pennebaker's film, it appears that the fans utilize Bowie to support their own refutation of traditional sex roles. If he can act like a femmey boy, it's okay if they also theatricalize their own appearance.

Todd Haynes's film reimagines glam rock and Bowie's place within it. Like Shelton Waldrep in his book *The Aesthetics of Self-Invention* (2004), Haynes posits Oscar Wilde as the spiritual godfather of glam rock, especially as *Velvet Goldmine* depicts it as being essentially about self-creation, the embrace of artifice and wit, and male peacockery—and media attention. In the film, an emerald brooch that Wilde wears symbolizes the lineage between Wilde and the character Brian Slade. The brooch is lost until Jack Fairy (a character partially based on Lindsay Kemp, or perhaps Jobriath, who looks a bit like Roxy Music keyboardist Eno) finds it in the dirt after schoolmates beat him up for being queer. The power of the brooch is clear—if you accessorize to the max, display your effeminacy, speak in clever epigrams, and act like a star, fame is yours—and fame protects you from virulent, violent homophobia. Brian Slade steals the brooch from Jack Fairy, and soon after, with the help of a manager who realizes that the route to stardom is paved by acting like a star—and inventing a character to play—fame is indeed his. Once famous, he can explain both his bisexuality and his open marriage to the assembled media, entertaining them with his Wildean wit.

The film is also a love story between Brian Slade and a character based on Iggy Pop, renamed Curt Wild (a moniker that alludes to Kurt Weill, Oscar Wilde, and Kurt Cobain all at once). While both Bowie and Iggy Pop deny a sexual relationship between them—and Bowie would not allow any of his music to be included in the film—the album *Aladdin Sane* is testimony to how spellbound Bowie was by the American rock god. Haynes's film emphasizes the difference between the cultured Slade and the raw Wild (it is rumored in the film that Wild was in part raised by wolves!) and how sexually appealing and romantically intoxicating Wild is to Brian Slade. Slade wants to save Wild from drugs and obscurity and to have his management team take him on, in part as a way to make sure Wild remains near him.

When Wild leaves him, Slade is unable to maintain the character Maxwell Demon and wants out of the glam rock scene he helped to establish. He stages his onstage death and is found out by the press to be a phony. After hiding out for a few years, Slade reinvents himself as Tommy Stone and hides any connection to Slade/Demon. Here Haynes comments harshly on Bowie's rejection of the bisexuality and opulence of his glam years when Bowie reinvented himself as the harsh, somber, coked-out persona that he named the Thin White Duke.

The narrative of the film is staged as a mystery—in homage to *Citizen Kane* in structure—with a journalist trying to find out what happened to Slade after his disappearance. The journalist was himself transformed by glam rock. His father finds him masturbating over photos of Slade and Wild kissing—and when he runs away to London, he is himself seduced by Curt Wild. Through interviews with Slade's first manager and his ex-wife (based clearly on Angela Bowie) the journalist realizes what has become of Brian Slade—he has become the more traditional pop singer Tommy Stone.

The plot in the film is complex, yet in many ways it only facilitates Haynes's depictions of the glorious excess of the glam years in the early '70s, when pop idols took on gender conventions and made a right mess of them, and did much of this by means of fashion, posing, and the utterance of witticisms. The costumes by Sandy Powell evoke the era of preening rock stars that became sex symbols not through macho posturing but through makeup and artifice, enabling a joyous display of effeminate masculinity. Their look may have been campy, but in Haynes's film the stars are always sexy, and, encouraged by drugs, they are seemingly open to sleeping with anyone. Haynes films an orgy scene as if it were a Roman saturnalia, imagining a realization of Bowie's lustful bisexuality.

Haynes also structures the film like a musical so as to provide ample room to dramatize Brian Slade's songs in imaginative fashion, delaying the narrative but providing fantastic illustrations of the glam aesthetic. They become like rock videos within the film and mirror Bowie's pioneering use of video in 1972 and 1973. Working with photographer Mick Rock, David Bowie made four promotional videos for the songs "Space Oddity," "John, I'm Only Dancing," "The Jean Genie," and "Life on Mars." They were made with no particular outlet in mind, but Bowie convinced his manager to fund Rock's endeavors. These videos predate MTV by eight years, but they anticipate the form of the rock video. They mix concert footage, lip synching in a studio or on a set, and choreography and hint at a narrative that does not necessarily coincide with the lyrics. Bowie and Rock's foresight was to realize that the pop song is no longer only a musical unit but also a visual one. Each song is a screenplay for the composition of moving images. Bowie's emphasis on video as a medium that expresses and sells a song paves the way for the era when fans will say that they have seen a song.

The video for "Life on Mars," done in May 1973, is particularly striking. It features Bowie in a series of close-ups, lip-synching to the melodramatic ballad that speaks of the chaos of earthly existence. Bowie wears a turquoise-colored suit. His face is pale, and his eye shadow picks up on the color of his suit while his lipstick matches his bright red hair. The video doesn't portray the song so much as it offers a vivid portrait of the singer, focusing intensely on the dramatics of his face. (Annie Lennox imitated this look in the '80s, when she dyed her hair red and sported a blue suit and tie.) Bowie's gaze into the camera (a pose he also assumed on the TV show *Old Grey Whistle Test* when he performed "Five Years") provides the video with intensity, a technique Sinead O'Connor used in her video *Nothing Compares 2 U*. The stare into the camera, as well as the use of multiple angles on Bowie's face and body, limits the drama of the song to Bowie, painting it back onto the corpus of the performer, and highlights his dilemma of living on earth, the most disappointing of planets in its predictability and everyday injustices. In this way Bowie uses video to highlight his alienation and make it entirely desirable, equal parts self-indulgent and expressive.

Haynes's film serves to remind us that part of Bowie's glam years was his embrace and exploration of various media for expression, as well as an expansive sexuality—even if he was not truly pansexual, he was certainly multimedia. This embrace and exploration of sexuality via media ensured that his music was accompanied by theatricality and videographic detail. By indulging in diverse modes of self-portraiture that highlighted estrangement, Bowie began to write the future of popular culture. He wrote it with a feather boa and a video camera.

CHAPTER 5

The Nightbird

GENDER AND THE FM DJ

THE BIRTH OF THE NIGHTBIRD

While Billie Jean King and other tennis players were changing and popularizing tennis in the late 1960s and early 1970s, distinctive voices and personalities were transforming the world of radio on the FM dial, providing outlets for newly popular artists like David Bowie. One of the most original voices was that of Alison Steele. She extended what was possible to do on air, experimenting with inventing a persona through her mellifluous voice, and she became emblematic of the changes that were occurring in the medium of radio in the '70s. Popular radio would never be the same again, especially as the medium has become more conservative and predictable in the last forty years. Like Bowie, she theatricalized her life and indulged in a legend that she authored. With her on-air persona seemingly fully lodged in her being, she broadcast her performed identity.

Alison Steele, also known as the Nightbird, worked at WNEW-FM in New York from 1966 to 1979. She became the queen of FM radio. Steele's title was new: women DJs were very rare on radio (indeed most DJs are still male), and FM was newly popular. Her story is related to the development of FM and the extension and revival of radio at a time when television's ascension in the 1950s was endangering the medium. Her story is also related to the change in the status of women in culture and the impact this change had on popular media—indeed, Alison Steele encouraged these transformations. Every night she began her broadcast with her own intro, varying it according to her mood. She intoned in a smoky, sexy voice that curtailed some of the harsher vowels of her Brooklyn accent. One of her favorite intros was "The flutter of wings, the sounds of the night, the shadow across the moon, as the Nightbird lifts her wings and soars above the earth into another level of comprehension, where we exist only to feel. Come fly with me, Alison Steele, the Nightbird." She invited her audience on a journey—a journey that mixed sexuality and spirituality.

Alison Steele was born in Brooklyn in 1937 and died on September 27, 1995, at the age of fifty-eight. Her father worked in vaudeville; her mother was trained as an opera singer. They both gave up working in the entertainment business when they had children, but the desire to perform was instilled in Alison. First she wanted to be a model, although when she was fourteen years old Eileen Ford of the Ford Modeling Agency told her that she should give up this dream. This rejection only served to fuel Alison Steele's ambition, although she decided she would work behind the camera. She talked her way into working as a production assistant in the television industry at the age of fourteen; she later worked as a producer and announcer for a variety of local shows, often lying about her age in order to gain more responsibility.

In addition to her career at WNEW, Steele also moonlighted with Armed Forces Radio in the late 1970s, focusing on interviewing and profiling rock bands. In her later years, she also comanaged a cat boutique in Manhattan with her sister. Before her death from cancer she returned to radio, this time on WXRK (known as K-Rock), in part to obtain medical benefits from her union. She needed expensive treatment for her cancer, although she never let her audience know this. Her shift at the time of her death was from 2:00 to 6:00 a.m.

In 1966, after a call for auditions to which over four hundred women responded, Alison Steele debuted on radio when WNEW decided to experiment with an all-female format. At the time WNEW played music that ranged from easy listening to cocktail music such as Frank Sinatra and Sergio Mendes and Brazil '66. The station's experiment in using female voices failed after a year and a half. The sales staff could not sell airtime. According to Nat Asch, station manager at the time, advertisers did not believe that a female voice could sell products, especially to a female audience (*Museum of Broadcasting Seminar Series*, "Radio Personalities"). This bias still exists—male voices continue to dominate advertising on radio, no matter the format.

But the station stuck with Steele (and not with the future talk show host Sally Jesse Raphael, who also had been part of this experiment in "chick radio") when it changed its format to freeform in 1967. Steele later insisted that Asch fired her; she just refused to leave. Nat Asch concurs—he said in a WNEW-FM retrospective that he fired her three times and he was later grateful that she ignored his terminations (*Museum of*

Television and Radio Seminar Series). She ended up on the graveyard shift, coming after the influential African American DJ Rosko, for which she was paid $125.00 a week. She was on the radio from midnight to 6:00 a.m. As her popularity and power within the station grew, she moved to a 2:00 to 6:00 a.m. shift in the summer of 1969; finally the Nightbird moved to a 10:00 p.m. to 2:00 a.m. shift in August of 1973.

THE NIGHTBIRD AND THE HISTORY OF RADIO

In the early 1960s, the FM dial was opened up due to a series of changes in the industry and public policy. These changes were encouraged by changes in the culture, particularly the increasing influence of young people and new dynamics in the recording industry, in which the album had become at least as important as the single. Unimaginable today, in the early '60s radio was still synonymous with AM.

Even though the transmission quality of FM was superior to that of AM, industry forces held back the popularization of the band. These forces sacrificed innovation for control over the existing market. As a result, FM's audience did not surpass AM until the end of the 1970s even though the FM bandwidth had been available before the Second World War. The first step in the ascension of FM in the postwar period was generated by a policy change. In 1961 the Federal Communications Commission approved FM frequencies for stereophonic broadcasting. As FM already enjoyed relatively static free broadcasting with virtually no incursions from nearby stations, this was a way for the FCC to encourage its usage and popularity. This change also benefited female DJs as it was long believed that higher-pitched women's voices didn't transmit well in mono AM. In stereo FM, the qualities of female voices could be accurately broadcast and enjoyed.

Today many media users tend to regard the FCC as a restrictive organization that penalizes broadcasters who allow performers to indulge in lewd (or expressive) behavior, such as the antics of Howard Stern or Janet Jackson. Yet some of the FCC's rulings have generated positive structural change in the broadcast industry. If the FCC's support of FM ultimately helped secure the dial for large corporations, it also encouraged eccentric broadcasters to experiment with format and diverse choices of music within a set—and at the same time play with the ways in which this music was discussed and introduced.

In 1961 the tone of the FCC changed with the appointment of Newton Minow, who famously accused the airwaves of being a vast waste-land. In 1962, the FCC ordered a freeze on AM license applications, as the dial was becoming too crowded. The FCC decided to promote the FM band. Crucially, in 1965 the FCC issued its nonduplication ruling. In cities with populations of over one hundred thousand, an AM station could duplicate only 50 percent of its programming on its FM sister sta-tion (many owners had stations on both frequencies and were broad-casting the same programming on each). This policy prompted station owners to quickly develop new programming. The ruling affected only 337 stations, but it encouraged an industry trend: between 1964 and 1967 more than 500 new commercial FM stations and 60 educational sta-tions took to the air.

In 1968 the FCC put another freeze on new AM station applications, this time for five years. This freeze further ensured that FM would be-come the official area of growth for the radio industry. The era of FM ex-pansion was now in full swing. In 1974 Congress attempted to pass a bill that would require car manufacturers to include FM in their car radios. The bill failed to pass, but the message was sent to Detroit manufactur-ers. Only 25 percent of cars at the time had FM receivers. This number would continue to rise during the 1970s, due in part to the success of the government agency in motivating the settlement of the FM dial. The FCC's actions in the '60s and early '70s challenged the stagnant radio in-dustry and inadvertently contributed to the rise of the FM DJ.

When the FM band opened up, 1960s counterculture moved in. This included a handful of forthright, assertive women, especially the Night-bird. Many DJs and station managers had been trained on college radio, and some were exiles from AM. The success of the AM exiles and col-lege-trained DJs shocked the radio industry into acknowledging the new possibilities of broadcasting. This is analogous to how wayward programmers inspired new ways to use the Internet in the early 1990s. By 1973, young people were tuned to FM music stations, and indeed many were using music stations as their primary source of news.

In the late '60s, broadcasters on FM commercial stations took advan-tage of some of the techniques that had already been developed by DJs that worked at the not-for-profit radio corporation Pacifica. These tech-niques became known as freeform, and this format stands in opposition to the station-devised playlist. With freeform, the DJ is given total free-dom to play the music he or she wants play—and to introduce and dis-cuss this music using any words and intonation. Freeform arguably be-gan with John Leonard at Berkeley's Pacifica station. He began experimenting in the 1950s with his choices of recordings, naming his show "Night Sounds." This show consisted of collages of music, poetry, and satire.

After the Pacifica Foundation bought a station in New York, Bob Fass's "Radio Unnameable" on WBAI-FM in New York brought freeform to the East Coast. Naming the show after Samuel Beckett's novel, Fass devised a spontaneous collage of interviews, sound clips, listener calls, and comedy that remains enormously influential.

Vin Scelsa, who started out at WFMU in 1967, was also a freeform innovator. Today WFMU is still a freeform station, a rarity for a station that is not affiliated with a college or university. Scelsa's popularity allowed him to retain control over his shows even when he worked at commercial stations such as WNEW. He is now at the noncommercial station WFUV. Vin Scelsa's show "Idiot's Delight" still has a cult following; he has been on the air in the New York City area for over thirty-five years.

On the West Coast, Lorenzo Milam was also a freeform pioneer. In his own estimation no one did more to lay the groundwork for freeform than Milam, a onetime KPFA staffer. He founded KRAB in Seattle in 1962, heralding an approach he called "Free Forum." He went on to found thirty other stations (known at the time as the "KRAB Nebula") in the West, South, and Midwest. Milam's approach seemed to deny the presence of the listener when he was playing difficult, unknown temple music from Korea, allowing for silences between songs, and including impromptu vocal asides. In 1985 Milam published his early writings on radio; this excerpt is about the philosophy guiding his Seattle station in 1963.

> Actually we may have a few listeners but we try to ignore them if at all possible. For we find that the thought of broadcasting into the void gives a certain spontaneous quality to our announcing and our actions. KRAB is, we suspect, too young to have its own mythology and yet, even after five months, there is a bit of apocrypha about the station— all of it stemming from the fact of our feeling ourselves free of the millstone of too many listeners. (17)

For Milam, DJs at his small nonprofit station were free from having to play to a distinct demographic and the demands of an invisible listenership that craves the latest hit played every hour. The display of the personality of the voice of the DJ was crucial, and the eccentricity of the DJ's musical preferences was paramount. The DJ wove new stories and experiences through mixes of recorded music. Style was not ordained;

rather it was created through experimentation. At Milam's station, ratings were all but ignored; the untainted expression of the DJ became the
station's identity. Similarities between DJs were created organically, not
imposed by management. Milam even advocated silence as a form of
transmission (akin to one of John Cage's famous performances in which
the pianist never plays the piano), allowing dead air to go live.

Two other pioneers of freeform who brought experimentation to
commercial stations were Tom and Raechel Donahue. Tom was an AM
DJ until his conversion, and he is usually described as an overweight,
pot-smoking hippie. One night in 1967 he complained to his wife
Raechel that he couldn't find a station that played the Doors (or any of
the music that was emerging from the San Francisco hippie subculture)
on the radio. He called all the radio stations in the Bay area until he
found one whose phone was disconnected. He located the owner of this
station and offered to take it over. He and Raechel brought their records
down to the station and began KMPX. He opened the show with the
line, "This is Tom Donahue, I'm here to clear up your face and mess up
your mind." Word spread, and the station found advertisers from some
of the stores in the neighborhoods where the hippies were moving in.
Donahue was soon asked to program a station in Pasadena, and his influence on other commercial broadcasters, including WNEW-FM, was
immense. Raechel Donahue also became a DJ on freeform stations (and
later became CNN's first entertainment reporter).

The freeform style is DJ centered. Given the freedom to play music
from any genre or era, creating unlikely linkages between songs, DJs
also inflect their shows with their personalities and indulge in the sound
of their own voices, mixing improvised monologues with displays of
eclectic musical taste. For example, the groundbreaking DJ Rosko remembers playing the Supremes after a Bob Dylan song after a Ravi
Shankar raga, and he would tell stories between sets based on his experiences and observations (*Twenty Years of WNEW-FM*). In the '60s and
'70s, freeform DJs played many long songs in succession without a
break and then spoke expansively during breaks. The FM format benefited from the growing popularity of the album, which provided longer
songs and songs that sometimes fit a theme or story that was carried
throughout the album. Such songs could then become recontextualized
in a DJ's set. The DJ repurposed the artist's song into his or her own narrative. Such shows verged on what might today be called performance
art or spoken word performance.

Alison Steele drew on the freeform style in devising her Nightbird persona. This allowed her to play the long album tracks that she favored—and even to play entire sides of albums by musical artists such as the Beatles, the Who and the Rolling Stones, who were recording concept albums. On FM in the late '60s and early '70s, the DJ's number of words per minute decreased; the vocal delivery used deeper tones and breathier intonations (often sounding self-intoxicated) and even allowed for a moment or two of reflective silence, long considered a sin on high-velocity AM.

The DJs often free-associated or pontificated about issues of the day in a spoken word improvisation, and they became conscious of what they were doing as an art form. Some evenings Steele's vocal intro to the show lasted fifteen minutes, reciting poetry, celebrating self-knowledge, and promoting inner peace to an anxious, sleepless audience. The music she played was in long sets, mixing symphonic rock, world music, jazz, folk, and other music in unlikely combinations. These sets became part of her own personal expression, reflecting her mood and perceptions, as well as her own musical tastes.

FREEFORM DJ AS ARTIST

The rise of DJs is connected to the artistic developments and shifts in the popular culture that supported new forms of expression. The raucous comedy of Lenny Bruce consisted of monologues that challenged limits and were structured for improvisation. Members of the art movement Fluxus staged events and performances in galleries that were clearly influenced by Dada and surrealism. Allan Kaprow produced happenings beginning in the late 1950s, which inspired human be-ins (the first one held in San Francisco in 1967) and 1960s protest strategies. In these events, the art became the people interacting with the setting and the site became a performance space. Much of 1960s art mixed the everyday with the extraordinary, privileging possibility and the creation of templates for the emergence of the aleatory over expertise and the celebration of the moment over the denouement of clear causal narratives. Examples of the quotidian meeting the spectacular included Yoko Ono coughing repeatedly in "Cough Piece" (1961)," Nam June Paik's collaboration with cellist Charlotte Moorman in "TV Bra with Living Sculpture" (1964) in which television sets become part of the musician's costume, and Joseph Beuys repeating sounds in "Ja Ja Ja Ne Ne Ne" (1970). Fluxus artists' work challenged audience preconceptions about the ordinary and the routine, as well as the necessity for artistic flair and virtuosity.

In addition, pop artist Andy Warhol, influenced by underground performer Jack Smith's experimentations, became notorious for filming his Factory regulars, giving them no motivations other than their already tangled web of relationships. Warhol also projected an eight-hour film *Empire* (1964) depicting the Empire State Building, creating an epic of nonmovement that was both boring and, at times, unexpectedly riveting.

Art making in the '60s was often shockingly mundane. In the dance world, choreographers involved in creating postmodern dance at the Judson Dance Theater claimed that everyday movements were part of the vocabulary of dance and insisted that anybody was a potential dancer. They used both untrained and trained performers in elaborate pieces that rejected both modern and balletic traditions of composition and relied as much on chance as on virtuosity and synchrony. In rejecting the accepted rules of composition, they invented a new tradition in performance.

These innovations in art suggest to us, looking back, that the freeform DJ and Alison Steele were part of a cultural break. In this break, the commonplace moment—revealed in all its elaborate glory—became prevalent as an aesthetic. Although the 1960s and early 1970s are often thought of as times of political rebellion and protest that involved social activism, in the arts this rebellion took the form of highlighting everyday life through media—the rebellion took place in form not content. Scripts were dropped in films, and traditional proscenium theater stages were replaced with performance spaces. Elaborate choreography for complicated dances was eschewed; movement was privileged. Paint and canvases became unnecessary. Seeing what happens when the microphone and/or camera are on and there is no specific plan in place became part of art-making strategies. These new forms of experimentation did not require conservatory training. Rather one had to be prepared to be able to see the perfection in the routine occurrence and believe in risk and chance.

This atmosphere of experimentation influenced all modes of artistic endeavor. The freeform radio DJ was part of this cultural shift, which allowed DJs to talk about themselves, to discuss the politics of the day and perceptions of consciousness, and to play widely diverse songs in longer sets. This was validated as the most expressive and relevant way for the DJ to communicate with his or her audience because cultural precedents had been set in other media (from film to dance to the visual arts) to indulge in the expressive, unplanned moment.

Steele was part of this conception of performance as she created her on-air persona and immersed herself in enunciation that emphasized the sultry sound of her character's voice, discussing whatever came to mind and playing whatever she was moved to play. Steele never rehearsed her shows, never knew what she was going to play, and usually picked out the poem she would recite on the day of the show. Her improvisations were based on the structure of the show, but she herself was never sure where she was going to lead her audience. She was an artist, creating an installation on the air.

Undoubtedly Rosko influenced the Nightbird's famous vocal signature. Rosko moved to WNEW after WOR abandoned its influential but short-lived freeform experiment in 1967 (this format lasted just over one year) at the station, signaling the beginning of WNEW-FM's golden era. Perhaps Rosko's antidrug message was lost when he repeated his opening lines: "reality the hippest of all trips . . . a mind excursion . . . the true diversion." Despite his words, his voice itself seemed to endorse drugs with its silky, deep tone that allowed for time between his words, inviting his listeners to space out. Alison Steele was also influenced by Rosko's DJ philosophy: he advocated never knowing what he was going to play on turntable 2 when he started to play a song on turntable 1. In other words, Rosko's technique let spontaneity and intuition define the music that the DJ plays. This was a technique that Alison Steele used in order to lend the feeling that she was present and active in response to her listeners. There was no set list before the show began.

She favored bands such as the pioneering synthesizer band Tangerine Dream, the Moody Blues (she helped to popularize "Nights in White Satin"), and the influential psychedelic band Soft Machine. For her vocal intro, she spoke over South American religious music recorded by Elisabeth Waldo (a violinist born in the United States who later devised a notational system for indigenous music of the Americas) that used pre-Columbian instruments, a rare recording she found in the collection of a friend.

The DJs went to great lengths to sound hip, keen to their listeners' concerns, and up to date in their use of language. The station encouraged its DJs to be known as on-air personalities, sensing that its attraction was not only in the music that was being played—its allure was also in who was playing it and the ways DJs introduced and arranged the songs. These on-air personalities on WNEW—Rosko, Scott Muni, Alison

Steele, and Dennis Elsas—became local celebrities. They branded the station through their diverse approaches to being a DJ, without intervention from consultants.

The station emerged from this milieu of experimentation and expansion and became New York's premier underground commercial rock station. The DJs developed distinct yet complementary on-air personalities, though there was a decided emphasis on ratings. Since WNEW-FM went freeform on Halloween night in 1967, its stature as one of the most revered and remembered stations has never diminished for those who grew up listening to New York FM radio. By 1973, there were over four hundred progressive rock stations in the United States (known as "underground radio" in the 1960s) while the number of classical music radio stations was decreasing.

The audience for freeform radio was primarily young and urban. They bought albums not singles; they disapproved of the higher pitched, scripted, and rapid vocal delivery of AM DJs. They wanted a DJ who sounded suave, mellow, and distinctive—not one who spoke in manic, well-rehearsed, station-manager-approved, frenzied outbursts. This audience wanted cool (and this from a medium that Marshall McLuhan had deemed was "hot" because, unlike television, radio intensifies the use of one sense and its transmittance is dense with information). The FM DJ worked against the inclination of the medium to support rapid-speaking, angry men like Father Coughlin (an anti-Semite who ranted during the Depression), Huey Long (a southern populist governor with a noted distrust of the New Deal), or the more contemporary example of a bellower, Rush Limbaugh. Such men tend to be right wing; they express their views by challenging the top of their tessitura (they use the top of their vocal range), fuming with outrage at a frenzied tempo. In contradistinction to the AM radio announcer, the FM DJ indulged in the sonority of his or her own voice, sounding mellow and relaxed rather than revved up or angry. Alison Steele would never sound as if she was on amphetamines or caffeine or on a political tirade. Instead she and her radio kin's voices seemed influenced by marijuana or other mild hallucinogens.

The freeform DJs reflected their audience's concerns and passions but also played a part in creating the taste and outlook of their listeners. John Dunne, a New York City fireman who grew up in Brooklyn's Bay Ridge in the late 1960s, acknowledges the central role of the FM DJ in his teenage years: "FM radio awakened the social conscience of my generation and the deejays were the arbiters of that consciousness. . . . I never thought before to question authority, or why we were fighting in Vietnam, or about racial injustice in America, but the music awakened that in me" (15). For Dunne—and many others in the New York City area—the DJs of WNEW-FM were among those who beat "the tribal drum."

Commercial freeform stations such as WNEW (WPLJ was also freeform for a number of years) in New York flourished for a few years. They enjoyed a close relationship with listeners. Yet beginning in the early '70s, their management gradually reinstated playlists and other controls on the DJs, signaling the end of freeform dominance. This in turn was a sign that the 1960s were over and the corporate-controlled mid-1970s media culture was being established. Alison Steele, though, still managed to thrive throughout the decade.

Station managers and advertisers did not control freeform DJs. Many DJs saw themselves as part of an emerging subculture of resistance. For example, in his account of the rise and fall of WNEW, Richard Neer recounts a story in *FM: The Rise and Fall of Rock Radio* (2001) in which Alison Steele refused to air advertisements for *Penthouse* magazine. In order to encourage her to change her mind, the station manager arranged a meeting between the fiery, opinionated, and apparently quite stubborn Alison Steele and Bob Guccione, the publisher of the country's second most popular soft-core pornographic magazine. For Guccione, Steele's audience was key to his magazine: it consisted of mostly young men, awake at night, listening to a voice of a woman. Steele refused to budge. Her reason was not a strongly held feminist philosophy about the magazine's exploitation of women. Instead, according to Neer, her dispute was aesthetic (140). She did not like the hairiness of the naked women photographed in the magazine, stating that she liked to have hair only on her head. She persisted and never aired the ads for the magazine. It is unimaginable that a music-playing DJ would have that kind of veto power today. Today the advertiser and station manager (as representatives of the corporation) exert ultimate power over media content.

Alison Steele was clearly conscious of cultivating her celebrity status and made great attempts to link her face and body with her voice. She appeared in the fashion pages of the *New York Times* on August 26, 1973, in an article titled "Good News, Women Are Going to Dress Up Again," in a bronze slinky outfit, accessorized not only with a bracelet but also with a wineglass in her right hand! She appears sophisticated, contemplative, and distinctive. She gazes into the distance, giving us a hint of the dreaminess of the Nightbird. But there is a difference between how she "appears" in sound and what she looks like in a photograph; in a photograph she is indeed fashionable and attractive, but she doesn't necessarily look like the Nightbird. The soft voice of the Nightbird does not match the harder look of this chic Manhattanite, Alison Steele. She was distinctive: she smoked dark Nat Sherman cigarettes and was known for her red hair, dark turtlenecks, and the small poodle that accompanied her to the station.

Ms. Steele also appeared at many local rock concerts, introducing the band. In 1973, she introduced the pop star Melanie, who was performing at Carnegie Hall. Usually at these events Alison Steele was very enthusiastically received, even though some in the audience had never seen her before. One event, though, turned into a fiasco and showed how different Alison Steele was from the Nightbird. In 1973, WNEW threw a benefit event for the radio station at New York University. As told by Richard Neer (206–7), Carol Miller, who was a newly hired female DJ, and Alison Steele both attended the event. Carol Miller was introduced first, and she was cheered. When Alison Steele was introduced, there were a few loud, discernible boos mixed with the applause. Neer recounts, "She stormed off with fire in her eyes; it was the first time she'd ever been upstaged by another woman and certainly the first time she'd been booed." At age thirty-six, Steele was already much older than her audience, and she always stood out in a crowd: after all, she didn't dress like an aging hippie but like a Manhattan fashionista.

As Neer tells the story, Steele got Carol Miller fired. Students from New York University called Steele's show to tell her that Carol Miller had incited their classmates to boo her. Steele went to the station's general manager and issued an ultimatum: either fire Miller or the Nightbird quits. Carol Miller was in fact fired, but it's not evident that this had anything to do with the onstage incident. Regardless of why Miller was laid off, Steele would fight hard to maintain her own position as the leading female at the station, even as she was known to be otherwise supportive of young women who were coming up in the business. Yet, as the diva of the station, she was not to be replaced.

While Alison Steele was emblematic of on-air personalities that inspired the popularization of FM, she was also unique, and not only because she was female. She created a character that was at once sexual and yet invoked a spaced-out spirituality—and maintained this dual role for many years. She navigated a male-dominated industry, surviving many changes in management, and she fought hard for her autonomy. She was outspoken, hung out with the guys, yet always made sure to defend her turf. She needed to do so: when *Billboard* magazine named her Personality of the Year in 1976, the station manager didn't even give her the evening off. She was tough out of necessity.

She had to endure much sexism, both from people who were supposed to assist her and from management. When she worked the after midnight shift, she was also named musical director, which meant little more than that she had to clean up and refile records. When she had to inform her colleagues of new records to play, she received flack from them.

> I had a terrible time with the guys. They resented it mightily that a woman would be in that position and they would certainly ignore my advice. And management never backed me up, which was so weird. I mean, they hired me to do the job, they would tell me what they wanted me to do, and then when one of the jocks would come screaming into the manager's office saying, "She can't do this, she can't do that," they would never back me up and say, "We told her to do it." (in Gaar, 103)

Steele recounts that when she asked for a stepladder in order to reach the top shelves, her boss retorted that he would just find a taller person for the job. Relatedly, as recounted in Sterling and Keith's history of FM, *Sounds of Change* (2008), when WBCN was looking for an office assistant in 1970, it unabashedly put out an ad for a "chick who can type" (132). Incidents like this made it difficult for Steele; she clearly made the choice to put up with the everyday sexism, but she remained assertive.

Steele turned the slot after midnight into one of WNEW's most important times. Although this shift limited the amount of listeners and hence served to justify her not receiving parity with her male colleagues, it also allowed her more freedom to design her own show and persona with less interference from the station management. She became legendary and influential; Jimi Hendrix wrote a song about her in 1971 entitled "Night Bird Flying." The lesser-known guitarist Roy Buchanan also wrote an homage to her named "Fly . . . Night Bird."

THE FCC AND THE FALL OF THE FM DJ

Sterling and Keith remark on the end of a "golden era" in FM.

> Experimentation was often encouraged or at least tolerated. FM's "alternative" role to AM (and sometimes everything else) peaked in the 1960s and early 1970s. Then, as the financial signs for the medium im-

> proved, the flexibility and experimentation began to disappear in equal proportion. Once the medium was seen to have the potential to make money (by rising in market ratings and thus attracting more potential advertisers), it could no longer be treated as a programming sandbox. (153)

FM and underground radio was the victim of its own success. Ever-enlarging mainstream corporations inevitably won out, seeing the transformation of a youthful counterculture into a demographic, whose taste and buying inclinations could be identified—and influenced.

Guccione's son, the publisher of *Spin* magazine, admitted to being a fan of the Nightbird, despite the fact that his father could not convince her to accept his magazine's advertisements. In an article in the *Los Angeles Times* entitled "When Innocence Died and Marketing Set In," he recounts moving to New York City in 1971 and becoming transfixed by the DJs and their eclectic tastes (6). He mourns the passing of the golden era of FM radio, and is less than pleased with the album-oriented radio that replaced the freeform. Guccione sees the beginning of the end with the Woodstock festival, when the sheer numbers of countercultural youths caught the attention of all, including those in the marketing and advertising industries.

Steele decried the increasing standardization of FM radio and found that there was no place for her creativity within this structure, especially by the early 1980s. In a roundtable discussion at the Museum of Broadcasting that occurred in 1989 she railed against those who had taken over the industry, their lack of musical knowledge, and the kind of control they had over the DJ, and music radio. She became embittered with the changes in FM radio, convinced that large corporations had ruined what was once an ideal space for expression.

The FCC, which played such a major role in enabling the development of commercial freeform radio stations, also played a key role in curtailing the independence of the DJ. In 1971, the FCC issued an advisory statement warning against stations playing music that appeared "to promote or glorify" drug use. Then on January 10, 1972, the *New York Times* reported that stations had "scrambled to ban such songs as 'Puff the Magic Dragon'" ("New Trends After Underground Radio"), which was long rumored to be secretly about marijuana and not a magical creature. Apparently the stations overreacted, and the FCC issued another statement indicating that its intention was not "to censor any specific records." Regardless, this shows the vulnerability of the broadcasting industry to any issuance from the commission. Policy matters and any utterance by the agency resounded across the industry and served to signal the end of the reign of the DJ.

The next statement by the FCC in 1971 had a greater effect in limiting the independence of freeform DJs. Citing an underground station in Iowa, the commission warned that the format "gives the announcer such control over the records to be played that it is inconsistent with the strict controls that the licensee must exercise to avoid questionable practices" (in M. Hall, 50). In making such a statement, the FCC was asserting that the autonomy of the DJ violated its regulations. The station management was duty bound to ensure that the station was acting in accordance with all FCC regulations, and the commission's statement suggests that the freeform format transferred too much power from management to the individual DJ. In issuing this judgment, the FCC advocated that the station management adopt a restrictive rather than a supportive role with its staff.

The FCC was thus acting to curtail the activities of the radio counterculture, which took to FM so unexpectedly and successfully—ironically with the initial help of the FCC's actions in the early 1960s. The statements of the FCC in the 1970s encouraged the end of the freeform format and the rise of station-imposed programming based on the research of outside consultants who surveyed the tastes of particular markets. And indeed the taste of young people had changed. After all, the mood of the country and many of its youths had become politically and economically more conservative: Nixon was resoundingly reelected, and popular music became less overtly antigovernment, returning to love songs or inner journeys as subject matter. Although there were over four hundred freeform stations in 1972, some were not doing well, and station owners began to look for advice in reaching a changing demographic. Appealing to hippieish sentiments was no longer a recipe for success; some newer listeners wanted to dance in discos, while others wanted to assemble in huge stadiums, light matches, and listen to corporate rock.

The success of the FM pioneers also paved the way for the standardization of a format. This format was imposed on DJs in many stations as underground radio was renamed progressive radio in the early 1970s and became album-oriented rock (AOR) by the late 1970s. In a sense the new DJs' success helped to bring about their own demise—the FM announcer showed media corporations that FM could be popular and profitable, and, starting in the early 1970s, consultants were brought into newly popular commercial stations to standardize the FM format. Also rock music became less rebellious and vital; it evolved into stadium rock with bands such as Yes, the Eagles, and Foreigner. This music fell more easily into a standardized format than the more eclectic and urgent music of the late 1960s and early 1970s.

One of the reasons that WNEW-FM was able to last longer using the freeform format, as Pete Fornitale (one of the freeform DJs at the station) suggested in a twenty-year retrospective held at the Museum of Television and Radio on October 30, 1987, was that the station was never run and staffed by counterculture types; the DJs were professionals first and foremost. The original freeform DJs (Rosko, Scott Muni, and Alison Steele) were already older than their listeners and had worked in radio for years. Muni was by this time a familiar voice in Top 40 radio, and Rosko had developed a following at WOR. Steele, who didn't have the same amount of experience in radio, had been working in the entertainment business for over ten years at this time. They were responding to the music of the time, and, like Alison, grew to love it, but they were not kids or especially countercultural types; each deliberately took on a role in order to appeal to his or her audience.

MYTHS OF THE NIGHT

In Western cultures, there are myths about the nighttime and darkness, especially the hours between midnight and the dawn. For some the night is for sleep; for others it is the time for passion and creativity. Or, as Patti Smith sang in "Because the Night" (written with Bruce Springsteen), "the night is made for lovers." The line is almost a quotation from Lord Byron's poem "So, We'll Go No More a Roving," which reads "Though the Night is Made for Loving." Lyricists and poets have long been enchanted with the possibilities and challenges of the night.

Night is the time for parties and outlandish behavior, when the rules of the day are altered to accommodate that which the moon provokes and the sunlight inhibits. What the day represses, the night says out loud. Many believe that night is when artists and writers do their best work. It is when bands perform at clubs and people dance into the wee hours enjoying their leisure; it is also when people feel their loneliness most sharply.

Michael Keith remarks in his book about late-night radio, *Sounds in the Dark* (2001):

> The so-called witching hours fascinate us. They are a time of legends and myths. We are told that the full moon can make people crazy, turning otherwise reasonable individuals into ranting fools and even raging, bloodthirsty monstrosities. We are beguiled by the moon in all its orbital incarnations and attach profound and symbolic meaning to them. For most of us, the hours beyond the stroke of 12 are curious and inscrutable essentially because these hours exist in an uncharted and unfamiliar region. (4)

Alison Steele played with these myths and celebrated the darkest hours of the night as the time when the mind of the listener was most open to hearing her music and incantations.

Late-night radio was an early development in the history of broadcasting. The broadcasting era began in 1920 and broadcasting after midnight began as early as 1922. For Keith, late-night radio was successful and appealed to its listeners because it provided companionship and the need for an intimate encounter. Many late-night listeners are at work; others are unable to sleep. The late-night DJs that Keith interviews in his book (and many of the women DJs cite Alison Steele as inspiration) speak of an affinity with their audience. For example, radio professional Elizabeth Salazar relays, "The biggest lesson I learned in terms of my listenership at that hour of the morning was that it was heavily populated by a sub- or counterculture. These are a group of listeners unlike any other. The bottom line is that lifestyles change during the graveyard hours" (in Keith, 12).

Alison Steele always professed an affinity with the nighttime hours and those who were sleepless overnight. In an interview with her colleague Dennis Elsas ("Reflections with Dennis Elsas," 1977), she remarked how she hated the morning and relished the opportunities that the night provided for her to read, ponder, and reflect. She also acknowledged that the night's intensity had its downsides; a flu is always worse at night, as is anxiety. In creating the Nightbird she understood that nighttime listeners needed an advocate who understood both their plight and their privilege. When she was devising this persona, she ran the idea past some her colleagues at WNEW; each of them told to her to abandon the concept, but she knew she was onto something. Her first night as the Nightbird, she received many calls of support and requests for songs. In the *New York Times* she was quoted as saying, "I never get lonely up here" (Dec. 9, 1971, 60). One reason she never got lonely is that she received many phone calls during her show; another is the bird's-eye perspective her berth provided her.

Alison Steele. (Photofest.)

Most of her listeners were in the age range eighteen to twenty-four, and most of these were men. On the microphone, she was cosmic cool, serene, speaking in a slow tempo in a breathy near contralto, hiding her accent with a mid-Atlantic cadence. Off-mic, she was a tough New Yorker, making no attempt to conceal her pronunciation. On air, at times she verged on sounding like a seductress, breathy and impassioned, yet rather than inviting sex acts, she spoke of astral travel, the cosmos, and peace. She eroticized the inner journey and made outer space alluring and textural. She provided companionship with her voice.

Clearly Steele's pioneer status is in part a reflection of the sexism of the larger society—she was only one of a handful of successful women on radio. Larger societal attitudes, not only the distinctive gynophobia of the broadcasting industry, kept women off the air. Yet part of the Nightbird's success is that she cooed in a sexy fashion, titillating her male audience, though she never giggled in a girlish, coquettish soprano in order to get the ratings. Nor did she ever rely on words of sexual innuendo even if her enunciation resounded with sexuality. Yet part of her success was because her voice was exotic within the realm of male tonalities. In the region of the radio, she was an "other." She moved through socially created borders that rested on stereotypes of the maternal, the virginal, and the whore. She invited fantasy.

The old sexist slogan that young women grew up with—and young men heard and repeated—seems to be at work in media: "little girls should be seen and not heard." Indeed women, as performers, were always more prevalent in television and film, and female personalities were historically far more rare on radio. Radio, of course, leaves the visual details of the performer to the imagination, and isolates the transmitted human voice, granting the voice expansive power to communicate and express, unleashing the imagination. The dynamics of the radio voice explain in part why women were exiled from the medium for far too long—the voice's signification could not be curtailed since the voice was not pinned to a particular, visible body.

Despite the imbalance of the genders in the medium, the history of women on radio is dynamic and interesting, of course, from the very beginning. According to Michele Hilmes in *Radio Voices* (1997), some of the radio "boys" in the teens of the last century, who were working on homemade radios, were in fact female. Many of the great stars in radio's golden era were female comedians and actresses. In the 1950s, a radio station in Memphis, playing soul and blues, adopted an all-female list of DJs (at a time when much of the more established talent in radio was moving to the newer medium, television). As we have seen, Raechel Donahue was a pioneering freeform force, working with her husband, and WNEW tried all-female DJs for one year as an experiment in 1966 and 1967. Women have long been involved in the history of American radio.

In the beginnings of broadcasting, female voices were more prevalent in radio drama and especially rare when it came to announcing the news. Researcher Hadley Cantril and others who were involved in radio research at Columbia and Princeton Universities surveyed the listening public and found that listeners did not find female voices as trustworthy as male voices, especially when it came to reciting world events (see Cantril and Allport). Where women were experienced as superior was in reciting poetry (one of the activities favored by the Nightbird). In a sense the audience entrusted men with facts and women with whimsy, a sexist attitude that arguably continues today in broadcasting as women reporters often cover human interest stories while their male counterparts travel to war-torn regions. In 2006, it was even a big event when Katie Couric became the anchor for CBS's *Evening News*, revealing the degree to which women—and their voices—are still excluded from doing hard news yet are desired for the recital of other words.

Alison Steele seized this contradiction. She developed an on-air personality that was sexual, poetic, and provocative of fantasy. Her voice was well suited to define the night in New York City of the late '60s and '70s. Nonetheless Steele suffered from the discrimination against the female voice even as she benefited from the particular power this voice has for provoking fantasy.

THE FEMALE ACOUSMÊTRE

In Hollywood film there are a number of films that feature a male character only heard as a voice-over. As Kaja Silverman notes in *The Acoustic Mirror* (1988), there is only one film (*Letter to Three Wives*) in which the viewer hears a female character's voice and never sees her body. In popular film and media, the mandate is clear for women: if you speak you must be seen. For a woman to speak without showing the contours of the body is transgressing into the domain of men. The voice of the disembodied woman is virtually taboo in popular culture, and because of this taboo it is particularly involving and engrossing, and often highly sexualized.

A voice with no visible origin can take on godlike proportions; think of the burning bush that converses with Moses. In fact, before the Renaissance, the appearance of God was always an audible occurrence (e.g., Joan of Arc never sees God, she hears Yahweh), as it was rare for God to be depicted in paintings and there was no conception of what this entity looked like. The need for women to be made visible, yet denied voice, especially by way of the camera or canvas, is well-argued by feminist theorists such as Laura Mulvey. Through the sequence of camera shots and angles, films are traditionally edited to link the viewer with the male protagonist within the film, so that the spectator sees the female from the perspective of the male lead. The female body is, therefore, often framed by a male character, and female speech is always affixed to corporeality. In popular film, the female voice can never leave its perceived point of origin, its apparent source. Unlike the Nightbird, the female in film can never fly from scene to scene like the male voice-over, who can also exist within the film in the privileged position of narrator. The female voice in film is matched to a visible body, unable to transcend the body and assume the position of narrator while remaining a character. The female DJ, however, has specific freedoms.

In *Audio-Vision* (1990), film theorist Michel Chion invents a term to describe a character that appears only as a sound and is never seen. He calls this entity an acousmêtre, or sound-being, a blending of the word *acousmatic* and the French verb meaning "to be" (*être*). An acousmatic sound is a sound one hears without seeing its source. Radio, like the telephone and the phonograph, is an acousmatic medium—the listener doesn't see the point of origin for the voices and music. Instead the user hears the sound of projected voices or recorded music. The Nightbird is thus an acousmêtre who exists via an acousmatic medium, the radio. This voice flies. Her counterpart, Alison Steele, is earthbound.

Within radio, the female acousmêtre, when heard, is restricted as well. She is heard in comedy, and in recorded or live music as a vocalist, but female voices are rare as newscasters and commentators, and as DJs—to say nothing of the paucity of women in management until quite recently. From the beginning, part of the explanation for this exclusion was about the transmission of voices: high female voices were thought not to transmit as well as lower alto or contralto ones, or baritonal male voices. But the real reason is the taboo on the female acousmêtre. The implication is simple: you can't trust a woman unless you see her, and yet one can trust an unseen man (with a godly voice). To disembody a voice is a privilege that should only be given to women in restricted fashion. The female acousmêtre has such rules and values projected on her through no fault of her own; she is exoticized, desired, but also mistrusted—from the get-go.

Hearing women's voices without seeing the matching body is thus a precarious affair, even if it is often an intensely pleasurable one. More is at risk and more is unleashed when the female voice is severed from its body. For theorists influenced by psychoanalysis, men's and women's voices have very definite repercussions. For example, the psychoanalyst Didier Anzieu speaks of the distinctive resonance of the mother's voice as if it were an enclosure for the child, a space that is created for the infant to reside in, providing protection, what he calls the "psychic envelope." (See Steven Connor's "Sound and the Self" [2004].) This theory draws its strength from the narrative of an infant's development: children discern voices before they can see shapes, so the voice of the mother is a desirable object before the mother's body is known to be separate from the infant. The female voice, in this theory, is reassuring and transformative and refers back to the original female voice, that of the mother. But for Anzieu the sonorous envelope can be restrictive of the ego's development.

Related to this notion of the maternal voice, in the film *FM* (1978),

which depicts the struggle of a progressive station to retain its autonomy within a corporation that wants to dictate what ads it should play,
the character based on Alison Steele uses the name the Mother. Like
Steele, she is slightly older than her audience and is troubled by her position covering the graveyard shift; also like the Nightbird, she has a devoted following. The film lays bare one of the tones of the Nightbird's
voice: as much as she was desired for her presumed and actual sexiness,
he Nightbird also was heard as a maternal figure—after all she takes
care of her listener. In the film, the Mother (played by Eileen Brennan)
coos into the microphone, assuming her persona, and addresses the
needs of both her listeners and the other DJs. The Mother tries to quit,
but she just can't leave; when the station members take over the station
and lock themselves in, broadcasting without commercials, the
"Mother" rejoins her "children." In this film, the disembodiment of the
female voice is inextricably linked to the maternal.

Kaja Silverman acknowledges the disparate meanings of the female
voice and its rarity in mediated spaces. Yet she is also critical of the psy-
choanalytic focus on the "sonorous envelope" of the mother's voice and
argues that it is a male fantasy of women that is imposed retroactively.
For Silverman the disembodied female voice is a discursive, involving
one, not one that creates an ensnaring, if intoxicating, web for the listener. Perhaps this mythologizing of the female acousmêtre as an entity
that will always hark back to the voice of the mother plays into the ghet-
toization of women's voices on acousmatic media such as radio. Kaja
Silverman's critique is a crucial one, especially when applied to the FM
DJ—after all she is enunciating words not just issuing forth with
phonemes or glossolalia (nonsense). The DJ is articulate, discursive, and
communicative. Her words—no matter the pleasure involved in hearing
them—are also parts of narratives that are meant to be followed, involving intelligence of listening at least as much as the desire to be taken
over by the sonority of the voice.

The peripheral status of the female voice on radio contributes to its
becoming a sought-after object of desire. It is laden not necessarily with
maternal memories but also with exotic flavors of difference and sexual
possibilities. The Nightbird's success as a beloved woman is related to
this allure, and the fact that she was so singular and unique is also related to the taboo on the female voice. The deployment of Alison Steele's
voice as the Nightbird, ever reassuring its audience that she understands its concerns, could only provoke fantasy. Alison Steele does not
provoke this fantasy herself; rather it was encouraged by the structure in

which the Nightbird was heard. Her listeners were poised at the edge of wakefulness and the passageway to dreams, presumably providing diacritical marks to the language of the unconscious. If the Nightbird was an exciting or tranquilizing voice, it was also one of intelligence and articulation, a voice that told bedtime stories. Although none of the stories were naughty or laden with double entendres, many heard a beguiling voice of seduction.

The enigma and power of the female DJ, a persona that Alison Steele created, took flight into other media and reappeared in other characters. Each incarnation refers back to the Nightbird, and each provides insight into the meaning and importance of the Nightbird herself. Two films released in 1979, John Carpenter's *The Fog* and Walter Hill's *The Warriors,* both feature female DJs. These films provide a counterpoint to Clint Eastwood's *Play Misty for Me* (1971), in which the female lead is a deranged, murderous fan of a male DJ who has rejected her.

In *The Warriors,* the African American actress Lynne Thigpen plays the female DJ. The film depicts a wayward gang in a New York City that, like the city at the time, was full of gangs in a dilapidated, almost lawless environment. The Warriors have been wrongly accused of killing one of the leaders of one of the main gangs in town who sought an alliance between all members. The call goes out via the DJ to capture the Warriors, who are running back to their safe haven in Coney Island. Lynne Thigpen appears only in profile in her radio station, a near acousmêtre with lipstick lips. She announces the whereabouts of the wayward gang to all listeners, encouraging them to find the gang and bring them to street justice. She speaks in street jargon and acts as a narrator within the film, reporting on the progress of the fleeing gang. The DJ magically knows the whereabouts of all the gangs, as if she sees all in her perch above the city. Even though she is denied an entire body, her soft, sexy tones speak powerfully of the need for revenge. Of course, the Nightbird was never vengeful, but as the DJ in *The Warriors* reminds us, she alerts her nocturnal listeners to presences that they might otherwise overlook. Although the female DJ is unseen, she sees all. She is a form of surveillance, with erotic overtones.

The B-movie actress (and daughter of Maude in the sitcom of the same name) Adrienne Barbeau plays DJ Stevie Wayne in *The Fog* (remade in 2005 with Selma Blair as the female DJ), who comes to operate a small radio station located at the top of a lighthouse in the haunted town of Antonio Bay. When fog rolls in from the harbor, it is the harbinger of murder, and Stevie Wayne uses her voice to save her child and alert the townspeople to the mist's deathly arrival. Ms. Wayne, like Alison Steele, is an object of desire. In one scene, we overhear two male characters discussing how sexy she is, though only one of them has seen her. It is her voice that produces the appeal, yet it is also her voice that provides her son with maternal protection against the vengeful ghosts of a drowned ship. Stevie Wayne (Steven and Wayne are two traditionally male names) is desired for the sexual possibilities of her smooth voice, yet she is also the all-powerful mother who will stop at nothing to defend her child. Like the DJ in *The Warriors,* her position on the radio gives her a privileged optical position, allowing her to see what others in the film can't see. As surveillance, she hovers above the ground in her station at the lighthouse. She, too, is a narrator in the film, but also an active agent, and ironically her ability to have her voice separated from her body gives her the ability to see more. It is as if her voice itself has vision. This, too, is the Nightbird's advantage. She is an entity that you hear, but she is able to translate what she sees to her audience. She provides word pictures to those who listen to the radio in the dark, foggy night. She has a perch; being on the radio allows the speaker altitude, releasing the voice to the ether, allowing it access to flight patterns.

Gregory Whitehead's radio play *The Loneliest Road,* performed for the BBC in 2004, features another incarnation of the Nightbird, a character named the Hungry Raven. The Hungry Raven links the monologues of the other characters, all of whom have traveled down the highway in Nevada that is known as the loneliest road in America. This road travels through desolate, unpopulated desert. The Hungry Raven sums up the spirit of the denizens of this highway and invites all to her environment, one that also represents the state of a forlorn nation. A radio DJ, she brings her listeners to this solitary, mobile place. She decries:

> Lonely drifters, dark strangers, luscious friends of the long night, around me a vast network of abandoned mines, and inside those mines abandoned dreams, and inside those dreams the spirits of the vanquished gather, and they dance the ghost dance, and they call out to the great warrior, who will come and end this agony.

She finishes her invocation by almost directly citing the Nightbird. She adds a sinister coda on the omnipresence of violence in the United States at the beginning of the twenty-first century under the Bush/Cheney regime: "And you can hear it all right here on WDOA in the United States of America, so come fly with me for I am the Hungry Raven, over and over and over and out."

The Hungry Raven is both a character and a narrator, stitching together the stories of those along the highway from a bough above. As Alison Steele said to the *New York Times* on December 9, 1971, she never gets "lonely *up* here" (my italics), indicating that her place on the radio lends her a perspective that gives her a panoramic view of what is beneath her. Whitehead's version of the Nightbird is sinister and ravenous, feeding off loneliness rather than offering shelter from it, but she shares the ability to see from an aerial perch. Whitehead's rendition, though, suits the landscape of America in one of its most recent manifestations, a Nightbird for the Bush regime.

What these disparate incarnations of the Nightbird allow us to see is that Alison Steele created a persona with archetypical dimensions—her voice evoked another body imagined by her listeners, one that had little to do with Alison Steele. Moving from being reassuringly maternal to being inadvertently seductive to becoming an unsettling narrator, the Nightbird was experienced in variegated ways that could both soothe and excite listeners: she was provocative. Through a force of will she came into existence in the early 1970s—and because of sexist barriers she could not have appeared until two crucial events occurred due to social pressure: the FCC insisted on the expansion of FM and the women's movement won legal victories. Although she had to fight to keep her place, the Nightbird proved to be both mysterious and knowable, roaming from her bough on the radio, inviting wayfarers of the night to accompany her.

CHAPTER 6

The Silence of Lance and Pat Loud

EVIL FLOWERS

Camera-loving Lance Loud was the oldest son of the family depicted in the television docudrama *An American Family.* Lance died just before Christmas in 2001 of liver failure brought about by hepatitis C and HIV. He was fifty years old. He had lived a hard life of both craving and escaping the limelight, indulging in drugs and then living on the straight and narrow, working frenetically and then retreating from the world. He was creative and witty and full of ideas, many of them completed, others not; like Alison Steele, Loud refused to be a has-been or rest on his previous successes. Lance was the first reality television star. He was also a journalist, singer, and performer in his later manifestations.

Like many reality stars that came after him, from Pedro Zamora (a heroic AIDS activist featured in the third year of *The Real World*) to Richard Hatch (the divisive winner of the first season of *Survivor*), Lance Loud was an openly gay man. Unlike David Bowie, his sexual orientation was not only an act; like Bowie, though, he was drawn to the demimonde of New York City that circled around Andy Warhol, much of it residing at the Chelsea Hotel. Loud's performance of self on the small screens of America was especially pioneering, paving the way for Zamora and Hatch and the standard inclusion of gays and lesbians in reality shows. More important, for many viewers, Lance was the first openly gay man they had ever seen. Lance both reinforced some stereotypes and, at the same time, challenged many preconceptions. He was never apologetic and never acted as if he felt any shame about his sexual orientation—or his outlandishness.

The show, filmed in 1971, premiered on Thursday, January 11, 1973, at 9:00 p.m. on PBS and ran for twelve weeks. Each episode was one hour in length. *An American Family* changed the medium of television, though its effect was not immediate. Years later the producers of *The Real World* acknowledged the show as an inspiration, but every unscripted drama that uses nonactors in situations or dilemmas devised by the producers owes a debt of gratitude to the show—as does any show that features gay characters or actors. In 2011, HBO presented a behind-the-scene depiction of the show, entitled *Cinema Verite,* and starring James Gandolfini and Diane Lane.

The twelve-episode series was edited from three hundred hours of footage and was filmed in 1971 in Santa Barbara, California, and New York City, where Lance, the oldest son, lived in the Chelsea Hotel. The show and the passionate response it provoked in purportedly revealing the truth of a large (five kids), white, property-owning American family, propelled Lance and his family into the media spotlight. They appeared on talk shows and game shows and were discussed and analyzed (and quite often harshly criticized) by experts and academics, as well as the rest of the viewing audience.

However, noted anthropologist Margaret Mead celebrated the show's innovative form—she wrote in *TV Guide* in 1973 that it was as "new and significant as the invention of drama or the novel—a new way in which people can learn to look at life." Even though her praise for the show is justified, as Jeffrey Ruoff notes in his book *An American Family: A Televised Life* (2002), she did have a connection to the show, as its producer, Craig Gilbert, had made a film in 1968 that portrayed her, called *Margaret Mead's New Guinea Journal* (Ruoff, 9). Another important cultural critic, Raymond Williams, supported the show and the possibilities of this new genre in his book *Television: Technology and Cultural Form* (1974), but he was not writing for the mass-market magazine *TV Guide.* The French cultural theorist Jean Baudrillard noted in *Simulacra and Simulations* (1994) that the show was an example of a media simulation and argued that the family didn't really exist at all and had in fact become a simulated entity.

As Ruoff argues, most of the public and the critics treated Lance and his family as if they were real people rather than characters in a film shown on PBS. The critics rarely disparaged the show for being too exhibitionistic or advocated for further use of this new type of programming. Instead they took issue with the family—and certainly Lance was singled out and attacked more than his siblings and parents. For example, Anne Roiphe, writing in the *New York Times Magazine* of February 18, 1973, referred to Lance as "flamboyant," "leechlike," and an "evil flower" (292). Even if one disregards the virulent homophobia of her descriptions (although it does link Lance to the innovative French symbol-ist poet Baudelaire, who wrote *Les Fleurs du mal*), Roiphe fails to under-stand a key aspect of the show and all of its participants. Lance's por-trayal is always an unwilling collaboration with the editor, the producer, the production crew, and the press materials that sensationalized the show. In addition, as Lance is not contrite about either his homosexual-ity or his outlandishness, he is subject to all sorts of homophobic re-sponses that insist one's gayness should remain hidden.

The Louds were the opposite of the Bradys of *The Brady Bunch*, a fa-vorite television family at the time (1969–74), especially among children (and the focus of much nostalgia to this day). The Bradys were also a large West Coast family (six children) that lived comfortably in a con-temporary suburban home. Of course, the Bradys were a fictional fam-ily consisting of two divorcees with three children each (of matching hair color) that lived comfortably within the sitcom world of network television. All of the family's comical problems were solved within thirty minutes each week, often with the assistance of their maid Alice. The Louds' problems were many: an adulterous husband, a wife strug-gling to find her identity, rebellious children who loved rock 'n' roll, avant-garde/queer theater, or modern dance (not to mention the fact that their house was in danger from the fiery Santa Ana winds). A script, or the obligation to provide a happy ending, could not solve such mal-adies. Americans saw what happened when a camera crew came to live with the family. Lance, his younger brothers Grant and Kevin (in a rock band), and his sisters Michele and Delilah (studying dance) had a vari-ety of responses to their parents' crumbling relationship and the effects it had on their complex set of sibling rivalries and alliances. Each reacted differently to the presence of the camera to record their moody interac-tions. Many viewers and critics forgot to mention that they were looking at a version of themselves. In denial, many decided that the family was at fault, not the culture. Such a family could not represent America.

COMING OUT/LEAVING HOME

Episode 2 is often described as Lance's coming-out episode. During this episode, Lance's mother Pat visits him in New York to see for herself how he is doing. Lance is not working: he is trying to get a job at an un-derground magazine, which is sure to pay very little. He is sharing a rather untidy room at the Chelsea Hotel with another man, Soren, and their cat (at the end of his life, Lance took in many cats). Soren and Lance live on the outskirts of the Warhol-influenced demimonde—and of course Andy Warhol depicted the poetic chaos of the hotel in the film *Chelsea Girls* (1966). Lance is friendly with Holly Woodlawn (memorialized in the Lou Reed song "Walk on the Wild Side" and the star of the Warhol-produced film *Trash* [1970]). He has come to New York to be among exactly this type of creative—if self-destructive—artists and performers that made the reputation of the hotel (writers from Mark Twain to Allen Ginsberg have lived at the Chelsea Hotel, as well as musicians from Bob Dylan to Sid Vicious). Craving fame, Lance moved into the epicenter of New York bohemia.

Although Pat is open-minded, her upper-middle-class Californian outlook clashes with her son's New York lifestyle. His lifestyle places esteem on camp, kitsch, and artistry that focuses on outrageous self-presentation. She enters into the belly of the beast by taking a room upstairs from her son in Manhattan's semiofficial home for troubled, talented artists. In the episode, we see how Lance loves living there amid its crazy residents. Pat sees her son's level of comfort there, but she can't help but judge the hotel's lack of cleanliness, lax management, and drug-taking denizens.

Lance and Soren bring Pat into their world. They take her to Jackie Curtis's drag queen show, *Vain Victory* (featuring numerous artists and performers that included Andy Warhol, as well as others affiliated with Warhol's world—Ondine, Holly Woodlawn, Candy Darling, and Mario Montez). They also go to a Broadway musical (*No No Nanette*), an Andy Warhol exhibit, and a discotheque. Pat tries to view Manhattan from her son's perspective rather than imposing her preconceptions on him and his milieu. It is a moving episode, with moments of acceptance and concern between mother and son—as well as awkward silences. These silences announce her conflicted responses to her son's surroundings.

Lance never "comes out" to his mother or his audience. He never tells her—or the camera—that he is gay. In fact, Pat probably already knows. According to filmmaker Susan Raymond, Pat had known since he was sixteen (he is nineteen during the filming of the episode). In her 1974 book *Pat Loud: A Woman's Story* (written with Nora Johnson), Pat writes that if Lance is homosexual he is also much more than that as well (97–98). Mother and son never talk openly about his sexual orientation during the show, though they refer to it (certainly Pat warns Lance that Soren may not be the best "friend" for him, though she never refers to Soren as his lover). What the episode does show, and why it is so groundbreaking, is a gay son who does not hide his life from his mother and a mother who accepts her son and his milieu, however reluctantly. The word *gay* or *homosexual* is never mentioned, though Lance does at one point say to his mother "Je suis fatigué," a French phrase meaning "I am tired." The word *fatigué,* as pronounced in French, ends with a syllable that sounds like *gay.* Lance is pronouncing a coded confession to his audience—and his mother. There are also a few moments in a sequence in which Lance and Pat are walking in Central Park when Lance darts away from his mother (and the sound technician). He says something that we can't discern as he moves away from the camera crew.

During the Central Park sequence, Lance talks about the loneliness of his teenage years, living with parents who didn't understand him, which made it hard for him to understand himself. If he never exactly comes out by uttering a confession about being gay, by his manner, his friends, his dress, and his taste Lance has already shown the audience that he is a young, urban, gay man of the early 1970s. He is attracted to art, performance, film, and the possibilities of self-presentation as a form of self-preservation against the kind of intolerance that is expressed by Anne Roiphe and many others.

A new glossy magazine appeared in New York in the 1970s that appealed to this exact audience of artistically and musically inclined urban men. *After Dark* never used the word *gay* to refer to its readers (though the word would appear in reviews of plays and films). Along with articles about the arts and reviews of plays and operas, the magazine featured nude photos of dancers and actors. It also contained editorial fashion spreads that could only appeal to gay men of the era, many of them shot in the gay and lesbian enclaves on Fire Island. The magazine reveled in the open secret of its gayness and always privileged the arts over politics.

FILMIC CONTEXT

Even though *An American Family* is often described as groundbreaking and the beginning of reality-based (or unscripted) television programming, it didn't come out of nowhere. It followed on fifteen years of influential documentary filmmaking in both the United States and France, a cinematic movement that did away with voice-over narration, the use of a musical score, reliance on interviews between filmmaker and subject matter, and other devices that became commonplace in nonfiction storytelling. In France, the cinematic movement became known as *cinéma vérité*. Jean Rouch was a leading proponent of this filmic style, which acknowledged the presence of the filmmaker and highlighted the interaction between the filmmaker and the people being depicted in the film. For example, Rouch's *Chronicle of a Summer* (1960) begins with a young woman recruiting people into the film by asking passersby in a busy Paris street if they are happy. It concludes with the assembled characters viewing the footage of the film in which they are featured and commenting on it and themselves with the filmmakers. An epilogue features Rouch and his sociologist collaborator, Edgar Morin, discussing the merits and drawbacks of their cinematic experiment.

Many American filmmakers took up the term *cinéma vérité* to describe their films, even though the technique commonly used by Americans was usually very different than their French counterparts. More appropriately, perhaps, American filmmakers used the term *direct cinema* (or *observational cinema*) to describe their approach. Simply put, direct cinema mandates that the filmmaker act like "a fly on the wall," never intervening into the scene he or she films and never adding any sounds other than those that occurred during the recording of a sequence. The premise of direct cinema is that the viewer and the audience learn about the subject matter not through what sociologist Daniel Boorstin, in *The Image* (1992), described as the pseudoevent so indicative of America (media interviews, press conferences, publicity events) but through the close observation of details and appearances that the camera and sound equipment can provide.

Direct cinema was made possible by changes in film technology that radicalized the possibilities for both fictional and nonfictional filmmaking (changes we take for granted now with handheld video cameras that record both image and sound). In 1960, lightweight 16mm cameras equipped with synchronized sound became available (developed in part by filmmakers Richard Leacock and D. A. Pennebaker). These cameras allowed filmmakers to claim that they could capture real life in near objective fashion, without having to spend hours setting up, moving in cumbersome equipment. These new cameras allowed the human subjects of a film to act almost as if the film crew was not there—or at least not there obstructing their movements or making them wait endlessly while a crew sets up a shot. New technology indeed did allow "the fly" to sit on the wall, though of course the filmmaker never entirely disappears and his or her presence transforms the milieu to be filmed, even when the equipment is not obtrusive. As Pat Loud describes in her memoir, the Heisenberg Effect went to work instantly. (Heisenberg was a physicist who argued that any phenomenon that is observed is changed by the way it is observed; here the communications medium is the mode of observation.) She writes that as soon as the cameras arrived the family members tried to become "charming, amusing, photogenic, and generally irresistible" (89).

Relationships between the filmmakers and the Louds developed. Filmmaker Susan Raymond (who worked as the sound person) became especially close to youngest daughter Michele during the filming of the show. Pat met producer Craig Gilbert for drinks, and he even became something of a confidante for her during production (there were some unsubstantiated rumors of an affair between the two). The Louds remained friends with Susan and her husband Alan; they did not forgive Craig Gilbert, however, for the way the show was edited and how PBS marketed the program.

Direct cinema focused on the untold stories of people outside the limelight, as well as celebrity figures. For example, *Dont Look Back* (1967) by D. A. Pennebaker portrayed Bob Dylan's first visit to England, Pennebaker filmed David Bowie's last concert as Ziggy Stardust (1973, discussed in chapter 4), and the Maysles Brothers' *Gimme Shelter* (1970) depicted the Rolling Stones and the free concert at Altamont. Earlier Robert Drew, a forerunner of direct cinema, filmed *Primary* (1960), which offered a view of the Democratic primary contest between Hubert Humphrey and John F. Kennedy in 1960. These films were attempts to get beyond the hype of celebrity and public image and move behind closed doors in order to show life backstage, providing the viewer with an angle on the real-life dynamics of living an authentic life under the seemingly constant gaze of the media.

Other examples of direct cinema focused on more mundane but no less important events, environments, and personalities. These films, which could be shocking exposés or more tame depictions of ordinary lives, included the work of Fred Wiseman in *Hospital* (1970) and *High School* (1968) and his film about a hospital for the criminally insane, *Titicut Follies* (1967). The Maysles brothers, who were often interested in celebrity, also filmed *Salesman* (1969), which depicted the decidedly unglamorous lives of traveling Bible salesmen and their desperate selling techniques. These films laid the foundation for *An American Family* in terms of both subject matter and filmmaking style. The show is part of an American tradition in media making, one that had emerged since 1960; in fact, *An American Family* can be viewed as made-for-TV direct cinema.

An American Family revises the characteristics of direct cinema in one important sense—length. Usually direct cinema films were feature length—90 to 120 minutes. *An American Family* lasted twelve hours. The effects of its duration and the way it was divided into segments were at least twofold. On one hand, the program became akin to a soap opera as "story lines" moved from week to week (and it focuses on a family that the viewer knows from the beginning is in turmoil). On the other hand its length allows certain events to be presented in their entirety, without editing. As a result, we see the entirety of a solo in a dance concert, not just highlights of it; we see all of Lance's footsteps as he returns to his room in the Chelsea Hotel after his mother leaves. While it is not exactly true to say that we see the family in "real time," there is a decided emphasis on representing sequences from start to finish. If the show was riveting, it was not because it was action packed; rather it was because the show's style allowed viewers to see how the family members moved through their home and experienced the passage of time. This was seen through a diverse set of interactions that emphasized the duration of actions and reactions. This technique was uncommon on television before this time and was not utilized after the show—unfortunately *The Real World* and the reality television that followed the MTV series privileges editing and the inclusion of video confessions performed by the characters (or contestants).

An American Family was the first, most successful attempt to bring a new documentary style to the formally conservative medium of television. Television began as a relatively tame medium that refrained from depicting key aspects of life—for example, it wasn't until 1957 that a toilet was seen on television, and couples were rarely seen in the same bed. Openly gay characters were rare on television, although there was a gay character in the short-lived sitcom *The Corner Bar* in 1972, and of course there were many gay and lesbian performers. Gay characters were more commonplace in mainstream cinema. Films such as *Sunday Bloody Sunday* (1971), *The Killing of Sister George* (1968), *Cabaret* (1972), and *The Boys in the Band* (1970) featured the lives of gay, lesbian, or bisexual characters. Although their lives were depicted as tragic, lonely, or stereotypically "bitchy," these films nonetheless acknowledged the existence of gay people, which television all but denied.

In documentary, short nonfiction, and experimental film, depictions or expressions of gay life were also more prevalent than on television. Pioneering films that were either directed by gay filmmakers or depicted gays and lesbians in complex ways included the experimental work of

Kenneth Anger in the 1950s and 1960s such as *Scorpio Rising* (1964), Shirley Clarke's *Portrait of Jason* (1967), and many of the early experimental films of Andy Warhol such as *My Hustler* (1965). In addition, a documentary about a drag queen contest entitled *The Queen* was filmed in 1967, and *Some of My Best Friends Are* (1971) depicted an evening in a gay bar. In sum, representations of gays and lesbians were becoming more prevalent in nonfiction and fiction film, indicating that filmmakers were responding to their increasing visibility and acceptance.

While representations of gays and lesbians were rare in the more closeted medium of television, shows such as *Bewitched* (1964–72) winked at their audiences, making fun of suburbia and heterosexual marriage. *Bewitched* featured the outrageously gay actor Paul Lynde as the bachelor warlock uncle and the actress Agnes Moorehead as the divorced witch mother. Gay actor Dick Sargent played the second Darrin—in fact, of the lead parts only Elizabeth Montgomery was heterosexual. The show was encoded with a gay sensibility but managed to keep its actors in the closet. If *An American Family*—and Lance Loud—went a long way in opening up the closet door, many actors still felt it necessary to protect their "privacy." Dick Sargent didn't come out of the closet until 1991 after a tabloid "outed" him. Paul Lynde never came out, although he was arrested for solicitation outside a gay bar in 1978 (which ended his guest spot on the *Donny and Marie Show*). Rumors about Agnes Moorehead's lesbianism were rampant in Hollywood (and Paul Lynde repeated them publicly, perhaps as a way to take the focus off him), but she, too, never discussed her sexual orientation openly.

Clearly in the 1970s—as today—it was easier to be a gay or lesbian reality television star than a successful openly gay or lesbian actor. After all, gay actors fear that they will no longer get leading roles if they are outed, whereas gay reality stars are ensured attention if they reveal their sexuality. For example, every season of *The Real World* has a gay household member—as well as a black roommate—both chosen not only for reasons of inclusiveness but also to increase the potential for interpersonal drama. One gay contestant on *Big Brother*, who was active in the rodeo circuit before his appearance, has given up the ropes to become a star in porno films, suggesting that gay male celebrities can get leading roles but perhaps not in PG-rated films. Leading men who are gay continue to hide the "truth" of their sexual orientation. It is easier to be a gay reality star than a "real" gay star.

An American Family not only broke new ground on television with its representation of a young gay man but also in its depiction of a divorce. In the first episode the viewer learns that the couple's marriage is now over, and in succeeding episodes the viewer learns about the circumstances of the divorce. The revelations in the last episode cause the viewer to rethink the entire program. The show's examination of a fraying heterosexual relationship occurred by chance—producer Craig Gilbert did not know this would happen when he "picked the family." Yet the breakup of the couple on the show reflected an important phenomenon in American cultural life. According to Sally Clarke of the National Center for Health Statistics (1995), the divorce rate increased by 40 percent from 1970 to 1975 and more than doubled between 1960 and 1975 (divorce rates have been decreasing slowly since 1981). Pat Loud's request for a divorce from her philandering husband was part of a real trend in the country.

The feminist movement in part motivated this trend. For some women, marriage—as a social institution, not necessarily due to the particular man—stifled female autonomy and identity. The rise of divorce was also motivated by economic and legal factors—beginning in the mid-1960s women were working outside the home more, so divorce became a more viable option for them. Also, changes in divorce law enabled this change: no-fault divorce became commonplace in most states in the 1960s, and many experts noted a correlation between the change in divorce laws and divorce rates.

Marriage was considered a patriotic act for women after the Second World War, encouraging the baby boom (the GI Bill also led to the growth of towns like Santa Barbara as white enclaves). Women in the work force were told to go back to the home so men could return to work after serving their country during the war. The loyal housewife was a culturally validated role in the 1950s and early 1960s, especially as seen in such sitcoms as the *Donna Reed Show* and *Leave It to Beaver.* Yet changes in the economic and legal structure of the country contributed to the rise of divorce. On January 22, 1973, the Supreme Court established the abortion rights of women in the landmark *Roe v. Wade* case. This decision followed on a 1965 decision to strike down the Comstock laws, ending state bans on contraceptives and thus ensuring that women had access to easy birth control methods, such as oral contraceptives like the pill, which, in 1960, had been approved by the Food and Drug Administration (FDA). By 1965, more the six million women were taking the pill. Pat Loud's divorce is part of the many changes of this era that afforded women a greater degree of control over their bodies. These changes enabled women to plan pregnancies and leave marriages in ways that were not possible before.

Pat Loud's independence from her husband also occurs after changes in the popular culture and political ideology inspired by some key thinkers and activists. Important books and writers fueled the feminist movement, such as Simone de Beauvoir's *The Second Sex* (first published in English in 1953), Betty Friedan's *The Feminine Mystique* (1963), and Germaine Greer's *The Female Eunuch* (1970). Each of these writers— along with politicians Bella Abzug (a Jewish woman elected to Congress in 1970) and Shirley Chisholm (a black congresswoman who ran for president in 1972)—became prominent in the media. *Ms.* magazine, funded by Warner Communications, was first published in January 1972 (in 1971 it was included as an insert in *New York* magazine). Its first editor, Gloria Steinem, was a public figure, if not an outright celebrity. Erica Jong's enormously popular novel *Fear of Flying* was published in 1973. This novel, which coined the term *zipless fuck,* detailed the pursuit of female sexual pleasure. It followed on both a feminist consciousness and a new openness in talking about sex, an openness that was inspired by the 1960s counterculture, as well as mainstream magazines like *Cosmopolitan,* which was increasingly geared toward an audience of women who were sexually adventurous, unmarried, and urban. In 1973, *Playgirl* magazine (discussed in chapter 7) was launched, featuring male frontal nudity and designed as a counterpart to *Playboy.* Although a significant part of its audience was actually gay men, it advocated a lifestyle for single women who were interested in enjoying a sensual life, hoping to create a new marketing niche.

The relationship between the genders in the late 1960s and early 1970s was becoming realigned, and women were gaining increased power both in the public sphere and in their ability to claim sovereignty over their own bodies. A new kind of woman was being addressed in popular media, and single women with careers were becoming more prevalent on television—from the black nurse *Julia* (1968–71) to the WASPy television producer in the *Mary Tyler Moore Show* (1970–77), with her best friend, the Jewish Rhoda Morgenstern, to the outspoken *Maude* (1972–78). Feminism and social change were in the air that Pat Loud was breathing, and the suburban, submissive housewife was no longer the dominant female image in popular media; the educated, independent woman with a career was replacing her. This woman lived in the city, not the suburbs, unlike the housewife of earlier decades.

Lance Loud. (Photo courtesy of Video Vérité.)

Lance—and gay men and lesbians in general—also benefited from this transformation of the social environment. Lance was not especially a gay activist in his life (though he later wrote for the *Advocate*, a popular gay publication); however, his openness has a relationship to the postwar gay and lesbian movement. In the aftermath of the Stonewall riots in 1969, when a gay bar was raided in New York City, gays and lesbians, like blacks and women, began to demand their civil rights. Yet important gay organizations such as the Mattachine Society (for gay men) and the Daughters of Bilitis (for lesbians) had already set the stage for activism in the pre-Stonewall era by asserting that a positive gay identity was possible and forthcoming. After Stonewall, the Gay Activist Alliance was formed in 1969 and the National Gay Task Force was established in 1973. These groups, with different ideologies, asserted the rights of gay people. One of the major victories of gay activists was that in December of 1973 the American Psychiatric Association removed homosexuality from the *Diagnostic and Statistic Manual of Mental Disorders* (DSM). Homosexuality was no longer considered a disorder. This signaled a huge societal shift in how homosexuality was to be treated by professionals and hence how it was viewed generally. For the clinician, being gay was no longer a malady of which one should be cured (unfortunately "transformational" ministries still exist that try to "pray away the gay").

In addition, although Andy Warhol was far from being a political activist, he brought an unprecedented amount of media attention to drag queens, gay and lesbian artists, and wayward debutantes, rendering them chic and fashionable—even if they were still freaks. He brought societal outcasts out of the shadows and asserted that they were superstars. In 1971 the hippieish cross-dressing theatrical troupe called the Cockettes traveled from San Francisco to New York. Although their performances were not well received, the critics raved about one of the group's stars, Sylvester. He later brought an African American gospel intensity to the burgeoning disco scene and celebrated an androgynous and yearning sexuality (see Gamson). In the early 1970s David Bowie (and later Elton John), as well as Suzi Quatro, paraded an ambiguous sexuality in their theatrical personae. Performers in popular culture were challenging gender roles—and audiences were loving it.

Thus, it was no mere coincidence that Andy Warhol inspired Lance Loud and Lance thought the American public would embrace him when he appeared on television as his fabulous self. Lance sent Warhol a fan letter when he was sixteen (after a number of letters, Warhol responded to him). In an essay included on Susan and Alan Raymond's Web site, written in 1973, Lance Loud writes of reading about Warhol when he was twelve years old in his father's copy of *Time* magazine.

> For the first time in my life, I knew why I wasn't happy it was because I couldn't even do or act the way I wanted to, much less make my living at it. And here was some guy who was going around and people were probably hating him and thinking he was crazy but he was having a great time of it all, he was having his cake and eating it too, and everyone else had to at least pretend to want a bit. ANDY WARHOL was my goal, ANDY WARHOL was my hobby, my hope, my guardian angel. (in Raymond and Raymond)

Lance dyed his hair silver in homage to his hero when he graduated from junior high school (Warhol was in his "silver" period—his studio and hair were painted silver). Later, in New York City, Andy Warhol became acquainted with Lance and would go see the Mumps, the rock band Lance formed. Lance also contributed to Warhol's magazine *Interview,* and Warhol appeared in a film Lance directed. Andy Warhol and

New York's artistic spirit represented freedom for Lance, and he came to New York as if he were a refugee from a repressive regime.

Pat Loud also came to New York to live after the series ended and her divorce was finalized. In episode 2 of *An American Family* we see that both Pat and Lance are exiles from the traditional heterosexual family. After all, Pat has temporarily left her husband and her other children in order to be with her firstborn, gay son in New York, perhaps not only to check on him but to take a break from her demanding family. She understands his desire for independence and self-creation, as this is part of what she craves for herself. In her memoir, Pat Loud writes very candidly about how Lance challenges her: "I admire his freedom and am frightened by it at the same time. I imagine a lot of other people must feel that way and that's why they get so indignant about him. In some ways, he's the future, and we all get a little unglued by that" (98).

VERSIONS OF REALITY

Jeffrey Ruoff, in his important book on the series, makes a crucial point about the creation of the show in relation to the history of public broadcasting. Ruoff writes, "From 1963 to 1970, the Ford Foundation provided NET [National Educational Television] with approximately eight million dollars a year, promoting high quality works on educational TV" (5). The Ford Foundation's support enabled the development of the show, and the foundation provided half the funding for it. The Corporation for Public Broadcasting (CPB) provided the other half. Ruoff notes the effect of Nixon's veto of the CPB budget in 1972: "After 1973, staff producers at member stations were bound, through ties to corporate funding, to conventional styles and non-controversial subject matter" (5). In sum, the show would have been impossible to produce a year later, and the freedom granted to the producer was indicative of a particular time period.

Although *An American Family* emerged at a time of creativity in public programming, it was also controversial and contested from the get-go. The show was Craig Gilbert's idea, and he was credited not only as producer but also with conceiving the series. However, the filmmakers Susan Raymond (who was a sound technician) and Alan Raymond (a cinematographer) claimed authorship of the film, as they headed the production crew. Most of the family turned against Gilbert and PBS— they were upset about how the film was edited and how it was being promoted and advertised by the network. During the filming of the show, most of the family became friends with the Raymonds and remained friends with the them. The Raymonds became the representatives for the family and directed the two subsequent films that followed up on the life of the Louds: a 1983 HBO film entitled *An American Family Revisited: The Louds 10 Years Later;* and a PBS film, *LANCE LOUD! A Death in an American Family* (2003). In both films the intimacy between family members and the Raymonds is evident; however, Craig Gilbert is not spoken of in such kind terms. In a *Museum of Broadcasting Seminar* that included family members, Gilbert, and the Raymonds, the squabble between the Raymonds and Gilbert and the family and Gilbert was all too evident (1988). The conflict that the show produced has not been resolved; Gilbert is blamed for the ways the show was received and for leading an unprepared family into the media crossfire for his own purposes. The family members do not forgive him.

Gilbert did have an agenda—he was looking for a particular kind of family when he was developing his idea. He wanted to use direct cinema techniques in order to portray an affluent, white American family during the turbulent times at the end of the civil rights period, during the Vietnam War and the counterculture it inspired. According to Ruoff (16) some friends recommended he choose an African American family as a way to bring visibility to a group that was underrepresented on television. Yet Gilbert wanted to find a family that looked as though it could have been part of a sitcom fantasy. He wanted to see how a family like this responded to real-life challenges and political tumult. According to Pat Loud, she was misled. Gilbert informed her that he was looking for a family to depict because he was fearful that families were falling apart all over the country (69). In fact, he was looking for a family that was suffering from all sorts of tension, and he came to Santa Barbara because of a book that was set in a fictionalized version of the town—crime writer Ross Macdonald's *The Underground Man* (17).

Associate producer Susan Lester recalls that they weren't looking for a family that featured homosexuality or divorce per se, but in the search to get beyond the appearance of a happy family they were trying to see the effects of the generation gap, the Vietnam War, and drug usage (Ruoff, 18). The family members felt producer Gilbert treated them as objects that he never really cared for except that they were proving his point about the end of the traditional marriage (Pat Loud argues that Gilbert's own marriage was failing and he was indulging in psychological projection in devising the show). The Raymonds, however, had taken the time to know the family and care for them. The tension between using this family as part of an agenda—to show the underbelly of the American Dream—and to depict the family as a sum of individuals seeking new identities is one that makes the series dynamic. It also makes episode 2 especially fascinating, as it depicts a clash of cultures.

Episode 2 begins with an establishing shot of the Chelsea Hotel in New York. We hear Craig Gilbert's voice, introducing it as the place where Lance, eldest son of the Loud family, is living and trying to get a job in the underground press. From this shot, we move to Lance's room, and we see him sitting on the bed. Gilbert's voice continues on the soundtrack, and he informs us that Lance is sharing this room with Soren Ingenue. This is the last we hear of Gilbert's narrating voice in the episode.

Lance is getting ready for his mother's visit. He appears nervous and changes his shirt three times before he sticks with an outfit. He jokes with Soren that maybe he should wear a suit, and the two laugh. The camera follows Lance around the small, cluttered room; the focus of the camera is Lance not Soren—after all Lance is a Loud and Soren is only his boyfriend and not part of the American family.

The next scene follows Pat Loud's arrival at the Chelsea Hotel. She is dressed fashionably with a white jacket and large blue sunglasses, and her dark, grayless hair is pulled back. The taxi driver carries her suitcase to the front desk. The camera work is fluid, following her movements and pausing when she stops, a trademark of Alan Raymond's camera use. He matches a character's speed with his own, never letting a family member "get away," and he shoots a character from a variety of angles and distances. When Pat or Lance slows down, so does the camera. Alan Raymond is skilled: he takes advantage of the moments in which a character is still by zooming in for a momentary close-up of the face or the hands. His technique mimics the movement of what he is shooting, but he never blocks the trajectory of the character.

In the next scene, Pat enters Lance and Soren's room (later she chastises her son for not coming down to meet her) and hugs her son. Immediately Pat has some choice comments about their lifestyle after being introduced to Soren, stating, "You boys need some policing." Although she is referring to the messiness of the room, she is also already criticizing her son's bohemian lifestyle. Lance avoids a conflict with his mom by pointing out a lithograph hanging on the wall; clearly he has experience in deflecting his mother's terse remarks.

The three of them settle into a discussion about current events. Pat mentions that there was a bombing in Eugene, Oregon (where Lance was born and raised as a child), and that the town passed a bill against the Vietnam War. Soren adds that he thinks Massachusetts, too, as a state, has officially protested the war. Lance tells his mother that he hears bombs in New York all the time and that he has become used to it. We are reminded that this is a time of extreme political activity in the United States—the Weather Underground and the FALN (Fuerzas Armadas de Liberacíon Nacional was a Puerto Rican pro-independence group) used bombing of property as a way to advance their political goals. It is clear that even though the Louds are affluent and can support their son in New York, they cannot keep him (and themselves) completely safe from social strife. One of the effects of the Vietnam War is the creation of a domestic front, where explosions, as well as mass protests, are commonplace. A Weather Underground slogan was "Bring the War Home," and to a large extent, domestic conflicts did mirror international conflicts—if the Vietnamese were struggling to gain sovereignty over their nation, women, gays, and blacks within the United States were also fighting to gain political power.

Lance asks his mother if she wants to go upstairs to her room on the eighth floor. Right outside the door is Holly Woodlawn (it appears as though Holly has been waiting outside the door so that she can get on film!). Pat is very cordial with Holly and her friend, telling the Warhol "superstar" that it is very nice to meet her. Pat's room is far more pleasant and light filled than Lance's; it has a bay window. But clearly Pat is less than comfortable in her surroundings. She is used to more luxury when traveling, yet she is going to make a go of it. Nonetheless, she can't help but comment on Lance's life and environment—and she lets him know that it would have been nice if he had met her downstairs and helped her to her room. Lance responds that he would have felt awkward waiting around the front desk with a man he finds pretentious and annoying.

After Pat is settled into her room, she accompanies Lance and Soren to the La Mama Theatre to see the Jackie Curtis drag revue show *Vain Victory: The Vicissitudes of the Damned*. Before they leave, Pat asks them if there are any supermarkets around where she can get some food to cook for them, and the guys tell her she doesn't need to do that. The next scene is a long excerpt from the play itself (filmed on another night by another film crew). Jackie Curtis's show is an irreverent, plotless, nearly tuneless musical that features elaborate costuming and the anti-acting style that the performers around Warhol favored. In this acting style, the unstated dictum is to pretend you are actually somewhere else, saying someone else's lines. The police raided the dressing room on opening night looking for drugs, and the show became the rage of the summer season in 1971.

Vain Victory may have been a downtown hit, but not everyone stays through the entire show. In the next scene, we learn that Pat, Lance, and Soren have also left during the intermission; we see them discussing the show in a coffee shop booth near Sheridan Square. Pat was taken aback by the show—she tells Lance and Soren that she was sometimes bored and at other moments made to feel very uncomfortable by its shock tactics. After all, Pat is not destined to sing along with the lyrics "this is a story, so touching, it must be told with a whip, a folktale of vicious simplicity involving two pyromaniacs, freaked out over a couple of hairdressers, who chain them to brown hairdryers." Pat was also annoyed at its lack of a discernible story. Lance and Soren don't defend the show too vigorously, but they do try to explain its lack of narrative as a style in the theater. Soren suggests that it might make more sense to people who take drugs (which doesn't seem to reassure Pat). Lance adds that he thought Candy Darling delivered some great one-liners and categorizes the revue as a transvestite variety show.

The next scene shows Lance, Soren, and Pat at an Andy Warhol retrospective at the Whitney Museum of Art. The exhibit is in a large space and features Warhol's early oversized silkscreens of duplicated and repeated images—cows, Marilyns, Elvises, and soup cans, as well as self-portraits. The three of them cling together at the exhibit, and the camera follows them around the gallery. Pat appears to like this work: after all Warhol's artwork is more palatable—and has gained more mainstream success—than the underground theater and film he often produced or filmed. The three of them move gracefully through the gallery as a unit, enjoying the experience. The Raymonds film the scene as a pilgrimage to view the work of a real master, one who is emblematic of New York City. Alan Raymond moves the camera behind Pat and Lance so that the viewer gets to see not only the scale of the Warhol artworks but also the ways in which Pat and Lance gaze at the portraiture.

The museum is a side of New York with which Pat is comfortable: elegant, clean, white rooms adorned with works of art that have already been approved, promoted, and proved worthy in the marketplace. Pat is not at ease in the harder-edged atmosphere of Jackie Curtis, even though, of course, this revue was also part of Andy Warhol's world. Warhol encouraged creative acting out in those around him, seemingly enjoying aesthetic displays of self-destruction, even as he himself appeared quite restrained. Pat, however, is more at ease with the restrained side of Warhol and New York.

In a counterpoint to the scene from the excursion to the La Mama Theatre, the next day features a sequence in which Lance and Soren hang out in their Chelsea hotel room, laughing with an unnamed young man in overalls (possibly the new boy toy of Holly Woodlawn). When Soren laughs, the young man asks him if he takes dope—he says that Soren laughs like someone who takes drugs. He also asks Lance and Soren if they've seen *Vain Victory*. Soren and Lance admit they didn't last through the whole show, and the young man laughs, saying, "no one stays to the second act." Pat calls on the phone, and Lance says to her, "Hi Cutie"—treating his mother like a friend. He tells her that he is in the room with the film crew. When he gets off the phone, Lance tells Soren that Pat is having dinner with Craig Gilbert. Soren sounds disappointed that they are not going to see her that night, and Lance tells him that she has been drinking. Although Pat bristled at media suggestions that she had a drinking problem, we often see her with a cigarette in one hand and a drink in the other, her sunglasses protecting her eyes from the camera. Indeed, as Soren and Lance walk with her to the corner to catch a cab to the show, Soren asks her what her favorite drink is. She states immediately scotch and soda and that she likes Dewars and J&B. Lance is not a drinker, and though we never see him taking drugs, drug taking is in the air at the Chelsea Hotel. Later in his life, he became addicted to speed.

The next scene is the famous sequence in which Lance and Pat walk through Central Park. This is often designated as Lance's coming-out moment. It is also a feat of filmmaking as Lance and Pat walk quickly through the park, almost as if they are trying to escape the Raymonds and gain themselves a moment's peace away from the film crew. Alan Raymond expertly keeps up with them, although there are moments in which Susan Raymond struggles to completely record their interaction at a discernible sound level. The background noise level in the park is high—and tells its own story. There are African-sounding drums in the background and the chatter of many other conversations, especially when the mother and son sit down at a café near the Bethesda Terrace. Central Park is a site of enormous activity and behavior—in the foreground and background. A young man who has climbed atop the Angel of the Waters fountain transfixes Pat and Lance. The camera captures their shift of attention. When the young man is told to come down,

Lance states that the man has been ordered out of heaven and as he descends carefully from the multileveled sculpture, Pat adds that the climber deserves a round of applause. The environment entertains and distracts them, and they find it hard to return to focus on each other; the camera captures this awkwardness.

In her book Pat recounts their interaction in the park: "We wander through Central Park and endlessly fail to communicate, throwing out bits and beginnings at each other like bait, hoping the other will throw back a fish." She adds, "Oh, that camera. That eye of half-truth. It scared me at first. I didn't know what to do with it. So I made like everything was all right, and when Lance and I were away from it, we talked. Sure we skittered around the real issues" (97). In this episode the viewer witnesses Pat struggle to become used to the camera's presence and also watches her responses to her son's performances.

Pat recognizes that Lance has star quality and not only because he is photogenic. She describes his attraction: "It's because he throws off his own special gamma rays, his own combination of brains and compassion and the sensitivity of somebody who knows what it is to feel more than most people do" (98). Such words could also be used to describe her—and there is no question that she and Lance are the stars of the series. They are the two figures that the media focused on, all but ignoring the social impact of the show and its effect on the medium of television.

The Central Park scene opens with Pat and Lance walking arm in arm through the park. She asks Lance to move out of the Chelsea Hotel, a request that she will repeat later. Lance defends the hotel and says he wants to stay there forever. They begin to discuss his childhood and teenage years, and as Pat indicates (97), their conversation is awkward, and each is unable to respond to the other's remarks. Yet we see that they are close by their insistence on keeping a physical intimacy between them. Lance states when he was young he "stood apart from anyone" and that there was "always something in me that I couldn't understand." He tells her that he was unable to judge his life "by the standards I was given." This is the nearest he gets to saying he is gay—that he experienced himself as different and refused to subject himself to society's opinion. Pat adds, "You were pretty hard to understand yourself." Lance then begins to suggest to his mother that his family could have treated him with more understanding. Pat doesn't argue with him but admits to having been confused about how to respond to him, as there were times when he barely left his room. There is no resolution in their conversation, nor is there total honesty. Instead there is inference—Pat can only suggest that Lance was a challenge to her even though she respects him, and Lance refrains from showing any anger about how he was raised. He lets her know that he is very reticent to see his father; when Pat tells him that Bill Loud is coming to New York, Lance blurts out irreverently, "Oh, how awful." He tells her that he feels sad because he can't help but feel that he has let his father down. Pat consoles him and lets him know that he shouldn't feel that way. She tells him she is happy that he has "found a place for you to do your thing."

They leave the table arm in arm again. Pat tells Lance to get to bed early so he can get up early (she wants to take him shopping, presumably to get some less flamboyant clothes that are more suitable for a young man). As they are walking by the park's model boat pond, Pat asks Lance if Jacqueline Onassis lives nearby. He tells her sarcastically that she lives "under the water in a glass house." Pat tells Lance that his grandmother is fascinated by the former first lady and reads about her in the tabloids. The scene ends with Lance stating, "Ah yes, the great American pastime," and they use a discussion about a celebrity as way to avoid discussing the very pertinent dynamics between them, even as they remind each other of the camaraderie between them. Of course they are about to become celebrities themselves, and they will be remembered for this very scene, one that ends with a discussion of fame.

The following scene consists of Pat receiving a tarot reading. The scene is filmed in tight shots of close-ups of faces, hands, and cards, and a few over-the-shoulder shots from behind Pat, looking at the tarot reader. Lance is in the scene, but he is remarkably quiet, allowing for the interaction to center between the tarot reader (a young man who may be a friend of Lance's) and Pat. It is an accurate, if vague, reading. He tells her that there will be changes in her financial situation and that she has major decisions to face in a few months. Both foreshadow her divorce. The tarot reader states that "something is ending." Pat is caustic. She retorts, "The world." And so it is—her world, as it has been structured, will soon end. The scene finishes as the camera zooms in for an extreme close-up on the tense face of Pat.

The next sequence celebrates the mother and son bond; Pat and Lance jump on the Number 1 train to Christopher Street en route to a discotheque. We see them dancing together—no expressions of concern or worry here, just the two of them moving to Mitch Ryder and the Detroit Wheels' song "Devil with a Blue Dress On." Lance prances like the effete rock star he will later try to become—he is wearing a flower-patterned shirt tied at his waist and tight blue jeans with no back pockets (he wears these jeans in most scenes). They are filmed in a long shot in the low-ceilinged room, and Pat looks like Lance's friend and not his mother. She laughs and smiles at some of his dance floor antics.

The comfort between them in the disco is contrasted with the ill-at-ease feeling between them in the next scene. Pat and Lance are in her hotel room. Lance lies atop the table in the bay window. Pat is sitting and complains about the television reception. She is drinking and smoking. As Lance poses, she compliments him and says, "You look like a statue, like a ship's figurehead." Then she begins to express her worry for him, telling him that he can't "depend on Soren." Lance agrees with her but tells her that "he's wonderful for company." He states quite honestly about Soren's flightiness, "I've learned it, but I'm slowly applying it."

In a sharp retort, Pat tells Lance that he is "a little old" to be depending on others so completely, and she is also perhaps speaking about how Lance continues to rely on his parents financially. Like the scene in Central Park, the conversation between them is not free flowing. Pat stops short of lecturing her son, and Lance never tells her to stop worrying about him so much. Instead he tries to deflect her criticism. This scene is placed against the kind of amity we see when Lance, Soren, and Pat leave the Broadway musical *No No Nanette.* The three walk arm in arm (Pat separating the two young men) to the corner to catch a cab. We then see Pat sitting on the couch in his room, a nightcap in her hand, and she tells him that she has had an enjoyable evening. Lance then asks her what shocked her most about her visit. She states her first day at the Chelsea. Lance compliments her and lets her know that he was nervous when she first arrived. Pat states again that she wished he had met her on her arrival. Before their interaction gets too tense, Pat asks Lance if the cat in the room ever goes outside. Lance tells her no but that the cat "would be elected the happiest person in the United States." He then adds, "I'd love to be a cat."

The next scene maintains the pattern of scenes, alternating between ones that show affection and connection between Lance and Pat when they are sharing an activity and the awkwardness between them when they are alone and trying to have a serious conversation. In these scenes there are moments of silence and a consistent failure to reach a resolution. Pat's suitcase is packed, and they are waiting around for her to leave—she is going to catch a train to Baltimore to conduct some business for her husband's company. Pat acknowledges how uneasy she feels and says that the waiting around is deadly. She reminds Lance of her demands: she wants him to write more often (she promises to do the same), and she wants him to move, if not out of the Chelsea at least out of the room. She also wants him to stop hanging out by the windows, as he had done in a previous scene. She comments on his red eyes and says he needs Murine eyedrops. Lance remarks that he wishes he had shaved and bathed first, and he appears laconic—as though he got "wasted" the night before.

He asks her for money but tells her not to give it to him right then but downstairs. Pat says she will give him some cash but she wants him to "use it for something less frivolous"—less frivolous one presumes than the extravagant clothing he favors. Pat tells him that he should continue to give New York a chance, even though he doesn't have a job (he thinks he might get one later that week through one of Soren's connections). She tells him to "have a good look at it, while you are here," and he reassures her that he won't give up without a fight. Still, he doesn't show much passion today. She reassures him and says that she will send him money to come home if he wants.

Lance carries her suitcase to the elevator. Downstairs Pat pays her bill and discretely gives Lance some money to hold him over. Outside the hotel, Lance hails her a cab, puts her red suitcase in the front seat, and hugs her good-bye. He tells her "thanks for coming," and she replies that "it was nice" and "good to see you." He closes the cab door behind her.

The camera then follows Lance as he bounds up the stairs in the Chelsea to his fourth-floor room—and again it is as if Lance is trying to escape the production crew, although they keep up with him. Yet Lance leaves his room door open for the Raymonds, and perhaps with his mother's voice in his head, he begins to clean up his room, hanging clothes that were strewn about on hangers and putting them in the closet. He turns on the television, switches channels, stopping at a station that is showing a war movie. We hear the voice-over from a film: "The Victory March through Paris. The Buck Privates have fought their war and won. Their reward: they are going home." The words are in decided contrast to Lance's situation; he has left home and won't be going back. The screen freezes on a close-up of Lance's face in profile.

The last scene gives a sense of Lance's silence and loneliness in New York, especially now that his mother is gone. Pat may nag at him, but she also animates him—he likes to perform for her. Although she is threatened by his camp behavior in front of the camera, she is also drawn to the way he can choreograph his outlandish nature and his inner freedom. Lance's sense of self is not one that he inherited from his parents. Indeed, he states in an unpublished 1973 autobiographical essay that he "divorced" his parents long before they divorced each other. Yet his mother is also a crucial person in his life, and he shows his enjoyment in presenting her with his version of New York in 1971. In turn, Pat knows that the city is a place where he can be accepted, but she can't help but worry about his future. She writes in her memoir:

> Frankly, I'm proud of Lance, of his candor, his daring spirit and his frontal assault on life. But by agreeing to do the series, we had locked ourselves into what now seems like two contradictory obligations—to be honest and to be a family at all costs. And for some reason (for some lousy reason, which is poisoning all of us) there's a hell of a contradiction there. It's as though to stick together and be a family and look like one, you have to kid yourself, to practice some form of self-deception. (100)

For Pat, being part of a happy family is now an acting job, a role that she can't sustain on camera. Despite all of Lance's searching, he is able to show his mother a way to be both inside and outside the family structure. Yes, he makes her anxious, but she can't help but respect him for the way he has resolved a contradiction that she hasn't yet been able to resolve. He has begun to gain an identity independent of his family—part of this identity is that he experiences a freedom in preening and prancing in front of the camera. In other words, he plays with his personae and does not rely on the filmmakers to find out the "truth" about him.

NONFICTION PERFORMANCE

In the essay "The Observed Looks Back: Performance in American Vérité" (2005), Vinicius do Valle Navarro uses the term *nonfiction performance* to describe what he considers to be a key aspect of American documentary films in the 1960s.

> Despite the effort to contain the documentary subjects' engagement in the filmmaking process, observational film allowed for—and sometimes depended on—the interaction between the cinematic apparatus and the people in front of the camera. (41)

For Navarro, this is a paradox, as filmmakers such as Robert Leacock, the Maysles brothers, and Frederick Wiseman set out to record people behaving within distinct environments that are not transformed by film crews and to see what happens when actual people interact without scripts. For Leacock his impulse is antitheatrical—as Navarro states, Leacock believed "cinema . . . should avoid the artificial quality of the theater—its pre-arranged scripts, which subordinated the actors to the director's commands" (38). In this view, film should observe reality and not distort it through artifice and storytelling devices. Yet, as Navarro rightly argues, despite their intentions "observational documentarists actually created the conditions for a performance-based cinema" (42).

This performance-based cinema is in clear evidence in *An American Family* and most obviously in full display with Lance's theatricality. Craig Gilbert and the Raymonds may have intended to show a real family and not the Brady or Partridge family, but the style of filmmaking that they deployed actually encourages the unabashed display of performance and its role in everyday life.

In 1959 (around the same time Leacock et al. began their experiments), sociologist Erving Goffman published *The Presentation of Self in Everyday Life*. This book used theatrical metaphors and terminology to analyze how people behave in particular situations and environments. For Goffman, every person constructs a "front," which is the technique that a person either consciously or unconsciously utilizes when making social appearances. A person becomes almost a sum of his or her performances, making distinctions on how to appear depending on the environment. For example, social actors decide that this is the me I show when I am at work, this is the me I show when I am with my friends joking around, this is the me I show myself when I am home alone, or this is the me I show the audience when I know I am being filmed. As Pat Loud admits, as soon as the camera crew arrived, she became conscious of her own acting—the camera allowed her the ability to see the degree to which she had also been acting all along.

In Goffman's way of looking at self-presentation, people operate under the advice and consent—or rejection—of social scripts, or what Goffman refers to as idioms. Goffman writes that

> when we observe a young American middle-class girl playing dumb for the benefit of her boyfriend, we are ready to point to items of guile and contrivance in her behavior. But like herself and her boy friend, we accept as an unperformed fact that this performer is a young American middle-class girl. But surely here we neglect the greater part of the performance. It is commonplace to say that different social groupings ex-

press in different ways such attributes as age, sex, territory, and class status, and that in each case these bare attributes are elaborated by means of a distinctive complex cultural configuration of proper ways of conducting oneself. To be a given kind of person, then, is not merely to possess the required attributes, but also to sustain the standards of conduct and appearance that one's social grouping attaches thereto. The unthinking ease with which performers consistently carry off such standard-maintaining routines does not deny that a performance has occurred, merely that the participants have been aware of it. (81)

We may all be improvising our lives, but our appearances are guided by expectations, learned behavior, and the restrictions that have been pre-ordained by the mandates of specific environments and time-bound events. We make decisions on what is appropriate to both reveal and conceal depending on the degree to which we are in public or in private—what we want our boss to know versus what we want our friends to know. The Raymonds, as filmmakers, consciously worked on their relationships with the Louds in order to be able to film the family in some backstage moments when they weren't so obviously putting on a show. Ironically, if one accepts Goffman's assertions, this is an impossible task. Observational cinema, despite its intentions, clears a space that is then occupied by the everyday performance of nonactors. *An American Family* reveals the show that a family puts on for itself, for its neighbors and friends, and ultimately for an invisible audience. Certainly Lance is given the freedom to perform like crazy in front of the camera. Paradoxically, this is the best way for him to be himself.

Lance also acknowledges his mother's successes in front of the camera crew (before she recognizes them herself). When Lance tells his mother that she fared very well in covering her shock at the Chelsea Hotel's residents and appeared natural (whereas he feels that he showed too much nervousness before she arrived), he is also telling her that she was able to give a good performance in front of the camera. Part of her performance is to try to show as much respect as possible for Lance and his milieu—that she is a hip mom from California who knows about the world of Andy Warhol—at the same time letting her son know in private that she is worried for his future. What we learn from her more private performances with Lance, away from Soren Ingenue and Holly Woodlawn, is that she is scandalized at his lifestyle and his cohorts. In part, she is still committed to showing the audience that she is a loving mother in a cohesive family who loves and accepts all of her children and is devoted to her husband. Yet, having the Raymonds around with camera and sound equipment serves to expose her facade to herself. This is why she refers to the camera as an "eye of half truth": it doesn't reveal the truth of a person; rather it frames the everyday theatricality of identity that is neither true nor false.

The theatricality and adaptability of the episode are recast in Cecilia Dougherty's *Gone* (2001), which uses dialogue from the show and resets the tale in a more contemporary New York. Importantly, Dougherty changes the gender of the couple in the episode, so that Lance (played by Laurie Weeks) and Soren (played by Frances Sorensen) become a lesbian couple visited by Lance's mother—what remains essentially the same is how the mother reacts to her child's queer artistic surroundings. *Gone* shows how the nonfictional transcript for the show works perfectly as a fictional script. In homage to the setting of the original and Warhol's split-screen film *Chelsea Girls* (1966), Dougherty's film is a two-channel video, which allows her to depict more of the milieu of the characters (and display disparate selves and surroundings). *Gone* also shows that a nonfiction event can be transformed and updated; the documentary veneer of the episode is peeled away to reveal that the second episode of the series is fundamentally a story between parent and child. As a story with quintessential characters and distinctive settings it is open to formal updates and radical reenvisioning—showing the impact of performers making use of a social script they have both inherited and memorized.

Relatedly, the classic performance-based documentary *Grey Gardens* (1975), directed by Albert and David Maysles, has also had a rather illustrious afterlife. Once a cult film renowned for the squalor and outrageous behavior of two forgotten female members of the American aristocracy, *Grey Gardens* has recently become a Broadway musical (2007) and an HBO fictional film (2009). Like episode 2 of *An American Family*, *Grey Gardens* is focused on the relationship between parent and child (Little Edie and Big Edie), and the transcript and the real-life drama in their performances easily translate into a fictional version. Both examples show the importance of acting in a documentary: self-aware performance in a nonfictional narrative is a sourcebook for fiction—after all, the extravagance of the performance of self has been there from the get-go, just waiting for a camera to come in for a close-up (or to compose a two-shot). Both of the Edies, as well as Lance and Pat, have used performance as a way to sustain very strained relationships and survive difficult circumstances. Susan and Alan Raymond are sensitive to the necessity of Lance's and Pat's performances (as were the Maysles brothers to the two Edies). The critics of *An American Family* saw Lance and Pat as indulgent rather than as deploying a strategy when the camera was present. That is, the critics did not believe that they knowingly used a strategy that protects them from breaking down in front of all of America and completely revealing (and inventing) all sorts of family secrets.

FOLLOW-UP

The Raymonds filmed two follow-up documentaries to *An American Family*. The first was *American Family Revisited*, which was done to mark the tenth anniversary of the program and shown on HBO. The second follow-up was filmed around the thirtieth anniversary of the program and entitled *LANCE LOUD! A Death in an American Family*. Each gives a new perspective on the family and the show and the lingering impact that the show has had on each of the members. The second documentary chronicles Lance's death and the effect it had on the family, and by extension the effects on the filmmakers themselves, who have befriended Lance. Lance had requested that the Raymonds film his final days.

The style used for the two documentaries is very different from the style used for *An American Family*; it includes the interactions between filmmakers and the family and abandons any attempt at pure observational cinema. The voice of Susan Raymond begins the film, and she acknowledges in her voice-over that the film is also about her relationship with Lance Loud. We also hear the voice of Alan Raymond asking questions to Lance and Susan asking questions to Pat. In *LANCE LOUD!* the Raymonds also paste in sequences from the series and edit in footage from previous filming that features Lance (they include the scene in Central Park between mother and son, a scene in the 1983 documentary in which Bill Loud states that he will never accept Lance's homosexuality, and a scene in which Lance sings and dances while he is riding his bicycle through Santa Barbara).

The Raymonds became part of the extended family of the Louds. They clearly have a fondness for Lance (they also wrote the obituary for Lance in the *Advocate*). Their fondness was probably always there, right from the start, from the moment they barged into his room at the Chelsea Hotel and saw him there with his boyfriend Soren (they had already been told by Gilbert that Lance was "flamboyant"). Lance recalls how Alan took him aside at one point during the filming of the series to warn him about how he was coming across. He had a sense that he might be subjected to harsh judgment from his future audience. But as Lance said, he thought he was acting "terribly avant-garde" to wear makeup and blue lipstick (he saves his most outlandish outfit for when he comes home to visit his family in Santa Barbara). He had no idea that viewers might deem him a drag queen or a narcissistic homosexual. He had no idea of this because between the milieu of the Chelsea Hotel and the relative acceptance of his family (except his father), he probably thought America would love him as well—after all, despite deliberate affectations, he worked at making himself lovable. And one of his endearing qualities was his ability to perform for the camera and to transmit his charisma, his "gamma rays."

Lance is brave in his attempt to portray himself in the Raymonds' final film about him, never hiding the excesses of his past. He admits that he likes to live in "reel time," which he says is the world the Raymonds provide for him through the recording capabilities of their film equipment. In other words, he imagines himself in front of the camera even when the cameras are not there. His life is one of display and self-presentation, and in a sense the cameras never leave him. At the end of his life, he is missing teeth and in obvious pain. He shuffles slowly, and years of drug addiction and hepatitis C have ravaged his now thin frame. Yet he keeps a modicum of autonomy in his nonfiction performance. We see him tend to his cats and gardens with dedication (he has to leave his tiny house behind when he moves into a hospice facility). We hear him tell his "cautionary tale" about drugs and the regret he feels now that he has come to appreciate life like he never has before—especially as he knows he doesn't have long to live. Another indication of Lance's forcefulness is that he has called the Raymonds to his bedside to record his last days, and they dutifully fulfill his last wishes. Indeed, the Raymonds continue to film after his death, interviewing Pat, Bill, some of Lance's friends and recording parts of Lance's memorial service, which includes a rendition of "Somewhere Over the Rainbow" sung by Rufus Wainwright. The Raymonds enable Lance's final words to reach the world—his words are of remorse but also of love. He talks of feeling connected to his family like never before. And though it is not stated, it is apparent that Lance feels connected to the Raymonds as well, as they have in a sense also been his family.

Perhaps the most moving scenes in *LANCE LOUD!* record the interactions between the Raymonds and Pat Loud and between Pat and Lance. When Lance is in hospice and his mother is visiting him, he asks her to climb into bed so that she can give him a cuddle. Pat is now a much larger woman, and Lance is nearly emaciated, but she gently wraps herself around him and cuddles him as they discuss family memories. Yes, they are both performing the mother and son bond in front of "the eye of half truth." Yet, enabled by the respectful distance given to them by the camera, we see that this is a scene of authentic intimacy, showing not only the comfort between them but also the ease they each feel with the Raymonds' presence, recording their interaction.

We read at the end of the film in a title that after Lance's death Pat and Bill Loud reconciled—ending thirty years of separation. We also read that this was one of Lance's requests. In a two-shot Pat and Bill Loud sit near each other during the service, with Pat in the row in front of Bill. It is an ironic moment: Lance's independence inspired Pat to leave her husband over thirty years ago, yet Lance had also become very close to his father before his death, and Bill's tears over losing his son— and not appreciating him enough when he was young—are very touching. Yet Lance very much wanted his family reunited, even if it was a family he, too, had once divorced in an attempt to ally himself with the idea of Andy Warhol's New York. In sum, in his last film we see that Lance has gone home again. This home is now queer friendly.

CHAPTER 7

Displaying Real Male Bodies for New Audiences

FABRICATED DESIRE

In the early 1970s new forums for the expression of sexual desire emerged that eroticized male bodies for a changing and increasingly visible audience. In each chapter, I have argued that the early 1970s featured new possibilities for gender through depictions of "reality" in popular media and at the same time nonfiction media provided new models for representations of women and gay men that fictional media did not. Here I present two examples as a coda to this contention. These two examples focus on the production of sexual desire and self-expression through the poses of staged bodies. Like the dynamic personalities who gained voice in the early '70s, both work to unsettle established regimes of sexuality, gender, and representation and to enlarge what is permissible in the mainstream.

One of the examples I conclude with is the gay pornographic icon Peter Berlin, whose real name, Baron Armin Hagen von Hoyningen-Huene, signifies that he is of aristocratic heritage. In 1973 Peter Berlin became a star through the release of the underground classic *Nights in Black Leather* (the title is perhaps alluding to the Moody Blues' "Nights in White Satin"), originally made as a final thesis project by a friend, Richard Abel, who was studying film at San Francisco State College. Berlin asserts that although he did not receive director credit, he was also the author of this film, as it chronicled his San Francisco life and he contributed to the film's artistic direction. Through Berlin's distinctive presence—and the alluring poster—the film became a pornographic vérité classic that depicted Berlin's erotic posing and his adventures in San Francisco. The film was a vehicle that celebrated his exhibitionism and his all-encompassing desire (or perhaps his need) to become an object of desire. He craved being looked at, either by a camera or a man, and ideally both. His films are a database of a yearning to be pined for sexually.

Unlike "Bruno," Sacha Baron Cohen's fictional character who is also gay and Teutonic, Berlin didn't come to California seeking his fame and fortune by being accepted by the mainstream. Berlin was content to become a sex symbol beloved—and be lusted after—by an emerging gay subculture. Berlin also asserted the artistic nature of his work and accepted that the homoerotic character of the images he produced (of himself) prevented him from becoming a superstar. Berlin wanted to be wanted, not by housewives across America but by gay men in New York, Los Angeles, Chicago, and San Francisco or the men who contemplated moving into the subcultures of these cities. He valued this audience's lust for him. It energized him and his propensity for the erotic pose.

Berlin also made a number of short, silent pornographic films that featured him and his lovers. Most famously, he followed up *Nights in Black Leather* with *That Boy*, a feature-length classic that he directed in 1974. With his film appearances and countless photographic self-portraits, as well as his appearances on the streets of San Francisco, clad in either black leather or tight white jeans, cruising (and ignoring) potential suitors, he succeeded in making himself—and his attire—a legend. Through his persona and stage name and the painstaking way in which he styled himself, Peter Berlin reveled in an unabashed and excessive, self-conscious narcissism that both invited and rejected admirers and suitors and placed himself astride the border between campy self-parody and ritualized erotic behavior. As much as he enjoyed being a person in motion, he seemed to prefer being a statue in provocative stasis— his pleasure was found in being desired and immobile as if in photographic suspension. He enjoyed restraint as much as release, and his wardrobe was always more revealing than his nudity. His filmmaking becomes a glorious exercise in reproducing this tension between motion and repose, release and restraint, self-love and yearning for another. Although he never made another feature-length film, his two films continue to influence gay pornography. Indeed, he continues to have an impact on the ways in which gay men accent their physique through clothing—for Berlin the contours of the thighs, the crotch, the abdomen, the buttocks, and the chest are articulated through the language of clothing. Fabric is akin to skin for Berlin: when it is stretched across the engorged, muscular body, the textile itself has erogenous zones and nerve endings.

MEN IN THE CENTERFOLD

The other example I look to in this chapter is *Playgirl* magazine, an erotic publication, featuring the display of men's bodies, oriented ostensibly toward women. *Playgirl* was first published in January of 1973 and reappeared later, in May 1973, under new management and editorship. By 1976 it had a respectable readership of 1.5 million. With articles geared toward women who considered themselves newly sexually liberated, and advertisements that ranged from cigarettes to makeup to clothing (especially underwear in the back of the book), the magazine became known for the full frontal nudity of its male models, although until the November 1973 issue penises were cloaked (by poses, hands, shadows, or some surprising props). The magazine continues today as an online publication with a subscriber base. Most recently it was in the news for its photos of Levi Johnston.

Playgirl also depicted romantic, precoital poses between heterosexual couples, usually with the male showing off his torso while the female remained fully clothed. The physique of the man was placed in the foreground, and the presence of the women in these photos served as a point of identification for the viewer. Fiction included light erotica (as well as short stories by renowned writers like Tennessee Williams). Experts wrote columns on topics that included cosmetics, making drinks, astrology, and, of course, relationships and sex. In the first few issues some of the advice columns, as well as the fiction, were printed on pink paper, differentiating them from the rest of the magazine and also perhaps making a link with a presumably "pink collar" readership. Later issues also experimented with font color, using a ruby red typeface against white paper. The designers for the magazine were clearly thinking of new ways to capture the reader through color and font, challenging the dominance of black type against white paper.

With its title, the magazine was obviously pitched to be the counterpart of *Playboy* magazine. *Playboy*, from its beginning, endorsed the proliferation of the postwar urban bachelor who was a connoisseur of wine, women, and fine living and defied the demands for conformity of suburban heterosexual masculinity. According to Barbara Ehrenreich in *The Hearts of Men*, *Playboy* advocated rebellion through lifestyle against the constraints of middle-class expectations for men of the 1950s to be respectable (and boring) family men (1987). Likewise *Playgirl* magazine endorsed a reader who could assert her independence and put her own needs and desires first, but it was not a mere imitation of the men's magazine—in tone, design, emphasis, and ideology—though many assumed it was a copy because of its title.

Indeed, one could argue that *Cosmopolitan* magazine, reinvented by Helen Gurley Brown in 1965, was already the female *Playboy*. Laurie Ouellette argues that *Cosmo* "articulated a girl-style American Dream that promised transcendence from class roles as well as sexual ones" (360). Although *Cosmo* was not a female mirror of *Playboy,* its impact on popular culture was similar—both magazines celebrated the lifestyle of single men and women. And both magazines supported the careers of their editors: Helen Gurley Brown and Hugh Hefner became spokespersons for outlooks that were strikingly similar; they shared beliefs about the privileged place for pleasure in the lives of middle-class aficionados, single men and women who believed they had good taste and were good in bed (and who deserved to be with equally good lovers).

Brown and Hefner were celebrities who made sure that the way they lived—at least publicly—matched their magazines' recommendations; their visibility was a crucial part of the "branding" of the product. Neither represented a small-town vision of America with traditional values advocated by *Ladies Home Journal* or the *Saturday Evening Post*. Instead *Playboy* and *Cosmopolitan* espoused an urbane existence in which the best things in life were enjoyed—to know about fine wines was not considered effete for a *Playboy* reader, and to watch sports was not unseemly for a reader of *Cosmopolitan,* as long as she kept her heels on. According to Ouellete, the evocation of upward mobility was a key part of the *Cosmo* girl's profile. The *Cosmo* reader may have started out as a secretary, but she became an executive assistant with a disposable income, and, armed with her magazine of choice, she learned to take responsibility for her own orgasm. She was upwardly mobile not only in terms of income and taste but also in terms of her sexual technique.

When *Cosmopolitan* was rebranded under Brown's direction, the use of the birth control pill was becoming prevalent. The pill had been introduced to the public in 1961, although certain states had bans on its use. In June 1965, the Supreme Court in the *Griswold v. Connecticut* decision struck down the state's laws banning birth control. Thus the stage was being prepared for heterosexual women to enjoy sex without fear of pregnancy and free from legal rebuke. Many have argued about the social importance of *Cosmopolitan* magazine and the change in the realignment of the genders that the magazine both encouraged and reflected.

Yet the arrival of the magazine coincided with changes in the legal status of birth control and the relaxing of the ways in which the state was empowered to control women's bodies. The use of birth control was no longer part of the state's purview, even if it remained part of the church's for those who adhere to its doctrine. Heterosexual women could now separate sexual pleasure (via heterosexual intercourse) from reproduction. *Cosmo* celebrated this change and was, in part, product placement for the pill.

In January of 1973 the Supreme Court handed down the historic *Roe v. Wade* decision, furthering women's control over their own bodies and restricting state power. Thus *Playgirl* emerged at a time when a major legal decision had empowered women. Such decisions, which were responsive to the rise of feminism, also fueled changes in media culture. Indeed, both *Cosmopolitan* and *Playgirl* followed directly on landmark Supreme Court cases that redefined the structural place of women in the culture, creating a social climate in which new demographics of women could be defined by elements within the mass media. Clearly the magazine industry was especially quick to appeal to this "new woman," and it was adept at defining the contours of these new niches by supplying the details of the lifestyle and outlook of the readership, encouraging it to indulge in the pleasures of looking—as well as purchasing.

Cosmopolitan, with its historic spread of actor Burt Reynolds in the April 1972 issue, paved the way for the male centerfold that became a feature of *Playgirl*. In this photograph, the hirsute actor is lying on his side facing the camera, his hand between his legs. Reynold's pose clearly differentiated the male centerfold from the female one. When female models are lying down in a shot, they are usually on their backs, looking up at the camera, in a pose that suggests a willingness to be submissive, of waiting for the male onlooker: the camera duplicates the missionary position. Arranged differently, the male centerfold is on an eye-level match with the camera and, when lying down, the man is on his side, with his face twisted toward the camera. His pose does not connote submissiveness. Rather it invites the viewer to a mutual caress, suggesting that the male is both available and active; he is ready to roll on top rather than lie back. The 1972 photograph of Burt Reynolds became a paradigm for shooting nude men as centerfolds, ensuring that the male and female centerfolds differ greatly in terms of how the male and female nudes are situated and framed. The female pose is indexical of passivity; the male pose indicates the ability to spring into action.

DEFINING THE PLAYGIRL

Part of *Playgirl*'s task, especially in its first issues, was to define the contours of the playgirl—what she does for leisure and work, her outlook, and especially her inclinations for pleasure. The magazine had to provide modes of looking at men's bodies as aesthetic objects to be desired and enjoyed as images. This scophophilia, this pleasure in looking, was thought to be the domain of men. *Playgirl* urged women to subscribe to a magazine that featured the bodies of men and centered on issues and expressions of a newly validated female heterosexuality, to indulge in a female gaze. Of course, a significant part of *Playgirl*'s readership has always been assumed to be gay men, suggesting a linkage between the erotic lives of gay men and straight women. After all, both share a camaraderie in discussing the finer points—and the flaws—of men.

The cover of the June 1973 issue sets the tone for the magazine and begins to define it and its reader. The title *Playgirl* appears at the top of the cover in an italicized, thick font in red, all lowercase except the initial *P*, which is especially elaborate. Under the title, the tagline in white small caps appears, nonitalicized: "The Magazine for Women." The background color of the magazine is a somber brown that allows the tanned model and the red and white type to really jump into the foreground. The cover image, set slightly to the left, consists of a man and a woman, though much of the woman is hidden behind the torso of the man. The man is presumably nude (save a necklace); he clasps his hand around the shin of his right leg effectively hiding—and drawing attention to—his crotch. He is a dark-featured Caucasian, strong jawed, and with a full head of black hair, although his body is relatively hairless. He is well built and looks to be in his late twenties. A blonde woman is partially draped over him. Her hands appear on either side of his décolletage, holding him gingerly; her face is perched along the right side of his neck and face; her eyes are closed or gazing on him. While the woman's presence is oriented toward him, he stares at the camera. Although much of his face is in shadow, he has the slightest hint of a come-hither smile—he looks as if he is about to enjoy the deliberation and assuredness of her seduction.

This cover differs from a *Playboy* cover—and not in the placement of the genders because the men's magazine would never include a man on its cover. In its first year *Playgirl* always featured a cover image with a couple in an amorous precoital pose—except the December issue, which features a joking couple surrounded by Christmas ribbon. *Playboy* only

The June 1973 cover of *Playgirl* magazine. (Image courtesy of Playgirl.com.)

featured women on its covers; to include a man involved in a seduction would have been sacrilegious to the brand. The man on the *Playgirl* cover is in the foreground; the female is placed as a visual permission slip for the viewer to gaze on the male. And this is what the female in the photo is doing; she is looking at the man with longing. The mise-en-scène of the photo invites the female spectator to identify with the woman in the image who is busy drinking in the beauty of the male in the image, and she clearly wants more. The viewer is encouraged to identify with the desire of the female in the photo; the male model's gaze out at the viewer serves as further provocation to indulge in the magazine—hinting that there is more inside the issue, including a nude centerfold.

The male reader of *Playboy* does not need any such permission to indulge in fantasy. He has already been trained to include women on the cover and in the centerfold as part of his reverie—the model moves into positions that already exist to please the male viewer, and the camera imitates the assumed dominant position of the male. For the *Playboy* reader by the early 1970s there were traditions to uphold. No such traditions existed for the male nudes and covers of *Playgirl*; there was no erotic infrastructure. Thus one had to be built. Mere imitation of *Playboy* would not work for a readership that had not been trained to derive pleasure in viewing men as purely immobile objects.

The cover lines (the text on a magazine cover) to the right of the image continue this provocation for the reader. Bordered in red, the cover lines read from the top: "Nude Centerfold, TV's Ryan Macdonald" then "Sexual Motivations, Compulsions of the Promiscuous Woman," "Hong Kong, A Playgirl's Paradise," and finally "Four Page Foldout, Our Man for June: Nude Lyle Waggoner." The emphasis of the magazine is clear: the word *nude* appears twice connected with men. The two other articles emphasize either sex (female promiscuity) or exoticism (Hong Kong as a paradise for playgirls). There is no mention of the many other articles that focus on decorating, entertaining, or testing whether or not you are a potential playgirl—these do not sell the issue like sex and men do.

The centerfold, Ryan Macdonald, appears alongside a pool. Sari Thomas, in her 1986 study "Gender and Social-Class Coding in Popular Photographic Erotica," notes that placing men outdoors was common for *Playgirl*, suggesting that this is more "reminiscent of the nudist magazines (popular in the 1940s and 50s) than of any of the heterosexual male publications" (109). (Shooting sex scenes outdoors also became a trope in gay male pornography, suggesting that such acts are not "unnatural" at all but an organic part of the masculinist landscape.) For the photographers and editors, it was important to stress male nudity as natural, hence the outdoor setting, and rather than using *Playboy*'s style as a template they used nudist and physique magazines of the pre-*Playboy* era as inspiration. The photos also seem untouched, not reliant on lighting other than natural light, and do not appear slick, although as the magazine progresses into the 1980s and 1990s the photos begin to appear more retouched. As Thomas notes, *Playgirl* men do not appear with "sexually-related props or sensual paraphernalia" (109) unless one considers a suede tool belt a sex prop (the December 1973 centerfold appears wearing only this male "G-string").

Not as muscled as the unnamed man on the cover, Macdonald, a soap opera actor, is perched on his right elbow as he smiles directly toward the camera, almost squinting in the brightness of the day. His left knee is raised, allowing his thigh to hide his penis but allowing the viewer to see his pubic hair. His chest is hairy and reveals some graying, indicating that this is not a man in his twenties but a man in his late thirties or early forties. The laugh lines around his eyes also show his age and indicate that there was no airbrushing of the photo. He lies in front of the pool (atop a rose-colored towel), which suggests relative affluence, but the overall look also connotes naturalness, as a Southern California topography appears in the background behind the pool.

The June issue also includes a special pullout photo section of the actor Lyle Waggoner (he appeared on the *Carol Burnett Show* from 1967 to 1978). The article about him describes him instantly in sexual terms: "He's the stuff of which sexual fantasies are made, a 6'4" hunk of gorgeous beefcake. Eyes: hazel. Hair: dark brown. Matinee idol's smile and boyish dimples." He appears outdoors in all the photos, twice with his wife, except in the large photo that is a pullout poster of him in the nude. He is reclining on a wooden chair, a cushion under his buttocks and his right leg crossed over his left in order to hide his crotch. His left elbow is on a desk, and his head appears against a dark-brown wooded wall. He is in what appears to be a den or a study, smiling at the camera. There is no attempt made to hide his graying temples, but his full head of blow-dried hair shows that care and time went into preparing his coiffure. He is a broad-shouldered man, but he is not cut and muscled from the gym; he is trim, but he doesn't have a six-pack from endless sit-ups and crunches.

Typical of male models of the era in being lithe and appearing limber, Waggoner would be atypical of models in the magazine of the 1980s and

1990s. Leit, Pope, and Gray studied the "Cultural Expectations of Muscularity in Men: The Evolution of Playgirl Centerfolds" (2000) and found that the centerfolds became increasingly brawny and "dense" with muscles during the 1980s and 1990s. The researchers assert that some of the physiques of the models in the 1990s indicate steroid usage. They hypothesize that the gradual change in the build of the centerfolds is related to "the growing evidence that the cultural norm for the ideal male body has become increasingly muscular over the years, especially during the 1990s" (92), citing also the change in the shape of male dolls like GI Joe during the same time period. They also posit that the magazine's secondary readership, gay men, may have had an impact on the increasing density of muscle coupled with decreasing body fat evident in the models, writing that "it seems likely that a certain number of homosexual men purchase *Playgirl,* and that these readers may have influenced the evolution of the centerfolds' dimensions" (92). Of course, it is impossible to measure how gay readership changed the centerfold, but a similar development occurred in gay male magazines, such as *Blueboy,* where the men have become increasingly more muscular since it began publishing in 1975. Arguably the musculature of the gay man becomes a kind of armor that symbolically defends one against AIDS and homophobia. Regardless, during the 1980s and 1990s the ideal male form became one in which the torso, especially, takes on more weight, thus reflecting the growing importance of gym culture with men becoming more bulky with less fat. Male fitness models lost their suppleness and everydayness as they became *über*men. Perhaps in the Obama era a leaner man with flexibility who does a perfect "downward-facing dog" rather than bench presses may become the ideal.

In *Playgirl's* first year of publication, two models used animals to hide their crotches in their nude shots. In the October 1973 issue African American action star Fred Williamson (one of the few men of color included) sits on the floor, his right leg bent and his left leg extended toward the camera. He holds a white kitten in front of him between his legs, providing a contrast in color and shape and bringing attention to that which the viewer does not get to see. Likewise in the 1974 centerfold, Euro-American John Ericson cradles a lion cub in his arms (the head of his penis is visible just beneath the animal). The use of these felines as props has many connotations: it signifies that the men—and their nudity—are natural; it suggests that, yes, these men may be animals (and have animalistic urges), but they are also kittens who will purr if the reader touches them in the right places—and can be domesticated by the right woman, as if to say that you can bring them indoors and they won't make a mess; and of course, these animals serve as fig leaves, bringing attention to that which is shrouded to the viewer. Although Fred Williamson is photographed indoors, Ericson appears outdoors in what appears to be a savanna in which a lion could be found—it is actually an animal park in California (another shot, one that features his buttocks and back, shows him near a leopard, and another shows him rather endearingly reaching his hands out to touch a giraffe's face).

George Maharis, July 1973's centerfold, is shot standing next to a bridled horse, again suggesting an equivalence between man and animal/nature (there is even an eye-line match between the horse and the model). At the same time the bridle, which Maharis holds, shows that the savage beast can be controlled by the "rider." These men may appear unbridled in their natural habitat, but in fact they can be restrained. Each of these centerfolds tries to reinforce that the nakedness of the man is natural and innocent, and thus there is nothing wrong with looking at these fine specimens of gentle, assured, and cultivated masculinity. These men may be most comfortable outdoors, but they are not beasts.

In a 1976 essay entitled "Male and Female Interest in Sexually-Oriented Magazines," researchers John Stauffer and Richard Frost studied a group of two hundred college-attending men and women in the Boston area about their responses to *Playgirl* and *Playboy*. I am not sure that the study has external validity (i.e., that one can generalize from its results to a large population) because the sample is generally younger than the usual reader and is from a distinctive location once known for its Puritan heritage. Nevertheless the results depict gender asymmetry when it comes to commercial erotica and displays of nude bodies. The survey may not reflect the opinion of all women of the era, but it does express the response of the sample group to erotica that is geared toward them.

Forty-six percent of the women gave high ratings to the centerfolds in *Playgirl*, whereas 88 percent of men gave high ratings to the centerfolds in *Playboy*. Of course, female dissatisfaction with the centerfold may have had to do with the quality of the photography but, coupled with another of the researchers' findings, we learn that men and women differ greatly in their acquaintance with centerfolds: 64 percent of men already owned a "sexually-oriented magazine" whereas only 28 percent of the women owned one (27). Thus young men are clearly more familiar with viewing nude women, whereas women do not have any precedent for viewing naked men. For most of the young women, the encounter with the centerfold was a new one. Perhaps this encounter was troubling for women: 80 percent said they would not buy a copy of *Playgirl* in the future, whereas 84 percent of the men said they would buy an issue of *Playboy* (28).

The researchers note that this statistic may be in large part due to fears of social disapproval—only 34 percent of the women believed that people in general would approve of their reading *Playgirl* (and again this may have much to do with their age and milieu). Even though a 1968 ruling by the Supreme Court declared that people were entitled to read and view whatever they wished in the privacy of their homes, women perhaps did not feel that this right extended to pornography—at least not in a dorm room, which offers only partial privacy. Social conditioning has much to do with the female response to erotica—they have not been given permission to indulge in this pleasure in the way to which men feel entitled. As much as gender roles had changed by the mid-1970s, at least according to this sample, most women did not feel that purchasing *Playgirl* was appropriate; presumably they would have felt embarrassed if their roommate or parent found a copy under the mattress.

When Stauffer and Frost asked the respondents to rate how sexually stimulating they found the nudity, predictably they found that men generally deemed the nudity more arousing than women did. Yet there were "some women [who] rated the nudity more sexually stimulating than the men did" (29). This latter group amounted to about 10 percent of the total sample of women, and they responded very favorably to the centerfolds in *Playgirl*. This group was presumably the target audience of the magazine, an audience it aimed to increase.

When asked how *Playgirl* could include material that was more sexually stimulating, the researchers comment on the women's responses.

> Most women expressed a desire for a more realistic, contextual representation of sexuality—one in which a relationship was clearly defined between the participants and could reasonably lead to nudity and sexual activity. (30)

In other words, the female respondents seemed to desire both more narrative, a story between the men and women depicted in an amorous pose, and a context in which to place the male centerfold, who was photographed alone. To look at a sole male body was not enough; the nude man in the center of the magazine should be attached to a story and a situation. Perhaps collegiate female viewers were trained as *readers* of the erotic and were familiar with the impassioned couplings of female heroines in romance novels (see Janice Radway's *Reading the Romance* [1991]). With such expectations placed on erotica for women, the editors and writers of *Playgirl* had a difficult task in front of them: to appeal to and define—as well as increase—its readership.

The magazine took on the task of defining its readership from the get-go. In issue 1 (June 1973) writer Marcia Borie defines the reader of the new magazine: "A PLAYGIRL is independent. Self-confident. Sensuous. Aware. Involved. Adventurous. Daring. Curious. Vital. Ambitious. Sensitive. Loving. Giving. Alive. Liberated. Free" (9). Importantly, Borie never explains this demographic or the new female in terms of her male counterpart, the playboy. She explains:

> A PLAYGIRL in the 1970's shapes her own lifestyle. She sets a tone which becomes her personal trademark. Invariably she begins with certain basics . . . Feet on the ground. Head in the clouds. Heart and body somewhere in between. To have one's head in the clouds, in this context, is to be above all the rest who choose to live down below, devoid of dreams, desires, passions. (9–10)

And so the playgirl is a desirous dreamer, in her body but also hovering above it, realistic but able to indulge her fantasies. Central and crucial to the playgirl, though, is that she is her own creation. She does not continue traditions; she begins new ones. The reader of *Playgirl* defines and refines herself and is not held back by her past.

Later in her manifesto, Borie explains the place of men in the magazine.

> And we will bring you MEN, romantic men. Yes, as a PLAYGIRL, you deserve a look at today's most exciting males. Men such as those you desire. . . . Men you wish to reach out—and touch. . . . Be with. . . . Experience . . . [and] love in any manner which is most pleasing to the individual you. (11).

Although men are the centerpiece of the magazine and are situated to serve as objects of desire for the readership, Borie gives them only a few lines in her introduction to the magazine. Gender politics are diffused; the assumption is that the reader has been able to liberate herself from sexist constraints and is already self-aware, and aware of her own bodily desires. The main message in Borie's introduction to *Playgirl* is the reader's autonomy, independence, and ability to reinvent herself.

Later in the first issue, writer Robin Richards offers the reader a quiz—"Are You a Potential Playgirl?"—modeled after the *Cosmopolitan* quizzes. Each of the thirteen questions has two right answers and two wrong ones. One answer, though, is "more right" than the other. For example, question 5 asks the reader if she would accept a promotion knowing that it will also require "a larger share" of her "in terms of time and energy expended" (70). Responses B and D are both correct. Response B recommends that the reader "carefully weigh the pros and cons" and gives the reader who chooses this response four points. However, response D is even more correct, providing the reader with five points and advising, "[H]ave a realistic talk with your employer. Find out exactly what the new position entails; ask for a week in which to decide" (70).

In this question and others, it is clear that the targeted reader is no hippie. She is involved in her career, and, although she is fun loving (especially when on vacation), she is responsible and her goal is to settle down with the right man. For those who don't do well on the quiz, Richards offers advice: "Take hold of yourself! You must learn to like yourself a whole lot more than you do right now." Later in the column, she suggests that the reader has found a friend in *Playgirl* and urges her to write to the magazine's self-help expert. In the course of the first issue, the magazine moves from a discourse of independence to one of self-help—meaning help that comes from an expert. The magazine has a contradictory ideology, and it literally moves within its pages from a posture that expresses the potential radicalism in the sexual expression of women in the early 1970s to a more accommodationist stance by the time it reaches the last pages. In the back of "the book" (magazine people refer to an issue as a book), the ubiquitous columnist that predominates in women's magazines returns, telling women who they should be and how they should appear, presumably for the pleasure of men. Still, in its centerfolds and depictions of amorous couples, *Playgirl* was groundbreaking, encouraging sexual exploration and fantasy.

BERLIN IS A STATE OF MIND

Just as *Playgirl* is not a mere copy of *Playboy*, gay pornography does not have the same roots and does not have the same logic as heterosexual pornography. Gay pornography that emerges in the post-Stonewall period has two antecedents: physique photography and the avant-garde and underground cinema of the 1950s and 1960s. Wakefield Poole, a gay pornographer (and a former dancer with the Ballet Russe) whose work appeared just before Peter Berlin's, was quite conscious of his intentions in his work. Poole remembers going to a porno cinema in New York and being both appalled and bored by the rather violent short film that was being shown in a loop (235). *Boys in the Sand* (1971), the film that he directed, which was inspired by this experience, was a filmed series of three sex acts that take place on Fire Island, starring Casey Donovan in each scenario. The setting itself becomes eroticized from the first scene as Donovan appears miraculously from underwater to seduce a lonely man on the sensuous beach. *Boys in the Sand* is basically a silent film—not only is there no dialogue, but there are also no intertitles—and it harks back to the poetic ruminations of Kenneth Anger and the early work of Andy Warhol. But it is also hard core—the sex is not simulated or suggested—and it includes interracial sex and, very briefly, the suggestion of fisting. It is a self-conscious break from the existing gay porn of the era, that devalued its characters and audience through low production values, simulated violence, and the use of runaways and drifters as performers. Casey Donovan was an all-American boy next door and clearly was not gay for pay. With *Boys in the Sand* as its title—and in its celebration of gay male sex acts—the film responds to William Friedkin's film *Boys in the Band* (1970), based on Mart Crowley's play, which highlights the claustrophobic bitchery of well-heeled gay men in Manhattan and keeps hidden the erotic value of their lives and sexual encounters. Much to Poole's surprise, *Boys in the Sand* became a hit, reviewed in *Variety* and the *New York Times*. Its success created a new paradigm for gay male pornography; and auteurs like Poole emerged in the genre, as did distinctive stars. Production values soared, and artfulness was mixed with explicitness. If there was a golden era of gay male pornography, one would have to say it was the 1970s.

Three stars emerged from the early part of the decade: Casey Donovan, Jack Wrangler, and Peter Berlin. They were distinctive and different from each other, but they also shared key qualities: onscreen they were men of few words, they were sexually insatiable, and by today's standards they were sexually versatile (i.e., they were willing to appear in a variety of positions available to a male couple). Not one of them could be called effete, and each adopted onscreen personae that related to their offscreen lives. Donovan, born Cal Culver, took the name Casey after the character he played in his first porno movie. According to his biographer, Roger Edmonson (1998), Cal became Casey—sexually insatiable and available, he often paid his rent by working as a sex worker. Although he strove to become a stage actor, he enjoyed his status as a sex symbol and worked as a call boy even after he found relative success, and he was known to be a regular in the Rambles, the area in Central Park known for cruising. His facade was that of the all-American boy with the golden smile, youthful looking into his forties, nothing limp wristed or sibilant in his masculinity, defying stereotypes in his manner and appearance, but perhaps endorsing the stereotype of the insatiable homosexual. Apparently there was nothing he would not try sexually on and off camera, a grown-up Boy Scout who knew all the knots and hankie codes.

Jack Wrangler, best known for his role in the 1976 *Kansas City Trucking Co.*, was not preppy like Donovan; instead he was the all-American stud with working-class appeal, easily able to convey that he worked as a trucker (even though in real life he aspired to become a musical theater star, and after his work in adult movies he did have reasonable success). Born John Stillman, he took the name Wrangler in homage to the jeans known for their ruggedness when he started doing a striptease in nightclubs. In interviews in the documentary about him, Jeffrey Schwarz's *Wrangler: Anatomy of an Icon* (2008), he is remarkably cognizant of the image he created and why it would appeal to the emerging gay culture of the 1970s. To a large extent this image was one he happily cultivated—he helped to create the so-called clone look of the late 1970s (tight nondesigner jeans, work boots, sleeveless plaid shirts). A man of few words, his onscreen same-sex desire was convincing—he was a grown-up high school jock who never went on to college and lived for locker room hijinks. Although he was relatively short, he loomed large on film. Whatever he did, even when he was the "passive partner" in a sex act, was manly. Proving his masculinity, he was able to move into heterosexual porn quite successfully and later married the chanteuse Margaret Whiting, though he never renounced his former gay life. In short, he was a musical theater queen who looked like the Marlboro Man.

Peter Berlin's image and persona were probably the most complicated of these three 1970s gay porn stars. First of all, although his career as a screen star was brief, he was also an auteur. Berlin was able to bring a vérité documentary style to his films, as if the camera were capturing the everyday existence of a real-life character. His character experienced his eccentricity as normative and his distinctive predilections as anything but pathological. His look was far more adorned than those of the other two stars (he shared as many qualities with Quentin Crisp, the very adorned English eccentric who animated the streets of New York City, as he did with Jack Wrangler) and did not conform to existing paradigms of American masculinity—indeed, he was foreign born and featured a German accent and a Teutonic appearance, perhaps evoking Lohengrin or the Norse god Thor.

Berlin's image was both carefully constructed and heavily accessorized. And perhaps most important, his performance was not focused on embodying the wondrous abandonment of sexual pleasure; rather it was centered on the tension and provocation of desire. For Berlin, the production of lust was tantamount and more important than the sexual act itself. He did not have to be good in bed in his films (he relied on the techniques of his costars); he was more expert in the creation of yearning than in gratification—he loved to pose and cruise. His acts of exhibitionist masturbation with entranced voyeurs always appear more impassioned than scenes of ordinary sex that involve touching between him and another person.

In the documentary *That Man: Peter Berlin,* directed by Jim Tushinski (2005), the writer Armistead Maupin recounts an amusing story about Berlin. Maupin met Berlin at a dinner party and believed he had struck up the beginnings of a friendship, finding the German far more approachable and amiable than he had imagined. Yet later, when Maupin saw Berlin in a cruising area, he made the mistake of walking up to him and saying hello. Berlin ignored him; clearly he would only acknowledge those he found attractive, and even then, in most cases he would reject a would-be suitor. He wanted to elicit the gestures and poses of being turned on, not a conversation. This was the persona of the public Berlin, the one who loved cruising. Privately, for most of his life, Berlin had a live-in lover who he probably was faithful to after his career in pornography was over. His lover passed away from AIDS, and Berlin continues to live in the flat they shared in San Francisco with his cat and photos—photos of himself, of course.

Berlin's *Nights in Black Leather* takes the form of a letter that the protagonist writes to his friends back home in Germany. The film has a strong nonfictional premise, and each section unfolds like docuporn. The protagonist is in Los Angeles, and he writes, describing his nocturnal life in San Francisco as he discovers the intricacies and eccentricities of the eroticized city. First he recounts getting a dirty phone call from an admirer, whose voice we hear admiring and imagining what he would do to "Helmut." Helmut/Peter is shown reclining on a velvet beanbag chair underneath a large spider plant as he hears the amorous voice adore him, concocting a fantasy starring him. Peter pleasures himself ardently and thanks the caller as he hangs up.

In the next sequence, Peter recounts meeting a dark-haired fellow after cruising him on the street. The two travel to the man's tent in the woods and quickly strip. They spend as much time chatting with each other about their mutual fondness for leather as having sex. The fellow laughs as Helmut/Peter uses the word *punch* instead of *pouch* when Peter tells him that he wants the fellow to see his leather jeans, which accentuate the crotch. As the sequence ends Peter confesses to being a leather freak. The camera treats both subjects as real people, not actors, and their interaction appears unrehearsed and actual, as if the camera just happens to be there, sticking to long and medium shots and avoiding close-ups of faces and body parts with few cuts.

In the third sequence, Helmut/Peter describes being at a typical San Francisco party; even though he is new to the city, his voice-over sounds as if he has been to hundreds of these parties and is tired of how predictable they are. The camera focuses on two drag queens seated on a couch, smoking pot and laughing. In vérité fashion we can barely hear their dialogue, but we do hear the pop song that is playing at the party. The fair-haired drag queen flirts with Helmut/Peter, but he appears disinterested and moves away. Then a slim, mustached guy with an exposed midriff and tight jeans sits down next to the drag queens. The dialogue continues to be barely audible. The blonde drag queen tells the guy, "You're cute." She pauses, then adds, "But then again, EVERYONE is cute" (a great line to my ears). The guy stands up to dance to the song, and Helmut/Peter joins him in a close dance in which they mirror each other's movements. In the final sequence of the scene, two couples are visible on the dance floor—the two drag queens, rejected but content to dance, and Peter with his new friend.

Helmut/Peter introduces the next sequence, in which he recruits a young man to play slave to his master. He begins by narrating in a voice-over an encounter he had with a man who was into Nazi regalia. In Peter's story this man claims that he and Peter are both Aryan, and hence superior. Peter chuckles to himself that he voted socialist in the last election in Germany and shares none of this fantasy—his fetish for leather is independent of right-wing mythology. By introducing the sequence with this story, he lets the audience know that role-playing involving dominance and submission is just that: it is performative and perhaps part of one's lifestyle. It does not determine the way one votes or the ideology one holds. In the documentary *That Man: Peter Berlin* he speaks passion-ately of his pacifism—he cannot bear that beautiful young men die need-lessly in a war devised by old men. Indeed, the idea of men wearing uni-forms provided by the state is repellant to him (his father died in the Second World War). Instead young men should be free to cruise the pub-lic parks of the city, dressed in sexualized gear of their own design.

The final sequence begins with Helmut/Peter retelling the events of another night out in San Francisco, of finding a leather bar in which sex acts appear to be as commonplace as conversation (it is quite a treat to see the nonplussed faces of some of the denizens of the bar as they in-volve themselves in Berlin-centric erotic entanglements). A rather en-dearing looking hippie uses a cat-o'-nine-tails rather lackadaisically on the buttocks of a young man performing fellatio on the protagonist. Later in the evening he meets an attractive couple who invite him home to watch them have sex. This scene stands out in the rest of the film—percussive Indian music that features tabla, sitar, and violin underlines the exoticism of the lovemaking and the scene is edited into sequences of a few seconds each (Indian music is also used in *Boys in the Sand* as embellishment during the interracial lovemaking scene). The lighting is dark, and at times it is hard to discern what sex acts are being performed and what parts of the three bodies are being filmed—it is a decided at-tempt to lend lyricism to the lovemaking, and it departs from the docu-mentary style of the rest of the film. It appears that Helmut/Peter does not watch the couple perform for him for long—after all, it is clear that he is far for more attuned to being watched, and halfway through the scene he joins in, becoming the centerpiece of the scene rather than the spectator. After all, Helmut/Peter is the star, not the onlooker.

The film ends with Helmut/Peter being approached by a young man with a dog as he finishes his letter to the German friend back home. He speaks of his being cruised as if it is occurring in the present instead of recounting an event in the past, and his tone is one of ennui, as if he is bored with being an object of desire. Yet at the same time, it is that which sustains him and keeps away the loneliness he might feel as someone new to the country missing his friends back home. The film itself cele-brates the demimonde he finds in San Francisco, a site that encourages him to fully investigate and engage his sexual personae.

In *That Boy* (1974) Berlin keeps the vérité tone but indulges much more in fantasy. The film also disconnects the voice from body by almost entirely abandoning dialogue and using voice-over instead. There is also an overarching narrative that connects all the segments in the film and a tone of longing throughout. A young photographer, who has lost his sight in an accident, recounts his obsession with the perfect-looking German. His remembrance is Proustian in its detail, and he recites a fantasy he had of photographing Peter in his studio. This tale, and the young man's vulnerability, fascinates Peter, and he rejects all suitors who can see him, presumably because the young man can "see" the real Peter behind the shiny facade.

In the fantasy sequence introduced by the blind photographer, Peter performs an endless striptease, removing his leather shorts to reveal a seemingly never ending sequence of black or white leather jock straps, finally exposing a see-through G-string as the final layer. The scene borders on being humorous and campy; it is only the voice-over of the photographer redolent with lust that rescues it from self-parody. The striptease also demonstrates Roland Barthes's emphasis in the essay "Striptease" in *Mythologies* (1957): the naked body is far less sexy than the corpus that remains partially clothed. This plays with the tension between skin and fabric, provoking a longing for what lies beneath, one that is often more alluring than the actual flesh. Indeed, by today's porn standards, Peter Berlin is not incredibly well endowed; he uses clothing and layers—and theatricality—to accentuate his size.

PORN DOCUMENTARY

In an important sense hard-core pornography shares a quality with documentary. In work that defines the parameters of documentary film, Bill Nichols (2001) emphasizes the indexical function of nonfiction films, using Peirce's notion of the semiotic term *index*. An index points to or indicates the presence of another object or activity (e.g., smoke is an index of fire, and a meow is an index of a cat). A film is not the actual experience it depicts, but it is an index of it—it points to an actual occurrence that happened in front of the camera and around the sound equipment. Hard-core pornography is a recording of actual sex acts; it is not a simulation, even though it may rely on camera angles, close-ups, edits, and soundtrack to provide a scenario with a sense of the erotic. When Peter Berlin is shown on film in a fantasy sequence having sex, it is a fantasy within the narrative frame of the film—the sex act actually took place—it is not imagined. Each of the fantasized sex scenes in *That Boy* serves a double function—it is a rendering of an encounter between two or more performers. Within the narrative, these fantasy sex scenes provoke a longing for an event that never occurred and will never occur as Peter rebuffs all advances from those who can see him. This provides a point of identification with the viewer, who will also never have the chance to have sex with Peter Berlin or any of the other performers in the film. A fantasy sequence hits home with the viewer—as it is footage of an event that both actually occurred and could never happen—at the same time. The indexical logic of documentary is kept in pornographic films, at least when it comes to the rendering of sex acts, yet it surrounds the recording of yearning bodies with narrative. Thus the context of indexical sex acts is fictional.

In Richard Dyer's classic article on gay porn, "Male Gay Porn: Coming to Terms" (1985), he asserts that "the narrative structure of gay porn is analogous to aspects of the social construction of both male sexuality in general and gay male sexual practice in particular." The formal aspects of gay male porn reflect the sexuality of men and inflect it as well. For Dyer, gay male porn is involved in the "education of desire"; that is to say, if porn bears a relationship to the ways in which its viewers have sex, it is in large part because porn is instructional—it is also "how-to," not necessarily in showing how to perform actual sex acts but in the importance of sex and sexuality to the identity of gay men. In portraying socially constructed landscapes that are depicted as ideal, they provide a tactical guide for viewers, especially in that gay porn views same-sex pleasure as normative and not abnormal; it is depathologizing.

Dyer does not laud gay male pornography as good or socially positive (though he does view it as less politically reprehensible than straight porn), nor does he strive to rescue it from marginalization as a genre; rather he is concerned with its formal characteristics and narrative structure. He argues that gay male porn is strong on story (unlike the photo spreads of *Playgirl*), not only on scenario, and that the narrative is masculinist in that it is geared toward the money shot—the visible ejaculation, which he calls "the coming-to-visual climax." He argues that even though porn is educational, in this emphasis it mimics existing tendencies of male sexuality: "The emphasis on seeing orgasm is then part of the way porn (re)produces the construction of male sexuality." Orgasm is the indexical proof of the sex act, granting the filmed event documentary verifiability; it also duplicates a tendency of male sexuality (at least under its current emphasis): guys like to watch themselves ejaculate—the pleasure is not only in the physical sensation but in witnessing its culmination as a visual spectacle of the body in performance.

Peter Berlin's oeuvre supports Richard Dyer's estimation of porn but

Peter Berlin in *That Boy* (1974). (Image courtesy of Peter Berlin.)

also differs from it in key ways. Certainly the cum shot is important in *That Boy* and *Nights in Black Leather,* and indeed there are story lines in each scenario, as well as one theme that ties each film together (*Nights* is the recounting of sexual escapades in a visualized letter and *That Boy* is an unlikely love story between an exhibitionist and a blind man whose memory of sight almost engulfs him). Indeed there is a compulsion to repeat in each of the scenes, which is that Berlin yearns to be adored for his visual appearance yet finds this adoration ultimately unsatisfying, urging him to try again with a sense of ennui and inevitability. It is only when he is forced to watch a couple (in *Nights*) and encounters his own desire for another in a desirable, vulnerable young man who can no longer see him (in *That Boy*) that he finds gratification. Each film indulges in Berlin's tendency to show off, to turn his body into an exhibition of self, and both films reveal that ultimately this narcissistic pursuit, while aesthetically sublime and desirous, reasserts his solitude. I would argue that in both films the narrative engine does not accelerate to orgasm but moves to unearth a longing, making clear that the desire to be looked at by someone who is desirous looking is an insatiable pursuit—it reveals the cul-de-sac of cruising (as if Sisyphus is checking out who is checking him out while he pushes the rock up the hill). The protagonist in *That Boy* is unattainable to all those who leer at him with lust (although each is able, within the narrative structure, to fully imagine an encounter). He only responds to the blind man, and for a hard-core gay film we spend considerable time watching them sit in a booth in a coffee shop, talking to each other (their conversation is not audible). Instead we hear Berlin's voice-over admit to his growing fondness for the boy, who cannot see how hot he is but remembers his sexiness through memories of his camera, an allegory of the filmmaking act itself and its inbuilt erotic interchange of voyeurism and exhibitionism.

Both Berlin films emphasize speech, even though they are elegies of the spectacle of the eroticized—and at times fetishized—male body. The use of voice-over (or a disembodied, yearning voice in the case of the phone caller) predominates and speech is disassociated from the body, as sync-sound is rare in both films. Instead, narrating voices fill up the space of the film (this is very different from *Boys in the Sand*, which in its desire to counter the endless banter of the men in *Boys in the Band* is virtually without speech and voice and arguably instead uses the loftiness of classical music to narrate and lend grandeur to the encounters). In *That Boy*, we hear from a variety of voices: a young African American man who stares at Berlin outside the gym, imagining seducing him in the locker room; the blind man recounting a fantasy of surrounding Berlin with photos of himself that he has taken; and finally Berlin's recounting of his desire for the blind boy (his character is not named, and he is called "the blind boy" in the credits) to be able to see himself in a mirror and masturbate to his own image. In the protagonist's desire for the boy, he imagines a narcissistic encounter for him, which only includes Berlin as the invisible director and not as an actor. Each scenario uses voice-overs extensively, showing that while much of gay male pleasure is visual, it also relishes storytelling via speech and voice to invent and embellish narrative, underlining details that heighten the ecstasy of the event. After all, speech acts are a crucial part of all sex acts, especially the performative utterance ("I'm coming") that precedes ejaculation. Berlin's pornography may shout the eroticism of his image, but he also speaks incessantly of the relevance of the voice in distinguishing an ideal sex act from an ordinary one.

If one were to look for an analogy for the narrative structure of the pornography of Peter Berlin, one could settle on opera in its alternation of aria and recitative (duets are rare, but they are there). Recitation leads to an aria, and the aria (always performed by Berlin himself) stands out from the narrative. For example, in the "aria" in which Berlin performs his striptease, the intensity of his performance allows the viewer to forget that this is part of the photographer's/blind boy's fantasy; instead it becomes a chance for Berlin to hit all his exhibitionistic high notes. The moment has nothing to do with the story and everything to do with providing the time for the tenor divo to reach his crescendo. Although Berlin ejaculates later in the scene, the money shot has already occurred: Berlin has succeeded strutting his stuff for an onlooker who will not succeed in having him.

In the documentary *That Man: Peter Berlin*, much of the footage is shot in Berlin's San Francisco apartment. He is surrounded by images of himself that he took with his camera during his youthful heyday (though Berlin continues to look great in his more advanced years and he has kept his trademark pageboy hairstyle). After his brief career in film, he focused more on still images and developed elaborate techniques for self-depiction in desirous poses. Berlin is remarkably conscious of the persona he created and sees this as an ongoing lived art project: he designed and made his own wardrobe, he picked out the right areas in which to cruise, and he turned his environment into a mise-en-scène. He also knew the distance between the persona he created and his own life. At home, for most of his adult life, he lived with his lover and professed to live what he described as a monogamous life. His desire was sated by self-presentation as an object of desire, unlike Casey Donovan, who lived a life of pornography and anonymous encounters both on- and offscreen. According to Peter Berlin, he was actually not that interested in sex acts themselves but found pleasure in what others experience as desire; sexual pleasure itself was never that fascinating to him. He craved yearning. That was transformative and enlivening; blissful gratification was only routine.

Peter Berlin appeared to live rather simply among a small circle of friends. He was probably shy. His excess and bravado were only to be found in the way he dressed and posed; he created a new paradigm of the desirable male—boyish but hypermasculinized and embellished with fabric, skintight nonetheless, reconfiguring the sexualized male body. His look had nothing to do with being preppy and all-American like Casey Donovan or a rugged, outdoorsy, working-class guy like

Jack Wrangler. In *That Man* filmmaker John Waters wittingly refers to Berlin as being almost like a cartoon character appearing on the streets of San Francisco. Waters finds him bordering on the ridiculous, but it is Berlin's conviction in his role and its relevance that saves the performance from becoming campy and self-parody. For Armistead Maupin, he was one of the most distinctive, colorful characters that populated San Francisco in the early 1970s, one that helped to transform the city from the home of hippies in Haight-Ashbury to the gay mecca of the Castro. Peter Berlin was a self-invention; born of German royalty, he gave birth to himself, sui generis, as a gay American sex symbol, a nonfiction star that starred in his own reality show in a milieu all his own.

THE RIGHT TO VIEW MALE BODIES

Both *Playgirl* magazine and Peter Berlin show the new ways in which men's bodies were highlighted and sexualized in popular culture in the early 1970s. This depiction was not analogous to the ways that female bodies had been displayed, especially since the audiences and their tastes were different, even as both these audiences—gay men and heterosexual women—had to undergo "an education of desire." Each had to take their desires and the pleasure derived in looking at naked bodies out from under the mattress and into everyday practice. Revealingly, the more overt sexualization of men's bodies in mediatized environments begins when women begin to gain a new level of autonomy over their own bodies, brought about by key legal decisions. But the objectification of men as fodder for the camera does not itself mean a redistribution of power between the genders; it is an indication of power shifts. Gay men and women benefit legally and politically when prudery subsides. Nonfiction media become enlivened with the inclusion of gay men and pleasure-seeking women.

In the early 1970s nonfiction media became a site where rebellious personalities explored their identities—and in certain instances, displayed their bodies in amorous poses. These personalities took their energy from political movements and changes in popular culture and told stories that are based on experience and are responsive to real and imagined audiences. They enlivened the media culture of the time.

Forty years later, nonfiction media have literally taken over—from user-generated content on social-networking sites to crowdsourcing and citizen journalism, the continued proliferation of reality television, and the rising popularity of documentaries at the box office, it is no longer exceptional to expect that nonfiction content has entertainment value, nor is it surprising that everyday people are as dynamic and engrossing as film stars or national leaders. After all, conflict and resolution seem inevitable no matter the form or genre. Yes, traditional stars continue to exist who have gained their notoriety from appearing in fictional films and television shows, but their celebrity is increasingly challenged by those who come up from nonfiction ranks—those who get their start on YouTube, MySpace, Facebook, or Twitter—and tell a story based on the supposed facts of their lives, as well as the provocations of their imaginations, and devise a performed persona that is equal parts revealing and fanciful. The exalted place of "real people" in contemporary media culture can be traced directly back to the early 1970s. As an audience, we are much more happy—and much more emotionally engaged—with a pop star that is seemingly elected by the American people than to one selected by artist and repertoire A&R people, agents, or publicists at a global corporation (even if the result in both cases is a corporately branded pop star).

Although the stakes are very different, we can draw analogies with political movements and popular protest. When the Iranian government censored state and corporate media during a rebellion in the summer of 2009, we responded to voices and images that were brought to us via YouTube and Facebook. Today citizen journalists and involved witnesses become crucial in providing information that otherwise would not be available; they also empower the speakers who become distinctive and crucial in the narration of the conflict. They become the heroes of the contemporary era through nonfiction media, intensifying the mediascape with real life tales of taking to the streets in defiance of the state. Because they are the "real people" of Tehran, their narratives are more compelling to us, and we feel that emergent media allow us access to individuals that traditional media might have ignored even if there were no censorship. Media users want to be involved with the creation, marketing, and publicizing of stars and political leaders alike; the audience wants to feel involved in the news and to respond via Facebook (hence the success of Barack Obama); we are continually implicated in the creation of nonfiction celebrities—celebrities who were never "discovered" but reap the benefit of appearing in a video that went viral. This is the promise of nonfictionality, a promise that emerged with such unlikely partners as the Senate Watergate Hearings and *An American*

Family. All apologies to George Herbert, who penned an oft-repeated epigram, but living well is *not* the best revenge; being in front of the camera is . . . and then posting the image online.

The extension of nonfiction media in the early 1970s encouraged the presentation of dynamic, flamboyant, exhibitionist, and pioneering personalities. These personalities challenged traditional representations of gender and enlarged what is permissible and popular in American culture. Through them, a diversity of sexualities and voices insisted on their prominence and relevance; these stars were convinced that they were speaking to a burgeoning audience that wanted to hear and see them explore the most extravagant corners of themselves, doing so in episodes and fragments of a mediatized reality. These refractions of self serve to characterize the decade and force it to reconsider itself in light of the contemporary moment. With their sheen and substance reapplied, these analog still lifes from the 1970s continue to come to motion in the digital present.

Works Cited

ABC News Special Report: Senate Watergate Hearings, John Dean Testimony, Day 2. Parts 1–5. June 26, 1973. Paley Center for Media. Catalog ID: T80:0549-T80:0553. Television.

Agamben, Giorgio. *State of Exception.* Chicago: University of Chicago Press, 2005. Print.

Allen, Robert. *Speaking of Soap Operas.* Chapel Hill: University of North Carolina Press, 1985. Print.

American Family Revisited: The Louds 10 Years Later. Dir. Alan and Susan Raymond. HBO, August 9, 1983. Paley Center for Media. Catalog ID: T88:0269. Television.

An American Family (episode 2). Dir. Alan and Susan Raymond, produced by Craig Gilbert. 1973. Museum of Television and Radio Screening Series: Lesbian and Gay Life on Television: An American Family, episode 2. January 18, 1973. PBS. Paley Center for Media. Catalog ID: B:32256. Television.

Auslander, Philip. *Performing Glam Rock: Gender and Theatricality in Popular Music.* Ann Arbor: University of Michigan Press, 2006. Print.

Badiou, Alain. *The Century.* Cambridge: Polity, 2007. Print.

Bangs, Lester. "Johnny Ray's Better Whirlpool: The New Living Bowie." *The Bowie Companion.* Ed. Elizabeth Thomson and David Gutman. London: De Capo, 1995. 123–26. Print.

Barnes, Ken. "The Glitter Era: Teenage Rampage." *Bomp* March 1978. Web. April 24, 2010. http://www.rocksbackpages.com/article.html?ArticleID=8326.

Barthes, Roland. *Mythologies.* Paris: Editions du Seuil, 1957. Print.

Barthes, Roland. *Mythologies.* Trans. Annette Lavers. New York: Hill and Wang, 1972. Print.

Barthes, Roland. *Le Plaisir du texte.* Paris: Editions du Seuil, 1973. Print.

Barthes, Roland. *The Pleasure of the Text.* Trans. Richard Howard. New York: Hill and Wang, 1975. Print.

Baudrillard, Jean. *Simulacra and Simulations.* Ann Arbor: University of Michigan Press, 1994. Print.

Beaufort, John. "Watergate as TV Drama." *Christian Science Monitor* July 7, 1973: 15. Print.

de Beauvoir, Simone. *The Second Sex.* New York: Knopf, 1953. Print.

Bewitched. ABC, 1964–72. Television.

Billie Jean King: Portrait of a Pioneer. HBO Sports, April 26, 2006. Television.

Boorstin, Daniel J. *The Image: A Guide to Pseudo-Events in America.* New York: Vintage, 1992. Print.

Borie, Marcia. "Reaching Out: What Is a Playgirl?" *Playgirl* 1.1 (1973): 9–11. Print.

Bowie, David. *Hunky Dory.* RCA, 1971. LP.

Bowie, David. *Space Oddity.* 1969. RCA, 1972. LP.

Bowie, David. *Aladdin Sane.* RCA, 1973. LP.

Bowie, David. *Ziggy Stardust and the Spiders from Mars.* 1972. Rykodisc, 1990. CD.

Bowie, David. *Life on Mars.* Dir. Mick Rock. *Best of Bowie.* DVD. Virgin/EMI, 2002. Video.

Boys in the Band. Dir. William Friedkin. National General Pictures, 1970. Film.

Boys in the Sand. Dir. Wakefield Poole. 1971. Wakefield Poole Collection, 1971–1986. Mercury Releasing, 2002. DVD.

The Brady Bunch. ABC, 1969–74. Television.

Brunsdon, Charlotte. *The Feminist, the Housewife, and the Soap Opera.* New York: Oxford University Press, 2000. Print.

Buchwald, Art. "America Loves 'Watergate.'" *Lakeland Ledger* February 25, 1974: 7D. Web. April 20, 2010. http://news.google.com.

Butler, Judith. *Gender Trouble: Feminism and the Subversion of Identity.* New York: Routledge, 1990. Print.

Cantril, Hadley, and Gordon Allport. *The Psychology of Radio.* New York: Harper and Brothers, 1935. Print.

Capo, James A. "Network Watergate Coverage Patterns in Late 1972 and Early 1973." *Journalism Quarterly* 60 (1983): 595–602. Print.

Chalou, George C. "St. Clair's Defeat, 1792." *Congress Investigates, 1792–1974.* Ed. Arthur Schlesinger Jr. and Roger Bruns. New York: Chelsea House, 1975. 1–18. Print.

Chion, Michel. *Audio-Vision: Sound on Screen.* New York: Columbia University Press, 1990. Print.

Chronicle of a Summer. Dir. Edgar Morin and Jean Rouch. Argos Films, 1961. Film.

Clarke, Sally C. "Advance Report for Final Divorce Statistics, 1989 and 1990." *Monthly Vital Statistics Report: Supplement* (Centers for Disease Control and Prevention) 43.9 (1995): 1–32. Web. April 5, 2010. http://www.cdc.gov/nchs/data/mvsr/supp/mv43_09s.pdf.

Connor, Steven. "Sound and Self." *Hearing History: A Reader.* Ed. Mark M. Smith. Athens: University of Georgia Press, 2004. 54–66. Print.

Dean, John. *Worse than Watergate: The Secret Presidency of George W. Bush.* New York: Warner, 2005. Print.

Dean, John. *Conservatives without Conscience.* New York: Viking Penguin, 2006. Print.

Dean, John. *Blind Ambition, Updated Edition: The End of the Story.* Palm Springs, CA: Polimedia, 2009. Print.

Dean, Maureen, with Hays Gorey. *"Mo": A Woman's View of Watergate*. New York: Simon and Schuster, 1975. Print.

Doherty, Thomas. *Cold War, Cool Medium: Television, McCarthyism, and American Culture*. New York: Columbia University Press, 2003. Print.

Dont Look Back. Dir. D. A. Pennebaker. 1967. Docudrama, 1990. DVD.

Dunne, John. "Album Oriented Rock: FM Radio Format." Term paper. College of Staten Island, City University of New York, 2001.

Dyer, Richard. *The Stars: Teacher's Study Guide*. London: BFI, 1979. Print.

Dyer, Richard. "Gay Male Porn: Coming to Terms." *Jump Cut: A Review of Contemporary Media* 30 (1985): 27–29. Web. April 20, 2010. http://www.ejump cut.org/archive/onlinessays/JC30folder/GayPornDyer.html.

Edmonson, Roger. *Boy in the Sand: Casey Donovan, All-American Sex Star*. Boston: Alyson, 1998. Print.

Ehrenreich, Barbara. *The Hearts of Men: American Dreams and the Flight from Commitment*. New York: Anchor, 1987. Print

The Exorcist, William Peter Blatty's. Dir. William Friedkin. 1973. Warner Video, 2000. DVD.

Farber, Jim. "The Androgynous Mirror." *Rolling Stone: The 70's*. Ed. Ashley Kahn, Holly George-Warren, and Shawn Dahl. Boston: Little, Brown, 1998. 142–46. Print.

Feuer, Jane. "Different Soaps for Different Folks: Conceptualzing the Soap Opera." In *Worlds without End: The Art and History of the Soap Opera*, ed. J. Simon et al. New York: Abrams, 1997. 89–98. Coincides with an exhibit at The Museum of Television and Radio. Print.

FM. Dir. John A. Alonzo. 1978. Starz/Anchor Bay, 2000. DVD.

The Fog. Dir. John Carpenter. 1979. MGM, 2005. DVD.

Forman, Pamela J., and Darcy C. Plymire. "Amélie Mauresmo's Muscles: The Lesbian Heroic in Women's Professional Tennis." *Women's Studies Quarterly* 33.1–2 (2005): 134–49. Print.

Friedan, Betty. *The Feminine Mystique*. New York: Norton, 1963. Print.

Gaar, Gillian. *She's a Rebel: The History of Women in Rock and Roll*. New York: Seal, 1992. Print.

Gamson, Joshua. *The Fabulous Sylvester: The Legend, the Music, the Seventies in San Francisco*. New York: Henry Holt, 2005. Print.

Garay, Ronald. *Congressional Television: A Legislative History*. Westport, CT: Greenwood, 1984. Print.

Gilbert, Matthew. "What's in a Pop Icon? Greil Marcus Figures Out What Makes Pop Culture Tick." *Boston Globe* November 18, 1991: 30. Web. April 24, 2010. http://pqasb.pqarchiver.com/boston/access/59289921.html? FMT=ABS&FMTS=ABS:FT&type=current&date=Nov+18%2C+1991& author=Matthew+Gilbert%2C+Globe+Staff&pub=Boston+Globe+% 28pre1997+Fulltext%29&edition=&startpage=30&desc=What%27s+in+ a+pop+icond%3F+Greil+Marcus+figures+out+what+makes+pop+cul ture+tick.

Gill, John. *Queer Noises: Male and Female Homosexuality in Twentieth Century Music*. Minneapolis: University of Minnesota Press, 1995. Print.

Gillmeister, Heiner. *Tennis: A Cultural History.* London: Leicester University Press, 1998. Print.

Goffman, Erving. *The Presentation of Self in Everyday Life.* New York: Anchor, 1959. Print.

Gone. Dir. Cecilia Dougherty. 2001. Single Channel Version. Video Data Bank, 2008. Video.

Greer, Germaine. *The Female Eunuch.* London: Paladin, 1970. Print.

Grey Gardens. Dir. Ellen Hovde, Albert Maysles, David Maysles, and Muffie Meyer. 1975, Criterion Collection, 2006. DVD.

Grey Gardens. Dir. Michael Sucsy. 2009. HBO. Televison.

Guccione, Bob, Jr. "When Innocence Died and Marketing Set In." *Los Angeles Times* August 14, 1994. Web. April 24, 2010. http://articles.latimes.com/1994-08-14/opinion/op-26956_1_corporate-rock.

Gutcheon, Beth. "Look for Cop-Outs on Prime Time, Not on 'Soaps.'" *New York Times* December 16, 1973: 173. Web. April 23, 2010. http://select.ny times.com/gst/abstract.html?res=F10C12FB385D127A93C4A81789D95 F478785F9&scp=7&sq=Beth+Gutcheon+&st=p.

Halberstam, Judith. *Female Masculinity.* Durham: Duke University Press, 1998. Print.

Hall, Mildred. "'Free Form' Radio Format Draws FCC Opposition." *Billboard* August 21, 1971: 1, 50. Web. April 25, 2010. http://books.google.com.

Hall, Oliver. "Greil Marcus: Interview with Oliver Hall." *Perfect Sound Forever* March 2005. Web. April 24, 2010. http://www.furious.com/perfect/mar cus2.html.

Harvey, Michael. *The Ziggy Stardust Companion.* Web. April 24, 2010. http://www.5years.com/mbh.htm.

Hebdige, Dick. *Subculture: The Meaning of Style.* London: Methuen, 1979. Print.

Hilmes, Michele. *Radio Voices: American Broadcasting, 1922–1952.* Minneapolis: University of Minnesota Press, 1997. Print.

Jong, Erica. *Fear of Flying.* New York: Holt, Rinehart, and Winston, 1973. Print.

Kanfer, Stefan. "Watergate on TV: Showbiz and Anguished Ritual." *Time* June 25, 1973. Web. April 22, 2010. http://www.time.com/time/magazine/ar ticle/0,9171,907444-2,00.html.

Keith, Michael C. *Sounds in the Dark: All Night Radio in American Life.* Ames: Iowa State University Press, 2001. Print.

Kellner, Douglas. *Media Spectacle and the Crisis of Democracy: Terrorism, War, and Election Battles.* Boulder, CO: Paradigm, 2005. Print.

Killen, Andreas. *1973 Nervous Breakdown: Watergate, Warhol, and the Birth of Post-sixties America.* New York: Bloomsbury, 2006. Print.

King, Billie Jean, with Christine Brennan. *Pressure Is a Privilege: Lessons I've Learned from Life and the Battle of the Sexes.* New York: Lifetime Media, 2008. Print.

King, Billie Jean, with Kim Chapin. *Billie Jean.* New York: Harper and Row, 1974. Print.

Kneeland, Douglas. "Ex-Counsel, Cool and Dogged, Reads 6-Hour Story to the Nation: Telephone-Book' Text Wide Expectations Admire and Respect' Not Many Chuckles." *New York Times* June 26, 1973. Web. April 23, 2010.

http://select.nytimes.com/gst/abstract.html?res=F20F1FF63959137A93 C4AB178DD85F478785F9&scp=17&sq=Douglas+Kneeland+Watergate&st=p.

Korreck, Erin. "Love-Love: A Content Analysis of the Media Coverage of Lesbians in Sports." Web. April 23, 2010. http://www.saintmarys.edu/~socio/Fo4SeniorSeminarstuff/ErinKorreck-paper.Fo4.doc.

LANCE LOUD! A Death in an American Family. Dir. Alan and Susan Raymond. Video Verite LLC, 2002. Video.

Lang, Gladys Engel, and Kurt Lang. *The Battle for Public Opinion: The President, the Press, and the Polls during Watergate.* New York: Columbia University Press, 1983. Print.

Lasch, Christopher. *The Culture of Narcissism: American Life in an Age of Diminishing Expectations.* New York: Norton, 1979. Print.

Leit, Richard A., Harrison G. Pope Jr., and James J. Gray. "Cultural Expectations of Muscularity in Men: The Evolution of Playgirl Centerfolds." *International Journal of Eating Disorders* 29.1 (2000): 90–93. Print.

Levine, Elana. *Wallowing in Sex: The New Sexual Culture of 1970s American Television.* Durham: Duke University Press, 2007. Print.

"Light My Fire." *The L Word.* Showtime, January 29, 2006. Television.

The Loneliest Road. Dir. Gregory Whitehead. 2004. Prod. by BBC3. Web. April 20, 2010. http://writing.upenn.edu/pennsound/x/Whitehead.html. Audio.

Loud, Pat, with Nora Johnson. *Pat Loud: A Woman's Story.* New York: Coward, McCann and Geoghegan, 1974. Print.

Mead, Margaret. "As Significant as the Invention of Drama or the Novel." *TV Guide* January 6, 1973: A61–63. Print.

Modleski, Tania. "The Search for Tomorrow in Today's Soap Operas." *Loving with a Vengeance: Mass-Produced Fantasies for Women.* New York: Routledge, 2007 [1982], 77–102. Print.

Milam, Lorenzo Wilson. *The Radio Papers: From KRAB to KCHU.* San Diego: MHO and MHO Works, 1985. Print.

Museum of Broadcasting Seminar Series. "Radio Personalities: Afternoon and Evening." April 13, 1989. Paley Center for Media. Catalog ID: T:16716. Video.

Museum of Broadcasting Seminar Series. "A Seminar with the Makers of 'An American Family' and Members of the Loud Family." February 23, 1988. Paley Center for Media. Catalog ID: T88:0320. Video.

Museum of Television and Radio Seminar Series. "The Third Annual Radio Festival: WNEW-FM and the Rise of Free-Form Radio." November 3, 1997. Paley Center for Media. Catalog ID: T:50942. Video.

Museum of Television and Radio University Satellite Seminar Series. "Worlds without End: The Art and History of the Soap Opera—the Making of an . . . Agnes Nixon Soap Opera, *One Life to Live.*" January 28, 1998. Paley Center for Media. Catalog ID: T:51417. Video.

Navarro, Vinicius do Valle. "The Observed Looks Back: Performance in American Vérité." In "Ordinary Acts: Performance in Nonfiction Film, 1960–67." Diss. Department of Cinema Studies, New York University, 2005. Web. April 10, 2010. http://tede.ibict.br/tde_busca/processaArquivo.php?codArquivo=349. 38–51.

Neer, Richard. *FM: The Rise and Fall of Rock Radio*. New York: Random House, 2001. Print.

New York Times. "In the World of Radio, She's a Rare Bird." December 9, 1971: 60. Web. April 10, 2010. http://proquest.umi.com.proxy.library.csi.cuny.edu/pqdweb?index=2&did=90705420&SrchMode=1&sid=1&Fmt=10&VInst=PROD&VType=PQD&RQT=309&VName=HNP&TS=1272122828&clientId=13029.

New York Times. "Dean's Wife Gives Him Tea and Advice." June 26, 1973: 30. Web. November 6, 2010. http://proquest.umi.proxy.library.csi.cuny.edu.pqdweb?index=3&did=90448904&SrchMode=1&sid=1&Fmt=10&VInst=PROD&VType=PQD&RQT=309&VName=HNP&TS=1289260926&clientId=13074.

New York Times. "New Trends Alter Underground Radio." January 10, 1972: 1, 46. Web. April 25, 2010. http://proquest.umi.com.proxy.library.csi.cuny.edu/pqdweb?index=0&did=79414558&SrchMode=1&sid=1&Fmt=10&VInst=PROD&VType=PQD&RQT=309&VName=HNP&TS=1272121229&clientId=13029.

New York Times Magazine. "Good News: Women Are Going to Dress Up Again." August 26, 1973: 365–66. Web. April 15, 2010. http://proquest.umi.com.proxy.library.csi.cuny.edu/pqdweb?index=7&did=90472092&SrchMode=1&sid=1&Fmt=10&VInst=PROD&VType=PQD&RQT=309&VName=HNP&TS=1272125026&clientId=13029.

Nichols, Bill. *Introduction to Documentary*. Bloomington: Indiana University Press, 2001. Print.

Nights in Black Leather. Dir. Ignatio Rutkowski (Richard Abel with Peter Berlin). 1972–73. Nights in Black Leather Special Edition. Gorilla Factory Productions, 2006. DVD.

Ouellette, Laurie. "Inventing the Cosmo Girl: Class Identity and Girl-Style American Dreams." *Media, Culture, and Society* 21 (1999): 359–83. Print.

Poole, Wakefield. "Revisionist Pornographer." *The View from Here: Conversations with Gay and Lesbian Filmmakers*. Ed. Matthew Hays. Vancouver: Arsenal Pulp Press, 2007: 233–41. Print.

Putting the Balls Away (excerpts). Dir. Tara Mateik. March 8, 2008. Web. April 10, 2010. http://www.youtube.com/watch?v=YrWWo4jM1-E.

Radway, Janice. *Reading the Romance: Women, Patriarchy, and Popular Literature*. Durham: University of North Carolina Press, 1991. Print.

Raymond, Alan, and Susan Raymond. "Lance and Andy Warhol." Video Vérité: The Films of Alan and Susan Raymond. Web. November 5, 2010. http://www.videoverite.tv/pages/filmllwarhol.html.

"Reflections with Dennis Elsas: Alison Steele." WNEW, New York. May 3, 1977. Paley Center for Media. Catalog ID: RB:16048. Radio.

Richards, Robin. "Are You a Potential Playgirl?" *Playgirl* 1.1 (1973): 69–71. Print.

Rintoul, Suzanne. "Loving the Alien: Ziggy Stardust and Self-Conscious Celebrity." *M/C Journal* 7.5 (2004). Web. April 24, 2010. http://journal.media-culture.org.au/0411/03-rintoul.php.

Roach, Joseph. *It*. Ann Arbor: University of Michigan Press, 2007. Print.

Roberts, Selena. *A Necessary Spectacle: Billie Jean King, Bobby Riggs, and the Tennis Match that Leveled the Game.* New York: Crown, 2005. Print.

Roiphe, Anne. "'An American Family': Things Are Keen but Could Be Keener." *New York Times Magazine* February 18, 1973: 8–9, 41, 45–46, 50–53. Print.

Ruoff, Jeffrey. *An American Family: A Televised Life.* Minneapolis: University of Minnesota Press, 2002. Print.

Sandford, Christopher. *Bowie: Loving the Alien.* Cambridge, MA: De Capo, 1996. Print.

Schlesinger, Arthur, Jr. *The Imperial Presidency.* Boston: Houghton Mifflin, 1989. Print.

Schorr, Daniel. "The Danger of Blurring Fact and Fantasy." *New York Times* August 7, 1977: D1. Web. April 20, 2010. http://select.nytimes.com/gst/abstract.html?res=FA0610F8395812718DDDAE0894D0405B878BF1D3&scp=1&sq=%22The+Danger+of+Blurring+Fact+and+Fantasy%22&st=p.

Searcy, Jay. "Sporting Goods Manufacturer Predicts Women Will Comprise One-Third School Sport Forces." *Sarasota Herald Tribune* August 16, 1974: C1. Web. April 23, 2010. http://news.google.com/newspapers?nid=1755&dat=19740816&id=5r8qAAAAIBAJ&sjid=72YEAAAAIBAJ&pg=2423,147614.

Semmerling, Tim Jon. *"Evil" Arabs in American Popular Film: Orientalist Fear.* Austin: University of Texas Press, 2006. Print.

Senate Watergate Hearings: John Dean Testimony, Day 3. Parts 1–7. June 27, 1973. Paley Center for Media: Catalog ID: T80:0615-T80:0621. Television.

Senate Watergate Hearings: John Dean Testimony, Parts 1–8. ABC, June 25, 1973. Paley Center for Media. Catalog ID: T79:0308-T79:03016. Television.

Shapiro, Peter. *Turn the Beat Around: The Secret History of Disco.* New York: Faber and Faber, 2005. Print.

Silverman, Kaja. *The Acoustic Mirror: The Female Voice in Cinema and Psychoanalysis.* Bloomington: Indiana University Press, 1988. Print.

Simon, Ron, et al., eds. *Worlds Without End: The Art and History of the Soap Opera.* New York: Abrams, 1997. Coincides with an exhibit at the Museum of Television and Radio. Print.

Smith, Patti. *Just Kids.* New York: HarperCollins, 2010. Print.

"Snapper and Chris Discuss Premarital Sex." *The Young and the Restless.* CBS, March 26, 1973. Paley Center for Media. Catalog ID: T:51612. Television.

Stauffer, John, and Richard Frost. "Male and Female Interest in Sexually-Oriented Magazines." *Journal of Communication* 26.1 (1976): 25–30. Print.

Sterling, Christopher H., and Michael C. Keith. *Sounds of Change: A History of FM Broadcasting in America.* Chapel Hill: University of North Carolina Press, 2008. Print.

That Boy. Dir. Peter Berlin. 1974. *That Boy* Special Edition. Gorilla Factory Productions, 2005. DVD.

That Man: Peter Berlin. Dir. Jim Tushinski. Water Bearer Films, 2005. DVD.

Thomas, Dave. *David Bowie: Moonage Daydream.* Medford, NJ: Plexus Publishing, 1997. Print.

Thomas, Sari. "Gender and Social-Class Coding in Popular Photographic Erotica." *Communication Quarterly* 34.2 (1986): 103–14. Print.

Time. "Hearts and Flowers from John Dean." July 9, 1973: 13. Print.

Tremlett, George. *David Bowie: Living on the Brink.* New York: Carroll and Graf, 1997. Print.

"Twenty Years of WNEW-FM (RADIO)." October 30, 1987. Paley Center for Media. Catalog ID: R:10469. Radio.

Velvet Goldmine. Dir. Todd Haynes. Miramax, 1999. DVD.

Waldrep, Shelton. *The Aesthetics of Self-Invention: Oscar Wilde to David Bowie.* Minneapolis: University of Minnesota Press, 2004. Print.

The Warriors. Dir. Walter Hill. 1979. Paramount Pictures, 2005. DVD.

Welch, Chris. *David Bowie: We Could Be Heroes.* New York: Thunder's Mouth, 1999. Print.

When Billie Beat Bobby. Dir. Jane Anderson. 2001, Miramax, 2005. DVD.

Williams, Raymond. *Television: Technology and Cultural Form.* London: Fontana. 1974. Print.

Woolf, Virginia. "Mr. Bennett and Mrs. Brown." *The Virginia Woolf Reader.* Ed. Mitchell A. Leaska. New York: Harcourt, 1984. 192–212. Print.

Wrangler: Anatomy of an Icon. Dir. Jeffrey Schwarz. TLA, 2008. DVD.

Ziggy Stardust and the Spiders from Mars: The Motion Picture. Dir. D. A. Pennebaker. Virgin/EMI, 2003. DVD.

Index

Page numbers in boldface refer to illustrations.